Single parents talk here about their l... starts earlier than the time of splittin... marrying, sometimes in childhood ... from widely varied economic and en... all of them, becoming single parents called into question... accepted social values – about money, sex, childrearing, responsibility, dependency. Most remarkable, perhaps, splitting up, though fraught with hardship, often proved to be a liberating experience. This engrossing and moving book tells too of the lives they live now, and offers both emotional support and practical advice. It also radically challenges many of the assumptions by which we live.

Catherine Itzin was born in Iowa in 1944, and has been living in London since 1966. Most of her work has been in the theatre. She has been closely involved in the establishment of the British Theatre Institute and the Theatre Writers' Union: she was founder and editor of *Theatre Quarterly* from 1970–77 and the regular drama critic for *Tribune* from 1972. She is the author of five books on the theatre. Catherine Itzin is a single parent with two children; she has recently taken on the full weight of the Inland Revenue, in a highly publicised test case, claiming tax deduction for her childminding expenses.

Splitting Up

Single-Parent Liberation

Catherine Itzin

Virago

Published by VIRAGO Limited 1980
5 Wardour Street, London, W1V 3HE

Copyright © Catherine Itzin 1980

ISBN 0 86068 109 2   Paperback Edition

Typeset by Malvern Typesetting Services
and printed in Great Britain at
Lowe & Brydone Printers Limited,
Thetford, Norfolk

For my children: Caitlin and Nicholas

Acknowledgements

First and foremost, I would like to thank the women and men who so generously gave their time and personal experience in the interviews. This book couldn't have been done without them: the book is for them and for all the other single parents and their children.

I would also like to thank the many people who helped with the transcribing of tapes and typing: Pat Carty, Carolyn Cisneros, Frances Lockwood, Sheila Malone, Alf Myers, Gail Robinson, Shirley Towner, Gordon Weller. Thanks, too, to Daniel Lang for his help with the research and to Gingerbread and the National Council for One Parent Families for their assistance. Special thanks to Douglas Hill for the idea of making something useful out of my misery. And to my friends and family for their patience and support.

Contents

Preface by Paul Lewis   xi

Foreword   xiii

New Perspectives on Single Parents   1

1. Eleanor   12

2. Alec   29

3. Christine   46

4. Tom   63

5. Ann   84

6. James   99

7. Doreen   112

8. Michael   134

9. Jane   147

10. Joe   163

11. Judith   176

12. Paul   190

Directory of Useful Organisations   202

Reading List   217

Preface

by Paul Lewis

National Council for One Parent Families

Every happy two-parent family is a potential one-parent family. Every year over 150,000 children under sixteen are involved in a divorce and there are now over 750,000 lone parents bringing up well over $1\frac{1}{4}$ million children.

Many lone parents soon enter a second marriage – though these marriages are known to be even more precarious than first marriages. But for many one-parent families, the end of the marriage is an important period of release and freedom.

Most of the characters in Catherine Itzin's book express their joy, despite the hardship, at being free. And not just free of a bad relationship. They feel free of the constraints inherent in any marriage – free to get to know their children better, to get to know themselves.

But this positive – and to many people surprising – side of becoming a one-parent family is outweighed in so many cases by the cruel practical difficulties which society puts in the way of one-parent families reaching their potential as whole, happy and well-balanced families.

One-parent families are, on the whole, poor families. Over half of all families at the poverty line are one-parent families and even those lone parents who work earn low pay – most of them are women – and face extortionate costs to have their under fives looked after all day or their five to ten-year-olds outside school hours.

Poverty has its effects on health – lone mothers are more prone to illness and disability; on housing – half of all homeless families are one-parent families; on children's attainment at school; and, if the mother becomes pregnant again, on the health of her new baby.

Even before the effects of poverty set in, the prospects for a humane ending to a marriage are damaged by the legal system. Wife is set against husband in a prolonged re-run of years of marital torment, all with a view to establishing rights to a weekly maintenance which, research shows, is seldom enough to make a real contribution to the family budget.

And when all these problems are too much and social work help becomes involved, too often children are taken into care. About half of all the children in care are from one-parent families, their blameless mothers labelled failures. And smug society takes over the parental rights, and pays a foster mother twice or three times as much as was given the real lone mother or father on supplementary benefit to care for their own children.

Poverty among one-parent families could be ended by the government acting on a five-year-old report on one-parent families – the Finer Report – and introducing a special social security benefit for all one-parent families. Such a move would cost no more than taking 1p off the standard rate of income tax. No government has yet had the courage to do it. Help for one-parent families is seen as under-mining the dominant two-parent family and with it the structure of society. But if the two-parent family is so weak an institution that it has to be bolstered up by a layer of poverty-stricken parents and children, perhaps it is time to re-assess its real strength and importance.

Throughout this book there are characters who have survived marriages destroyed by sex or work or selfishness, and emerged as new people and new, whole one-parent families. One man said he'd made real friends for the first time and was closer to his children.

Perhaps this book will help us all to see one-parent families not as a growing problem but as the vanguard of a revolutionary change in the structure of society.

Foreword

The stories in this book – of marriages splitting up and the people setting up as single-parent families – originated out of my own self-help efforts. Caught in the crisis of my marriage breaking down and desperate for moral support, practical advice and a new perspective, I thought it would be helpful to talk to people in similar circumstances – to hear how they had coped, or not; how they had solved their problems; how they had come through it and survived. Because, at first, you don't cope – or just, perhaps, by the skin of your teeth. Because you wonder if you *will* survive, and how, and at what cost.

There is, at the time, a terrible sense of isolation. I remember phoning Gingerbread the week my husband left. (Gingerbread was the only organisation I'd heard of then.) A very pleasant person answered: 'What can I do for you?' There was a long silence before I stuttered a few inarticulate phrases about being on my own, needing advice, and so forth. The short answer to their question was, 'Help.' But I was hardly, then, in a position to identify my problems, let alone any possible solutions Gingerbread might have helped with. I needed to talk about the immediate trauma – worries about the children and how they would manage without their daddy, where and how we could live, on what we could live – and to talk out the anger, hurt, frustration. Everyone else – ie. normal people, for even if you think you oughtn't you do feel abnormal – is happily married and securely nuclearly nested. Or so it seems. To them what you need to talk about is in a foreign language from another country – at least, culture.

It was pretty quickly clear that the first, last and only resort was to rely on myself. But I started to look around me, quite naturally in the circumstances, with 'unmarried' eyes. And I discovered that once you cease to see the world through married-tinted glasses, you suddenly find a startling number of single-parent women. So-and-so, whom I saw regularly in the park with her two children, was in the same boat in the same stage of sinking. Slowly, shyly, almost ashamed, we acknowledged our mutual concerns. So-and-so's mum from my son's playgroup – likewise. A woman I'd met on the PTA at the local school – likewise. And when I went to my daughter's teacher to tell her the news and to ask her to keep an eye on my daughter during the crisis, she told me that over half the children in her class were from single-parent families! A male colleague to whom I confided my situation (only out of economic necessity, for there is great pressure to conceal the awful news) revealed that he and his wife were splitting up. And so the network widened within weeks.

It was my desperate need at that time of crisis to share experiences that led me to consider talking to women (the men came later!) in similar circumstances, with a view to publishing what they said, on the assumption that if it would help me, it could be put to the use of helping other people too. So the stories came to be told, representing their view of what happened in their lives.

Individually, the people talking in this book come from very different circumstances economically and emotionally; the circumstances of their splitting up were very different; and they hold very different attitudes. Some – Eleanor, Alec, Christine, Doreen – were simply left by their partners. Judith initiated the separation. Tom's split was politically as well as personally motivated and he spent six years living with his wife and her lover before resigning himself to separation. He and his wife then carefully organised their separation in the mutual interests of themselves and their children. Paul was a single parent before the child was even born. Some of the people are more analytical than others in relating their individual experience to external structures – the women more than the men. But collectively, they are the 'voice of single parents' as Ronald Blythe's *Akenfield* is the 'voice of a village'.

Perhaps people in the process of splitting up, or who have split up, or who are wishing they could split up, will find in these stories some moral support. Perhaps married readers will be stimulated to give a passing thought to not being married (to their single-parent brothers and sisters) – better yet to analyse the conditions and contradictions of their own marriages. All readers will find in these stories drama, even melodrama, misery, but also joy. For despite the hardships, these single-parent people are – without exception – happier as single parents than they were married, even the 'happily' married.

The interviews were conducted over a period of two years. When the 'contributors' were asked to 'approve' their part of the manuscript for publication, they were also asked to comment, if they wanted. These comments are incorporated into the introductions to each story – and they are often fascinating. Some people have read themselves with amazement: they found it rather like reading about a stranger, they had changed so much. Others were amazed by how they 'saw' themselves objectively. Tom, for example, thought he sounded like a male chauvinist when he had always regarded himself as progressive and enlightened in his views about women and marriage. Doreen burst into tears when she read her story: she couldn't believe how much and how foolishly she had suffered. These retrospective comments offer yet another perspective.

The quotes which occur throughout the text are taken from the following publications: *The Finer Report* (Report of the Committee on One-Parent Families), HMSO, London 1974: Simone de Beauvoir, *The Second Sex*, Penguin, Harmondsworth 1972: Lee Comer, *Wedlocked Women*, Feminist Books Ltd, Leeds 1974: Rosemary Simon, *Breaking Up, A Practical Guide to Separation, Divorce and Coping on Your Own*, Arrow Books, London 1974. The book is prefaced by an introduction which draws some general, and deliberately provocative conclusions from the experience of the people included. And it is appendixed by a list of organisations single parents might find useful, and a reading list of literature on marriage, child-rearing, splitting up and single parents, for these were the sorts of things which I found practically and emotionally supportive at the time of the crisis.

Catherine Itzin, London, 1980

New Perspectives on Single Parents

People who get married don't expect to get divorced. Married people who have children don't expect to become single parents. Yet the fact is that there are three-quarters of a million single parents (660,000 women and 90,000 men) looking after over $1\frac{1}{4}$ million children. One in every ten families is a single-parent family. This is a significant minority of the population.

'Splitting up' – especially where children are concerned – is still universally regarded as a disaster – the end of the world, not the beginning of a new, certainly different, possibly better one. No one would deny that it is fraught with difficulties and hardship. But what is becoming increasingly apparent is that splitting up and single parenthood is often a liberating rather than a debilitating experience, not only for women, but also for men, and for the children involved. To present the phenomenon of splitting up from this radical perspective was one of the main purposes of this book – with the intention that it might encourage a change in attitudes if not actualities. And the best argument for an alternative view seemed to be the personal experience of people who had gone through the process of marriage, children, splitting up and settling down as single parents, who had themselves undergone a change in attitudes.

Thus *Splitting Up: Single-Parent Liberation* is a collection of stories in narrative form, edited from interviews with women and men, with children, whose marriages and conventional family life had ended. It is simply people talking. But in each 'story' the 'character' of the speaker comes across clearly and strongly: from the 'voices' comes a powerful sense of each reality. In each case the stories start earlier than the time of splitting up, usually with meeting and marrying, settling down and having children, and sometimes with childhood background when that is particularly influential or relevant. For it is now commonly appreciated (or it ought to be) that the seeds of discontent and breakdown are planted within a marriage, if not earlier, in that the patterns of childhood behaviour and of the parental marriage are often (painfully) repeated. In addition, some of the 'problems' are inherent in the social system itself, in conditioned expectations and in the institution of marriage. An accumulation of all this experience, to varying degrees, operates in any marriage and determines what happens at the time of splitting up. Thus the stories are as much a comment on marriage as divorce.

The main emphasis in the stories is on the period of splitting up, the events leading up to it and the circumstances in which it occurs. They emphasise the subsequent process of becoming single parents: the problems, how they were resolved, or not, and the positive aspects – something that can only be described as the liberation which so often occurs. The people who tell their stories represent a cross-section of age, class and education. Some married young, some later in life: some had been single parents for some time, some had only recently split up.

The book was originally conceived as being solely concerned with women – the single-parent women who are, of course, in the majority and who face obvious difficulties. But it soon came to seem a fairer reflection of reality – there are two partners in any marriage, marriages end for better or worse – to balance the book with stories from men. Not just those statistically few men who are left with children to look after, but those who leave their wives with the children and still try to function as parents. In other words, to present the other side of the story. Men left on their own with children face similar practical problems to women, but usually with different expectations. Men who leave have different practical problems, but share the trauma of separation and the need to resolve in some fashion a future relationship with their children. There is still the widely held notion that men who leave their wives and families are monsters: but they are often forced by the system to behave in ways they would not otherwise choose.

Certainly, as with the women, the splitting up calls into question just about all accepted social values connected with marriage, money, child-rearing, sexual role conditioning and role playing. So another purpose of this book was to throw those values into a perspective they do not normally have, a perspective which only splitting up where children are involved would seem to offer. The 'norm' is still regarded as the nuclear family marriage, despite the divorce statistics and the occasional choice by people to attempt alternatives. These stories, at least, suggest the need for a revised concept of 'norm'.

Another purpose of the book was to shed light on the emotional trauma and social crisis of splitting up, surviving with (or away from) children after the separation, and starting afresh. And the stories reveal, movingly, the very real problems faced by single-parent families in a society that does very little to accommodate them. In the process (between the lines, as it were) they also reveal the shambles of social, psychological and educational conditioning; the sham of society's assumptions about marriage, and the economic and legal sanctions which support the assumptions. The stories cry out the need for change – changes in attitudes, changes in law, changes in the welfare system, and ultimately changes in the social system itself.

Many Problems, A Few Solutions

Whatever the circumstances, women or men left on their own with children suffer severe hardship, both practical and emotional. They are persons without status, often lucky to subsist. Rosemary Simon, in her invaluable book *Breaking Up*, covers all the practical matters of separating, divorcing and setting up on one's own. In doing so, she shows precisely how disadvantaged single parents are, and especially women. She explains how to make the best of a bad deal, but she leaves the reader in little doubt as to precisely how bad the deal is. There are problems with property, housing, maintenance, pension and National Insurance rights, childminding, domestic help, Social Security and the iniquitous cohabitation rule, health, poverty and the poverty trap. As a social worker who works for a London borough says: 'Unsupported parents are the most vulnerable sector of our society. Eighty per cent of my case load are single parents.'

And the stories in this book are a catalogue of the difficulties, sometimes of hardships. Judith, having left her husband, was homeless for a time with three children. Doreen was lucky, but only at the last minute, not to lose her flat. The circumstances of his separation forced James to leave his children to manage on their own in Hampshire while he worked in London, calling once a week or fortnight to see how they were getting on. But many of the problems are purely practical, or economic: they could be solved.

In 1969 (a decade ago now!) a Committee on One-Parent Families was set up by Richard Crossman under the chairmanship of Sir Morris Finer to investigate the 'problems of one-parent families in our society and to examine the nature of any special difficulties.' The Committee's brief also included 'to consider in what respect and to what extent it would be appropriate to give one-parent families further assistance, having regard to *the need to maintain equity as between one-parent families and other families* and practical and economic limitations.' (The italics are mine.) The Finer Report was published in 1974 and left little doubt as to the severe hardships suffered by single parents and the degree to which they were unsupported by society. Finer: 'There are of course other disadvantaged groups, but in terms of families with children . . . there can be no other group of this size who are as poor as fatherless families, of whom so many lack any state benefit other than supplementary benefit or Family Allowance, whose financial position is so uncertain.' The Finer Committee made no less than 230 recommendations for reform! The Committee had identified a need on a grand scale and considered it appropriate to remedy the situation, also on a grand scale. In the *Finer Report – Action and Inaction*, published in 1978 by the National Council for One Parent Families, the deplorable state of inaction on the Finer Report was made clear: 'To date over half these recommendations have been rejected and fewer than one-fifth have been implemented.' The Report was debated only on four occasions in the House of Commons and once in the House of Lords. The longest debate in the Commons – $5\frac{1}{2}$ hours in 1975 – was adjourned because of time, and even the innocuous motion – 'That this House takes note of the Report of the Committee on one-parent families' – was not passed! One could reasonably ask why not.

Implementation of Finer's 230 recommendations would provide a minimally secure status for single-parent families in our society. This does not seem much to ask. It is of profound social importance that the recommendations should be legislated for. If they were, the basic material needs of single parents would begin to be met. It would be a small but significant step forward.

Single-Parent Liberation

On one level the stories in this book serve to confirm the fact that splitting up is a trauma and that single parents suffer, often unnecessarily. At the same time, on another level, the stories reveal something which is less widely realised, or at least less publicised. And that is the exceptional strength acquired by women and men in this situation. Set against the many problems is the positive way in which the constraints imposed by the situation 'liberates' people, how this kind of practical adversity deconditions much of the sexist conditioning which governs the way most women and men live.

Certainly the men and women in this book describe themselves as 'better' people. In most cases they are (as Christine says) 'profoundly grateful to have had the opportunity to grow and develop – to become "people" as opposed to role types or stereotypes, however painful the process.' And for all the real problems, these women and men seem reluctant to relinquish their newfound status as a 'person' *or* their independence by repeating the pattern of marriage. So yet another purpose of this book was to reinforce for people their positive sense of identity in a situation which is usually portrayed, and perceived, as negative: to suggest to the world at large that a change in attitude might be in order. Certainly, this 'liberation' gives good grounds for examining the assumptions about single parents, about marriage and divorce.

Most people still expect to get married and to have children within the marriage: marriage and the nuclear family are still the norm. The main motivation for marriage is love, 'falling in love'. Though assumptions about marriage have been seriously questioned in the past ten years or so, marriage is still regarded as a romantic, happy-ever-after, solution-to-everything venture. Children will 'naturally' have two parents, a mummy and daddy: they will all live together as a happy nuclear family. Society promotes this image of marriage and the family from the cradle. It is assumed. It is inevitable. Without exception, these were the expectations of the people in this book. They are typical. This is the norm to which they – and millions of others – have conformed.

Most marriages are still based on the expectation that the husband is the breadwinner and the wife is the housekeeper, the childbearer and childrearer. There are obviously variations on the theme, and in the wake of the women's movement and the consciousness it has raised, the whole subject of marriage and family has been much more widely discussed and analysed. But the pattern prevails. Before children, both partners may work and may share the housework in some fashion. As often as not, though, both partners may work and the wife still do all the housework as well. Very few marriages reverse the roles entirely so that the woman works outside the home and the man works inside it. And even when actual domestic work is shared, the husband is usually ultimately responsible for earning the living and the wife responsible for running the home.

The woman is almost invariably dependent on her husband – legally, financially, often in practical terms, sometimes emotionally, and, perhaps most insidiously, psychologically. On marrying, she loses her name and becomes the other half of her husband's. From that moment onwards, the pattern of marriage can be seen as a gradual erosion of her identity and individuality. What is less obvious or acknowledged is the extent to which this pattern forces men into roles they might not freely choose either.

After children, if not before, the overlapping of roles and responsibilities becomes more clearly separated. Biologically the woman has the baby: sociologically, she mothers. There are few fathers who mother. Women may go to work soon after having a baby, but they are still firmly bound by the responsibilities of motherhood, and still too by domestic responsibilities, even if the actual work is shared or jobbed out. Married mothers usually end up doing two jobs – their 'work' and their housework. And still they are regarded as the 'weaker' sex, even when they are functioning in this dual sex role.

These, basically, were the patterns of the lives of the people in this book. Significantly, marriage assumptions started operating and controlling the people in their relationships even when they were aware of the potential pitfalls and struggled against them. Not everyone was caught unawares. And whatever other factors were operating, it was a pattern that both the women and the men found repressive and frustrating. More obviously the women resented the freedom they lost, the restraints of children and domesticity. Less obviously the men were frustrated by the roles they were forced to play, or in some cases by the frustrations of their wives. Splitting up for them was a means, albeit a drastic one, of breaking free. In the case of Tom, this was done consciously. In the other cases – and for most of the women – the people discovered the freedom after the fact, but came to be conscious of its meaning and to value it highly. And, of course, they came to question their previously held views and values.

New Perspectives

Both the women and the men came to realise how arbitrary was their decision to marry, how little consideration they gave to it before embarking upon it, how little they understood the effects it would have upon their lives. They came to understand how marriage had trapped them in rigid roles and frustrated their personal expectations. They came to realise how little thought they had given to having children and how monumental the consequences. They appreciated the trauma of splitting up, whatever their circumstances, and realised how ill-equipped they were to cope in practical terms. For the men faced often for the first time with cooking, cleaning, and childcare, this was an extremely significant factor. For the women it involved a realisation of the limitations of their earning power.

Both men and women were able to analyse their sexual relationships and needs more objectively, to acknowledge the extent to which their married sexual relationships had been unsatisfactory, often over very long periods. There was a feeling amongst most of the women that the men were inadequate at coping with marriage and children, unable to accept responsibilities during or after the marriages. The men and women were unanimous in condemning the inadequacies of the welfare system. Generally, the women were better able to analyse themselves and their relationships than the men.

All of the men and women were able for the first time to see clearly the extent to which the marriage contract had been an economic one, some to appreciate the political implications of that fact. In 1974 in a very provocative book entitled *Wedlocked Women* Lee Comer explained how women and men are conditioned from birth through childhood to accept nuclear marriage as normal, and effectively trained to play their parts in it, without questioning it. She did this by showing the concept of family to be an integral part of the economic social structure:

> For the purpose of capitalist economy, the very best arrangement a man can make, regardless of his class or education, is to:

(1) take a wife who will care for him and see to all his needs and bear and rear his children.

(2) live with them in a small isolated group and preferably away from his first family.

(3) be intent on improving his standard of living, thereby committing himself to overtime or professional ladder climbing, both of which require long hours away from home, and a patient uncomplaining wife.

(4) be prepared to move house and town from time to time.

(5) support a wife and growing family.

For the purposes of capitalism, the best arrangements a woman can make go parallel to the man's. Her goals must mirror her husband's. She must be prepared to work long unpaid hours in the home while he improves his lifestyle. But as well as applying herself wholeheartedly to the husband's and children's needs, she must also be prepared to work outside the home for 'pin' money (ie. low pay), but not to identify with her work role. She must only see her job as significant insofar as it adds to the family spending power and gives her something to do when the kids grow up. Her work must never give her independence, because his mobility depends on her dependence on him. Where he goes, so must she. So that if she is laid off at work or is subjected to bad working conditions and pay, it will not matter too much. Thus, two basic needs of capitalism are met. A motivated work force, and a secondary, casual work force.

Whilst this is a marxist analysis of marriage, whilst some of the specific characteristics of the structure Lee Comer describes have changed since she wrote the book, and whilst it may seem a gross exaggeration of marriage and family life as most people think of it or live it – or think they live it – it provides a perspective on marriage that is totally obscured by the usual romantic representation of it. And it is a perspective that people splitting up are forced to face. The men, perhaps, most acutely: Michael and James barely managed to survive initially as members of the work force without the support system of their wives. The women found themselves suddenly unsupported and realised with a shock the extent to which they were dependent on the breadwinner of the marital unit: few were in a position to be self-supporting.

In important respects, one of the 'liberating' realisations of splitting up, for the women especially, was coming to understand their economic position in the marriage and their new one outside it. Most of the women sought economic independence (however unsuccessfully) and relished what they acquired. It contributed to a positive sense of identity. If one accepts, as Lee Comer argues, that marriage is part of the economic base of society, then changing that base, as splitting up does, will mean inevitable changes in the structure of society itself, and is conceivably threatening to its stability. This is important to bear in mind when considering the other implications of splitting up.

What happens with splitting up is that just about every pre-conception about women and men, women's and men's roles, women's and men's capabilities are called into question in one fell swoop. There is no division of labour along sex lines, because there is no division of labour. A woman left on her own with children has to carry on with everything she as a woman and mother is expected to do, and in addition take on everything the man did and is expected to do. The same is true, in reverse, for men. It is a proposition with radical implications. A whole lifetime of division of roles and responsibilities and expectations is called into question. It is more than a total reversal of women's or men's situations: it is an instant accumulation of both women's and men's situations into one person, who, in managing to do it, becomes what can only be described as a 'superperson' in terms of society's accepted idea and image of women or men.

These are the really radical implications of splitting up and becoming a single parent – what it means personally, socially and politically. The implications have perhaps been ignored, because it is a transaction which challenges fundamentally many of society's most fervently held beliefs and values: sexual role conditioning (eg. men ought to do one thing, women ought to do another), marriage, nuclear family values, childbearing and childrearing, education, work – basically the whole role of women and men in society. These consequences of splitting up are so profound that they demand a re-examination of the assumptions by which most people live, and they clearly indicate the need to evolve alternatives.

But that re-examination and the alternatives would also have profound consequences – ultimately threatening to the structure of our society as it is now. Even the implementation of the Finer recommendations would have radical repercussions far beyond creating a reasonable standard of living for single parents. In this respect it is worth noting the terms of Finer's brief: 'the need to maintain equity as between one-parent families and other families.' For if single-parent 'familyness' was a status as 'secure' and respectable and economically attractive as marriage, for example, people might start questioning the values of marriage. Single parent familyness might become quite as desirable an option as marriage, perhaps more so for some people. How many women – men too – marry and stay married because there are so few other viable choices? Single parent familyness, as a properly serviced status, would have a profound effect on the self-consciousness of single parents: it would also have a profound effect on the social consciousness of everyone in society. With the full implementation of the Finer recommendations, single-parent families would begin to acquire a new and possibly even desirable status in society. It is this, more than the practical considerations taken in isolation, which would threaten the existing social structure. To recognise, to accept and to accommodate the radical implications of single-parent familyness within the social structure would force revolutionary changes in society.

I have possibly over-argued the case to make a point, with the intention of being deliberately provocative. I realise that most people view splitting up and single-parent life as overwhelmingly disastrous from every point of view. There is no doubt that people need other people, need close permanent relationships, and wish to have children. What these stories indicate is that it is by no means clear how such needs and responsibilities can best be met and maintained. They also show that there are still many myths as to what marriage *is*.

Though it might seem otherwise, I am not arguing against marriage, but suggesting that there are advantages and dis-advantages to marriage, and advantages and disadvantages to being a single parent. But at present the disadvantages of marriage are played down, which can lead to confusion and suffering; and the advantages of single-parent familyness are largely ignored. Perhaps this book will slightly redress this imbalance.

The people telling their stories here, because of their experiences, are, at the very least, aware of the question that needs to be asked – how, given the need to love other people and care for our children, can we best organise and structure relationships to accommodate these needs? They may not have come up with the answers. But if one links the stories with the reforms proposed by the Finer Com-mittee, there are some ingredients for a radical revaluation of our society, if not a few tools for change. And it is time this was recognised. Perhaps these stories will provoke others to ask some important and necessary questions.

1. Eleanor

Eleanor comes from a working-class background. She married at nineteen and separated at thirty-five with three children under seven. At the time of the interview Eleanor had been on her own for five years: she had passed forty and her children were approaching their teens. She is not remarried nor in a serious relationship at the moment because of what she describes as a 'lack of commitment and general sharing of interests from men'. She says she might consider remarrying, 'but as each year goes by the thought of all the time it takes to know someone, and the compromising, makes it seem unlikely.' Eleanor and her three children are now living in carefree chaos in a council house in North London. Eleanor works part-time in a shop, and she enjoys the independence it gives her.

Of her situation now, Eleanor says: 'This interview was taped two years ago and I read the typescript of it reluctantly, fearing that I would be embarrassed. I was – and horrified, ashamed and amazed as well. I think in fairness to myself I should say that I don't think I am as mindless as I appear to be, or quite as obsessed with sex and money. There were periods of affection and humour between my husband and myself even in the thick of the affair I was having. And he was not as passive as I suggest. We talked endlessly about our situation, but seemed helpless to solve it.

'This interview was an uninterrupted flow of memories and impressions which came flooding out from me after a hesitant start and I suppose reflects the confusion that I was still struggling to emerge from. It's this confusion that I find horrifying, as well as my awful self-indulgence at the expense of another human being, in fact at the expense of several. I did suffer badly from guilt and remorse for a long time after the split, but gradually came to see things in what I think is a fair perspective.

'The divorce was hard to bear, but I wanted my husband to be happy. I felt he deserved a break. I wanted his new marriage to work. I don't know if it has. They have been together about five years now and I sincerely hope and pray that all is well, but I don't know. We have a polite, rather restrained relationship now and we keep off of any personal or past problems. The other man left finally about three years ago, having told me for the umpteenth time what a lousy mother I was, etc. I recovered as usual, eventually.

'The situation at present is that my children are well and don't appear to be screwed up at all. They are as happy as any other kids that I meet. I am a lot happier these days. I earn enough money to supplement my maintenance and it's not too much of a struggle to survive compared to the dreadful strain of life when I was married. I pay bills, we have holidays, I've a few good friends. Life is simple and fairly enjoyable.

'I still get depressed now and again, who doesn't? But I'm basically optimistic. I hope and pray that I never ever behave so badly towards anyone again, even though I know that I was only 50 per cent to blame. I bitterly regret the pain I caused my ex-husband and wish him well. I still have a great affection for him, although I know we could never live together. I seem to have written off the other man rather brutally. He obviously has his needs and problems too and I can just about manage to feel a little sympathy for him, but it's an effort.

'I think what I like most about my life now is the fact that I am in charge of it. The worst thing about my marriage was the important part that money and sex played in it. I couldn't control it. It was controlling me.

'The main problem that I have these days is being rather a push-over for any man who seems to take a kindly interest. I think I'm still looking for a closeness with a man which I haven't really found since my husband. I'm aware that I'm rather vulnerable and still indulge in wild fantasies about current relationships from time to time which are not realistic.

'But my life is without problems and I am basically happy.'

Well, when I met Harvey I was about sixteen. Very, very green; yes, very green and very flirty, and unaware, and dreadful really, you know. Anyway, I met him at the local youth club dance where I used to go with a friend. And there he was looking terribly arrogant and not very likeable with his feet up on a chair . . . and I didn't like him at all at first. He went out with a friend of mine for a while, and then she dropped him and I went out with him. We just kind of . . . we were very close actually, and we were . . . I don't know. It started out as the usual kind of infatuation. Once I had started going out with him we got very close, you know. I had lots of boyfriends before, in a teenagery kind of way, but he was the first person I really related to. Not physically intimately, but mentally intimately – we got very close. I suppose we loved each other, we must have done. I assumed that's what it was. I've never had the same kind of intimacy with a man again.

I suppose he must of been in his early twenties. Yeah, 'cause when I married at nineteen, he was about twenty-five. Something like that. Although he seemed much older somehow, and when I look back and remember how young he was, well . . . What happened I think is that I was looking for a daddy, I'm sure of it, you know, because I leaned on him terribly heavy, you know. And when we finally did get married, we were completely involved with one another. We leaned on one another; we were not aware of anything outside; it was sort of young lovers, you know, although we hadn't had any physical . . . er . . . love at all, and we didn't have for five years into the marriage.

We kind of tumbled around and everything, but I was completely unaware sexually and he was too, although I didn't know at the time. And it didn't matter because I didn't know what I was missing. And I didn't really care, you know.

We had a white wedding. It was ridiculous. We bluffed our way through the whole thing, you know. The reception was in a boozy old pub near where I lived, and it was all dreadful . . . all the relatives came and it was all absolutely horrible. There was no money and after the reception we went off to a hotel in the West End to a big dinner and dance, you know, and that was quite nice. Then we went back to our bedsitter in Muswell Hill where we had this bitch of a landlady, who turned out to have left us a little rose in a jar and a hot water bottle in the bed. We went to bed and it was a complete and utter flop – nothing at all. You see, if I'd been a more sophisticated lady, I wouldn't have chosen a purple see-through nightie, I would of done the white virginal approach. It was all dreadful, really dreadful, it was an absolute disaster. And, of course, I didn't know if he was impotent because I had turned him off, or impotent because he was impotent or what. But nothing happened from that point onwards for five years.

We did talk about it, at first you know, but it wasn't terribly serious for a long time. And it didn't really worry me much for two or three years. We groped about, we enjoyed ourselves, we would go dancing a lot. He was at art school, and you know, it didn't matter that much somehow. We sort of loved each other, we wanted to be with each other and although it was an irritating thing which wasn't quite right, it was in the background all the time. It wasn't that important, it didn't swamp the relationship, you know.

But, as time went by, I got round to knocking twenty-five and still nothing had happened. I was beginning to get a little screwed up, you know. And I was beginning to look at ladies with babies in prams with enormous malice. Then a friend of mine who got married a few years later than me wrote and told me she was expecting a baby and I was terribly fed up. I thought, oh my god, I'm going to be a virgin for the rest of my life. I was a virgin when we got married. He said he wasn't, but I think he was. He must have been, though he always said he'd been with another woman. But I don't think he could have been because he was terribly inexperienced, you know. I'm sure if he had been an experienced man, something would of happened.

We finally consummated it five years later, in Cardiff, in one tremendous evening with a great deal of growling and grunting. We finally made it, the big break, and I couldn't believe it. He'd actually gone to the doctor's, you know, after we'd had years of nattering about it in the early hours of the morning, and worrying about it, then shouting and screaming as time went by. Anyway, it finally happened, and it was okay. It was never great, but it was all right, a bit passive, but it didn't matter, because we were still having fun – we were going in for dance competitions – and we were still very involved with each other, very close.

Marriage is the destiny traditionally offered to women by society. It is still true that most women are married, or have been, or plan to be, or suffer from not being – Simone de Beauvoir

---

We were both working and dancing a lot and that took up all our time. It was an exciting sort of life, but there was hardly any money. There were stressful periods but we were still close, even living with various parents in between jobs. There was an awful lot of stress and anxiety which was probably not helping the impotent bit in the beginning. It's very hard trying to make a living as an artist. And I was all the time leaning heavily on him, wanting to be with him all the time. For security. Because my own father was a nonentity as a father. I mean he didn't exist – he was a weak man, completely dominated by my mother. He didn't play any part at all in my life really. So I suppose I must've been looking for a daddy, and I leaned on him, I wanted to be physically with him all the time. I must've been a tremendous burden on him actually, now I look back on it. Although it didn't seem so at the time. And that's why I feel guilty.

Anyway, we came back after Cardiff to Crouch End, and I discovered that I was actually pregnant. I went to the doctor's and he said I was, and I went weak at the knees, and sort of staggered about. I was terribly pleased. Terribly happy. I was so shaky, and I couldn't believe it. I sort of sat back in the sitting room in Crouch End, with a cup of hot chocolate, trying to calm down. It was fantastic. And that was Joanna. The whole pregnancy was absolutely beautiful and I was glowing with health. We were ever so happy. We had a lovely little flat and the baby was born at home. It was a beautiful summer's day, and the french windows were open. The whole thing was fabulous, you know. And we went on happily for a few months.

Then the money trouble started again. There had always been money problems but at that time I just put it down to bad luck and other people's faults – like rotten estate agents and landlords. From the beginning there were money problems. I wasn't aware at the time. I wasn't interested, you know. I was ever so kind of ignorant and sweet, in some ways green as grass. But anyway, we had to move up to a dreadful place in Willesden . . . with Joanna who was five months old. And from that period on things started to get a bit dodgy, you know. There was no money, and I was getting run down in health, and Harvey was getting odd cleaning jobs and selling the odd bits. It was almost continuously stressful. There didn't seem to be much good going on, because now that we had a child I couldn't go with him, you know, when he went dancing. And I didn't like him going off dancing because it meant I would be on my own, and I needed him for a daddy. So that's when things started going wrong.

Then we found we were living in Hackney over a greengrocers. Joanna was about eighteen months old, and I was expecting Adam. Sex usually carried on, but it wasn't very exciting . . . well it was okay, and I didn't know what I was missing anyway. I mean I didn't care, you know. At least I was normal and had a baby and that was enough, you know. At least we had consummated it finally. When Adam was born we moved to Barnet, a little run-down terraced house with a garden, and we were quite happy there for a while. Comparatively speaking. There were money problems as usual, we were always a bit short of cash. You see, he had the cheque book and he just gave me the housekeeping money.

As time went by sex got worse for me. He didn't seem to want to, and it happened very rarely. In fact, it wouldn't of happened at all if I didn't bring the subject up, which caused rows and which meant nothing happened. The sex scene got really bad for me, and nothing much was going on. In fact, it had been slowing down and getting a bit dodgy for a couple of years after Joanna was born. 'Cause he didn't want to know while I was pregnant and for six months after, and in between it was getting bad. I was thinking he must've had a low sex drive with me. I think he may be all right with his new wife 'cause she is totally different to me – small and dark and cuddly and independent.

By now I'm getting really pissed off with this bad sex scene, you know, and I started to think maybe I *was* missing something. Because this friend of mine who lived just across the road had just recently got married and it was all happening . . . wallop, bang every night, you know . . . randy scenes, orgies. And she was really ramming it down my throat twice a day, you know, and that wasn't helping. Especially when it was all grinding to a halt at our house.

I was beginning to get a bit restive, thinking well, you know, something's wrong here. This friend of mine had a New Year's party and I was really fed up. Mini skirt's had just come in and I thought, oh sod it, I'm going to get a bloke. I had never done anything like that before. I'd flirted with people. But I'd never ever dreamt of actually going up and doing anything. I think it had got so bad – there were terrible money troubles, debts, electric cut off, gas cut off, no sex, and money, no nothing – and I was really fed up. I thought, bugger it, I'm going out and have some fun. So I went to this New Year's party and Harvey stayed at home looking after the kids.

He knew I went to the party 'cause she only lived across the road but he didn't know I was on the prowl. Anyway, I looked around and I thought, 'I'm going to pick the randiest looking bloke I can find'. And I saw this absolutely crazy looking man sitting in the corner, so I went over and got him. And that was it, the beginning of the end.

I wish I hadn't done it though. I thought I'd had enough, I wanted something to happen, I was bored to death, I was frustrated physically – and depressed. And I was probably doing it to get at Harvey, as much as anything. Maybe I resented him or something. God knows what it was all about. I wish I hadn't done it, though, hadn't met Fred. Because that went on for ten years, that affair, by which time I had Emma, the last one. I think . . . I hope . . . that she is Harvey's. I think that she is Harvey's – she certainly looks like Adam. As far as I'm concerned she is Harvey's . . . I'm quite sure of it, but I don't really care. And I didn't care then. It never occurred to me that maybe Harvey would care that perhaps Emma wasn't going to be his. Which probably sounds awful. When he said – once when Emma was about a year old – that he'd always had doubts about Emma, I said, 'What do you mean, you don't love her?' Quite aggressively and in great amazement.

Harvey knew about the affair from the minute it started, well within a few weeks, because I told him. Because I wanted him to say 'You must stop', but he didn't. It was more, 'Oh well, if he can give you what I can't, carry on', which was the worst thing he could of possibly done. On the other hand, I doubt if I would've given up, because it happened that the sex thing with Fred was absolutely unbelievable, it was completely fantastic. In fact, he turned out to be the worst thing in the world that could have happened to me. He was not only married, but I felt he was altogether dishonest with me about his past relationships. I felt misused and degraded. But it didn't matter to me because the sex I was getting was incredible. And I had never experienced anything like that before. That kept me going for a long, long time, putting up with all sorts of dreadful feelings with this bloke.

His wife came to the maternity hospital when I had Emma. She turned up with a friend to see me. It was dreadful. It was the first time I'd met her. And I wasn't interested in Fred at this time. I'd had another baby and it was Harvey's as far as I was concerned. I didn't really want to know about Fred. You know, when women have just had a baby, they're not interested in all that. They're just mothers, you know, and the whole thing is hormones and glands and oestrogen, and blokes don't come into it. So I said to her, 'Oh well, I don't want to know about Fred, and I'm sorry and it's all over and all that.' And she said she had just had a baby herself a few months before, and she had lots of baby clothes and she said, heavily, 'Would you like some?' And I said, 'No thank you.' She was really rubbing it in, you know. She knew. He told her the whole thing, which I thought was absolutely awful. He'd told her where I was and all about it, which is just what I couldn't be bothered with, having just had a baby.

When I came out of hospital I didn't want to know Fred and Harvey was very distant because he thought Emma wasn't his. I knew it at the back of my mind, but I was still annoyed with him for not being a loving dad and bringing me lots of flowers and being a proper husband, even though I'd been having this affair. See how confused I was, and screwed up. I wanted both: I wanted Harvey to be supportive, the daddy, give his permission, look after me. In fact when I used to go out with Fred I used to say, 'How do I look?' and 'I won't be long, I'll be back early', and that kind of thing. I didn't mean it to be hurtful. I'd just given up by that time. I didn't mean it to hurt him but he'd taken on the father's role for me. Although I didn't realise it, he'd become my father, not my husband. The sex thing stopped with him and he became the daddy – the children's daddy and my daddy – and I was going out with my boyfriend, with Fred, you know. What happened as a result of that strange twist around was that any kind of physical contact between us became really screwed up in my mind. I found it taboo. I couldn't touch him or anything. It all went wrong, and that was the last nail in the coffin.

Anyway, I came out of hospital and then a few months later I suddenly started to get the feeling that I absolutely had to see Fred. It was an obsession – I had to. So I phoned him up, and it all started again. His wife found out and it all ended in a big row; it was sordid and dreadful. Then he left his wife and eventually they got divorced. In a way she was better off out of it. She was a head teacher, very efficient, super-mum type. I think he needed her, but probably didn't love her. He was such a loony.

I didn't want to leave Harvey. He was my dad, you know, my dear old dad, so the last thing I wanted to do was leave Harvey. He was part of me, you know. For all that I didn't want to leave him – or him to leave me then – we were having the most dreadful savage rows all the time . . . really physical fights and the kids were getting upset. I was particularly vicious. I mean I was a complete and absolute cow to him, because . . . oh, I don't know why I was doing it. Maybe I wanted him to have stopped it, just to do something. I don't know what was the matter with me. I know I was behaving badly and he was getting more and more distant. And, of course, we were still having a lot of trouble with money.

I had the three children to look after, so I couldn't get out much. They were all babies, you know, little toddlers. And I loved them you know. I wouldn't have wanted to leave them, because I needed them too, you know. I needed my kids at that time far more than they needed me, I'm sure. In fact, I've only just recently come out of that, so that I'm allowing them to get away from me a little bit. I'm not being quite so possessive. But I did need them so much.

It was getting worse and worse. We were married fifteen years up to the point when we separated. The first five years of that were nice except that we hadn't consummated the marriage; the second five years were beginning to get a bit stressful, during which time I met Fred. And the last five years were hell. God knows what damage we did to each other and the kids. They've survived, but only by the skin of their teeth.

Then Carol turned up – the other woman. Harvey had given up trying to be an artist; he'd taken a social worker's course, and was still dancing, still taking part in dance competitions. And he met this girl called Carol. The name kept cropping up, but I didn't think anything of it at the time. I was too busy with my own besotted affair. And it didn't occur to me that impotent old Harvey would ever find another lady. I used to say to a lot of people, 'Oh well, that's one thing that never will happen', I said, 'I'm enough for him for the rest of his life.'

Then he started coming in very late, about two or three in the morning or perhaps never coming in at all. Which he'd never done before. This really got me down, I couldn't cope with it all. It was really painful. You see, I could dish it out, but when I was getting it back, that was something quite different. And it really made me miserable and sick. This went on for a while and then it became more and more obvious that he was spending time with Carol. I'd kick him out as soon as he'd come in and say, 'Go back to her, go on, piss off'. In the end he said he couldn't stand it any longer, we had a big row and I told him to go. He went, and didn't come back and that was it.

Of course, immediately I realised what I'd done. I didn't want him to go really, despite the fact that we were savage to one another, miserable and unhappy. He still was part of me, and when he finally did go, it was like having a physical part of me pulled off, an arm wrenched off. It was agony. And when I had to clear all his things out . . . I really can't even bear to think about it even now . . . it was a most dreadful terrible business. So I obviously was very involved with him and I suppose I must've loved him, but we just couldn't live with each other. I suppose we had used each other up . . . or something.

I felt awful and I treated myself as if I was ill. I used to sit in bed and have glasses of hot milk. I'd cope with it by thinking, well today's not too bad, we'll float along today and hope that tomorrow is a bit better. It it's not, well, you know, I just took it day by day. I planned a trip to South Wales with some friends to . . . well . . . I had to give the kids something to look forward to. Like stepping stones through the years. So as soon as one treat was over, we had another one to look forward to. There was always something pleasant on the horizon to help us cope with this awful thing that happened. Anyway, we survived it.

He was all right about money. At first he gave me just about enough to live on, and then he got more successful and became a social worker and got more money, so he's been giving me more. So we're not badly off for money. It's not a lot, but we can manage on it and he does the best he can. He's quite kind for money, you know. Then he wanted a divorce, so we had a divorce. That was all rotten and horrible. It was straightforward and simple but it was nasty. That was about four years ago, I suppose, the divorce.

The affair with Fred was still going on then but it was beginning to fade out. He left finally for the last time last May, and I haven't seen him since. That whole thing went on ten years solid right the way through everything. He was a destructive man for me, and it was very painful with him too, you know. So it's been a fraught period. But having come out of it all and having to be on my own and look after the kids, I'm a much better person now. Although it's been very painful getting here, I feel that I am a much better person having been through it all, you know.

I don't think I'd ever be so destructive again myself, and I'm terrified of ever repeating all that again. I'm rather wary of getting involved with anybody intimately again, not at the moment anyway. Now there's the odd bloke around on a casual sort of basis, and I feel calmer and safer that way at the moment. I don't really know if I could cope with going into a really one hundred per cent intimate relationship with a bloke again. At the moment. I'm scared I'd make a mess of it.

At first I was terrified of being on my own, so Fred moved in immediately, which was a disaster. Because I wasn't able to accept him as a replacement for Harvey. But I was scared of being on my own. I'd never been on my own before, 'cause I'd come straight from home into marriage, you see, and the idea of being alone in the house and having to cope . . . I couldn't bear it. I was really scared of being alone, so Fred came and then he went away almost immediately, because I was crying a lot and he didn't want to know. He kept on coming back and going and coming back . . . this went on for a year. And it was screwing me right up, you know.

I was in a terrible state about Harvey and a terrible state about Fred, so the first year was just terrible. You know, sort of awful.

I wanted Harvey back. This was before the divorce. But he wasn't going to come back and I gradually realised that. There was a strange thing . . . one night shortly after Harvey had gone, I'd gone to bed – Fred was with me – and I was lying in bed feeling terribly miserable and I felt almost a kind of psychic slippping away. I knew that I'd lost him, that he'd gone, although we hadn't been divorced or anything by then. I just knew it was over. I suddenly felt a kind of slipping away of him, in a spiritual way. It was a very strange feeling, but I knew what it was.

There have been several surveys into the effects of divorce on family health and all of them reveal that divorced women, in common with mothers on their own, are at special risk . . . Robert Chester, senior lecturer in sociology at Hull University, found that the overwhelming majority of the 150 divorced women he interviewed claimed that marriage breakdown had taken its toll on their health. Again, nerves, nervous tension and depression were the most commonly cited complaints. Typical manifestations included crying, sleeping problems and weight loss— Rosemary Simon

---

He came once a week to see the kids. And that was pretty agonising for the first year. I used to hope he'd come back, so I used to brush Emma's hair to make her look pretty, and send her up the road to meet daddy and try and entice him back. I did everything – all the tricks. Make the place look nice, all shining and beautiful. And I'd make myself all neat and clean and pretty, and make sure the children were all beautifully dressed, to show him how lovely we all were, and how could he bear to leave us, sort of thing. But it didn't work – too late.

That year passed. We went from one stage to another, with exciting, nice things for the kids. Kids will always respond to treats. So we were up to our necks in puppies, kittens and trips to the seaside for the first year. The kids were very close to me. Harvey loved them but he was a detached dad. He wasn't one of those very intimate kissy sorts of dad. He loved them but he wasn't intimately involved with them every day like I was. I was really the mum and I was solid, and I think that helped them through. I never left them for a minute. They were always with me, except at school, where I met them and brought them back. We were together, they slept with me, they ate with me, they were with me one hundred per cent. Every time I used to cry, they used to get me toilet paper to blow my nose; we were all in there being miserable together sort of thing. They were very comforting, and they said, 'Don't cry mummy.' I'd be sobbing away, and they'd do something funny and we'd laugh and cry together. We got through the first year like this.

In the second year, once I'd stopped fighting it, it was even worse. Because the depression and the remorse and the realisation of my true situation hit me. The fact that he was actually gone, we were going to get divorced . . . I couldn't believe it. It seemed like a sort of game and I couldn't believe it was really happening. It had all been like a mad sort of game to me up to then. It hadn't really seemed to have any reality. I was slowly destroying the man in my life, the husband, but it didn't seem to occur to me in a strange kind of way. I didn't want to think about it. The true reality of the situation came home to me in the second year. And I realised that I'd got to have to stand up and start looking after myself and everybody else. So I started to pick myself up and stand on my own two feet. Until then, I was leaning and flopping on everybody in sight.

That was when I started to grow up and be a proper human being, without actually sucking somebody dry. You know, one dreadful thing happened just before we split up. We were having terrible rows and I found a little diary of Harvey's – in tiny repressed sort of writing, about me, saying whenever will I get rid of this gut-sucking bloody bitch. It was like a knife going in. I didn't realise I was a gut-sucking bitch, but I was, of course. I used to write things on the mirror like 'Fuck off'. He saw it when he came in. It was hideous. I can't believe that I was so foul. I cannot believe it really, the way I was carrying on and the way we were behaving to each other. We were just like a couple of savage animals tearing each other to bits, and the kids were right in the middle of it.

The first thing I did when I decided to pull myself together was to get us out of where we lived which was crumbling around us. So I started getting all militant with the council. I said, 'Right, that's it, I'm going to get us out of here.' That was my project for the second year. So I started getting really heavy with them. I'd never done anything like this before. I used to live through Harvey. I used to send Harvey out to do everything while I stayed at home. This was a symptom of the screwed up state I was in, I think. I stopped being a person, especially towards the end. On a Saturday, for example, I would sometimes get up and sit at the kitchen table, and I would stay there all day, not even get up and do the shopping or look after the kids. I suppose I was in a state of depression actually, although I didn't realise it at the time. I lived totally through him. I used him to do everything. As soon as he went out of the door, I stood up and started doing things; as soon as he came back through the door I stopped being a person. It was really pathological – I was crackers, I'm sure of it.

Anyway, the whole of the second year was concerned with getting us rehoused here. I felt triumphant when I'd done it. That was nice, and I was beginning to get used to being on my own. The third year of the separation I gradually started feeling freer and less troubled. There were more good periods than bad. Now this is the fourth year of the separation and the second year in the new house, and I feel quite a nice person. I'm feeling in charge of myself. I'm handling the money fairly well, we have holidays, I've got a fairly nice social life. I'm in control of myself and I feel quite happy really.

Since Harvey had always handled the money I was surprised when I seemed to go into it all right. As I never had the chance to handle the money, I didn't know whether I was good or bad at it. But I found it quite simple to do, I didn't find it difficult. I thought, well I'm not so bad, you know, I can do it. I suppose that contributed to my feelings of well-being.

I'm glad that we're not living together any more, I'm glad that it happened. I wish we hadn't destroyed each other. I wish I had been a better and more understanding person. I wish I hadn't married at nineteen. If I'd waited until I was twenty-five, it may never of happened – all that terrible business, you know. I suppose I was looking for a father figure, a classic story, I'm sure. And he didn't want to be a father figure, and he couldn't cope with being leant on heavily. He probably needed a mother figure, you know, and as I couldn't do that, it was a disaster. I'm glad that it's all over. I'd liked to have had a happy marriage and it didn't happen, but I'm all right now. He's married again and he's happy, I think. He seems to be. I'm nervous about getting into another relationship. I don't know if I'll ever achieve that again. It's a horrible thought, that I may never. On the other hand, it's nice to have experienced it. I just wish I wasn't so scared about getting into somebody else. But maybe that'll pass, maybe I'll feel more confident next year, about coping with another relationship properly.

On the other hand, I'm beginning to think maybe I don't need anybody – to live with anyway. This is what I'm recently beginning to think. I'm thinking, do I really need a bloke, I mean to live in the house. I thought I'm not all that miserable now I'm on my own. In fact, I'm not even worried about sex at the moment. I think I'm probably losing my sex drive, which will be a blessed relief. Do I really need a bloke saying, 'Well I'm watching football this afternoon'. I was thinking to myself, I don't have to watch football if I'm on my own, I can watch something else. Do we need the hassle? And I'm beginning to think that perhaps I don't. The only thing that bothers me is what is going to happen to me when I'm about sixty-five and still on my own. Should I keep an eye for the future – when I'll need somebody, maybe when I'm old. Or should I be confident and just surge ahead and be my own master?

Certainly another relationship would be based quite differently. We would be individuals within that relationship. I am a person. I would never submerge myself again in a relationship. I don't think I'd be inclined to submerge my personality again. So if I went into another relationship, it would be an equal sort of thing. I wouldn't contemplate anything but an equal respectful sort of thing.

Many young households give the impression of being on a basis of perfect equality. But as long as the man retains economic responsibility for the couple, this is only an illusion – Simone de Beauvoir

---

I've become independent, my own person, and it means a lot to me. That's been a hard one, that has, and I value it. I wouldn't want to lose that. If I was to have a man living here or get married again, it would have to be on an equal basis where we were individuals. I wouldn't expect to take too much from him and I would hope that he wouldn't take too much from me. But whether two human beings can live like that, I don't know, because I think that people are inclined to take from each other. I don't know if you can have a totally balanced relationship, or whether it's the way of the world that one person submerges slightly to love a dominant partner. That's what bothers me. I don't know if I'm prepared to do that. I like being me – now that I am me – one hundred per cent. And that also makes me wonder whether I'm fit to live with any more. I'm no longer so flexible, although I'm more tolerant and more understanding. I'm not prepared to give up so much, you know. I'm not prepared to be the supportive partner in the sense of staying at home while the husband goes out and has all the fun. I don't think I want that really.

At the moment the idea of taking on anybody . . . well . . . I'm not terribly keen. Because it's far too complex and I'm not that sure of myself yet. Although I am standing on my own two feet, I'm much more cautious. One of the nice things about being young is you don't think about all the possible troubles. You just go into things. You don't think. If you thought, you'd never do it. If you thought what could happen in ten year's time, nobody would do anything. That's one of the nice things abut being young, that you don't realise what can go wrong. But one of the equally nice things when you're older is you can see what can happen if you take the wrong course of action. So I'd be a lot more careful now.

I'm extremely tolerant these days with men. They just come and go. I don't give them any trouble. I don't ask for anything, they don't ask for anything. I don't need anything, I don't want anything, I don't ask, so there's no pressure in it. A friend of mine thinks that I'm degrading myself. But on the other hand, if I don't feel degraded, I am not degraded by letting blokes just come and go. I don't mean hundreds: there's one or two who come, maybe stay the night, or watch television, have a beer and go home – see them next week or in three months time. That's the scene at the moment. My friend thinks I shouldn't let them do it, that there should be a deeper relationship. But I don't want it particularly. I don't care if I have it or not. I don't mind just going to bed with them. I quite enjoy it, you know. It's not absolutely fantastic, but it's quite pleasant. Sex is a passing pleasure. I'm like a contented cow chewing the cud at the moment. Nobody's bothering me. I'm not bothering anybody, and I'm okay.

Postscript

Eleanor's story is quite extraordinary in several respects – not least that her marriage went unconsummated for five years. That fact alone – not to mention the fact that she says her sexual relationship with her husband was later erratic and unsatisfying – makes some sense of the long-term, obsessional, degrading affair she carried on for half of her fifteen-year marriage, and about which, in retrospect she felt so guilty. The extent of the emotional dependence between herself and her husband was also extra-ordinary: so extreme that they both could endure a very long period of trauma and unhappiness before becoming able to bring themselves to break the 'parent/child' bond – for that is how Eleanor, at least, came to view their relationship. And the extent to which Eleanor 'broke down' after the separation, to which she was unable to cope at all initially, indicates the abnormal degree of dependence on her husband. This was a common reaction amongst the women in this book who split up and raises the question of how much women may be conditioned to be dependent, or how little they are conditioned to be independent. Eleanor is not uncommon amongst women in marrying young, substituting a husband for parents as emotional and economic support. (She was not untypical either in having nothing to do with earning any of the family living or handling family financial matters even when her husband seemed not very successful at it either.) Eleanor is unusual only in the extremes to which her need to be dependent drove her – and her husband.

For Eleanor splitting up eventually came to mean 'growing up' – 'I started to grow up and be a proper human being,' she says. It was almost as if growing up was delayed by marriage, as if marriage provided an escape from becoming independent. After splitting up, Eleanor says 'I've become independent, my own person and it means a lot to me.' Why didn't she do it earlier? Why does this happen to so many women?

What comes across very clearly in the interview and in Eleanor's response to it (in the introduction) is the extent to which she blames herself for the failure of her marriage – at least *feels* guilty, *feels* it was her fault, despite the fact that she *knows* her husband must also have been at least half responsible. She had some grounds for feeling guilty – in her affair and the way she handled it with her husband – but her response neverthe-less raises the question as to whether women are more conditioned to taking the blame? From the story it is clear that she and her husband were equally locked in a mutually damaging relationship. But Eleanor seems to have difficulty in appreciating this and still lets her guilt condition her life, eg. her confidence in forming other relationships. At the same time she has become aware of some of the patterns of her relationship with her husband and struggles to achieve a sense of security that she won't repeat them. Like most women left with children, Eleanor was ultimately admirable in shouldering the responsibility for looking after herself and her children and building a new and what she regards as better life. The loss of a certain kind of security in marriage – with the accompanying suffering and hardship – does not for Eleanor or for the other people who experience it, seem a high price to pay for the gains in personal growth. As Eleanor concluded: '. . . having come out of it all and having to be on my own and look after the kids, I'm a much better person now. Although it's been painful getting here, I feel that I am a much better person having been through it all, you know.'

2. Alec

Alec is working class. He lives in Luton in a council house with his two sons. He is a car worker at a local factory. He married in his mid-twenties. His wife left him twenty years later, leaving him with two children aged fourteen and ten. At the time of the interview he had been on his own for three years. He was in his late forties, both of his sons teenagers.

Among his 'likes' he describes meeting people, especially witty people, talking and discussion with intelligent people. He dislikes people who close their minds to anything new or radical without at least saying why. Part at least, of this 'world view' is a direct consequence of his situation which he says 'has opened my eyes to a new way of life. I think I'm a better person for it'.

He is now in a serious relationship and intends to remarry because 'I believe in making my position clear to society. I am awaiting completion of mortgage acceptance so that I can remarry. My fiancée is the teacher of whom I spoke in my interview. We require a larger house so that both families can live together. Also a fresh start was judged a better prospect: new partnership, new house, new beginning. The lady concerned has become very dear to me and has helped and guided me during some bad times. My children like her also.'

When I first met my wife, I'd just come out of the army. I was in my mid-twenties then. She was fairly young, about eighteen. She had come from a family . . . a step-mother and a father who had very little influence on her. He was a really repressed sort of man. He was very much under his second wife's thumb. My wife also was very much under her thumb. Her stepmother was very demanding, expected her to help with the younger children, expected her to be the little mother – she was very much repressed. What followed after, in our marriage, looking back on the thing, dates back to this.

We both worked in the local factory. I was a paint-sprayer and she was in the office. I used to see her come around the factory daily. Two girls came down daily, and me and my friend used to have lunch then. So we decided we'd go and chat them up one day, and take them out. So the first one came down, my wife, and I asked her for a date. And it went on from there. I found that I liked her very much. I've always been very much of an overbearing type – I tend to be a bit overpowering. And she'd always been a very quiet, shy, reserved little girl, you know, so whether I overwhelmed her or not, I don't know. Anyway, I went out with her, and then we got married. Her mother didn't take kindly to me, because we're both strong characters.

Anyway, I married my wife. Until then I was just a typical young fellow who was quite happy just going along, no worries, no cares. I thought whatever would happen would happen. This is quite common with young men. I've always been attracted to women like my wife – small, dainty, very, very feminine. And I've always been more of the traditionalist in male things . . . traditional roles, you know, the man and the housewife and that kind of thing. She keeps the house and I get the money. That was the pattern and I seemed quite comfortable and she seemed to fit in quite well.

We had a very quiet wedding. We had a honeymoon in the Cotswolds. Rained every day for a week. But we didn't care. And then we moved round from small flat to small flat, like, because we had very little money. We didn't live together before we got married. In those days . . . you know what things were like . . . it wasn't done. Of course, we were sleeping together before we got married, but weren't actually living together, you see. Anyway, we moved around from flat to flat for a while, until we scraped up enough money to buy a house. We lived in Dunstable for three years. It was a nice little house, but we didn't like it very much, and it was miles away from anywhere. It was a new estate, very quiet in the winter and very, very cold, but we had each other, and we had no children and no cares.

We were both still working down in Luton and we used to drive down every day so we spent very little time in the house, drove every morning to work. She worked just down the road from me, so we'd drive to work early in the morning and in the evenings after work I'd pick her up from where she worked and have a meal out, or go to the cinema. And then we'd drive back to the house, just to sleep there. We didn't see people a lot. Weekends we used to work a lot, because we had no children and the money wasn't too bad in those days. So we had a pretty good life.

Then I started getting asthma pretty bad. I know now, of course, it was because I was allergic to dogs – we had got a couple of dogs. It got really bad. I started to have injections. At the time we were living in a very damp area, very misty, very damp and very cold as well. So we decided to sell the house and moved in with *my* mother who lived in Luton. I suppose it seems silly – saving for a house and then selling it to live with the family. But I was a bit younger then, and I didn't look at it that way. The point was we didn't spend much time in that house. We spent a lot of time going out. My mother had a few spare rooms so we felt, why not move in with my mother? I didn't have, at the time, any idea what that would do to us. And it was convenient, and there seemed no other way. So we came back and lived with my mother and then we decided to start a family.

The housing scene can best be described as chaos – Rosemary Simon

My wife told me afterwards that she never really wanted to sell that house, that she didn't want to leave, but she didn't say it at the time. Or if she did say it, she didn't put it into words strong enough. *I* decided. I was very headstrong in those days. I've got more restraint now. Anyway, I decided, and we came back and were living with my mother. Of course, it's okay when you've just got two people living with a parent, but when there's three and one of them is a little child, that's when the complications start. We stayed with my mother for three years during which time we had our first child. Then we decided we'd have to get away and find someplace of our own. So we went to the council and were given a small house, not as big as the last one. By then it was lovely to get our own place. At my mother's was where we first started to have arguments. However, when we got our house, we were feeling very happy. At that time my wife wasn't working, and I was the sole support. We didn't have a lot, but we seemed to be happy, we seemed to have enough. We settled into a pretty conventional life. I was husband, she was mother and housewife. But we seemed very happy. At least I was, when the kids were young. I imagined my wife was too, but obviously she was looking at life from a different point of view than I was. Then our second boy came along – Derwent. I thought up the most of the names. Then we moved to another house nearby which was bigger.

The boys were getting bigger by this time and my wife decided she wanted to go out and work again, bring some money into the household. I thought this was a very good idea, I was quite in favour of it. So she went out working for a small local company, part-time, in the evening, checking records. And while she was there, she learned of vacancies in the Personnel Office, so she did that for a while. She's very good at that sort of thing – she was assistant to the manager there, a very good friend of mine at the time. Still working part-time, though eventually she was working full-time. The boys were between eight and twelve when she went working full-time in the office. Anyway, it came along then that the firm was moving from its place in Luton to its present address. And the manager, her direct boss, and my friend . . . he plays a big part in this . . . decided to take on pub work, hotel work. And he left. So, naturally the choice fell upon my wife to replace him. She was well qualified, she'd been at it for a long time, so they put her in his position. I don't think they gave her as much money for it. But to all intents and purposes she was running the office, doing his job, the supervisor.

In the meantime, this manager went into club work, know what I mean? You get the big fella, he's got a sports club, tennis court, bar, gym, that sort of thing and my friend's job was to run the bar and have groundsmen working for him. It was a place just outside Luton. We went across to see him a couple of times, to see how he was doing. And he was really working very hard. He usually had two people helping him but one hadn't turned up. So we helped out. I worked behind the bar, and my wife helped. He said I could do it regular and I said great. So every Saturday night for the next couple of years, I used to go down and help him out. And when he went on holiday I used to take over for him as relief steward and run the whole place myself for two weeks.

As a spin-off of this, there was a club next door that belonged to a big national building society. The steward was retiring there. It was very well paid and you got a house with it. I fancied that job very much. So I asked a friend if he could introduce me to a building society person, to see if I could get it. Of course we got a good report, good recommendation. One of the features I could see of moving was I could pack in this lousy job, get a nice club, with nice accommodation in a nice area, open spaces to bring my kids up in. But my wife was very interested in her job, getting very involved with it. And it was about this time that the arguments began to start. There were lots of things which began to cause this. My son, who was about eight, nine, started to get into trouble. We began to have lots of trouble with him. My wife was working long hours as well, and I was working long hours down at the club and in the old job, putting in lots of time. But despite this we had a pretty good life, a new car every few years, we went abroad every year for a holiday, we went to Malta. Everything seemed to be going well. We had no debts of any kind, we didn't need to borrow money. We had money in our pockets. But, as I say, she was working all the time – she used to work on Saturday afternoons, she used to work Sunday as well. And I got up and accused her of giving us up to be a success, even though I was the one who used to push her along. When she got the job as supervisor, she said she couldn't do it, and I said, 'You've got to push yourself, get hard and do it.'

Anyway, we were both still working Saturday nights at the club. She was helping out, but I used to do more than she did because she was not much interested in bar work – hard work, long work, but good money. She used to go and talk to the customers. A fella used to come into the bar and my wife used to meet him. I didn't take any notice – he seemed like quite a nice guy. I even went to his house a couple of times with him, and his wife – they'd been married about five or six months or so. We went out for dinner a couple of times with them to a restaurant. They used to embarrass us, him and his wife, they'd be arguing like mad. Not quite English, you know. We used to talk in whispers, especially eating out.

I couldn't see it, it was right in front of my eyes but I was right stupid. My wife seemed to think a lot of him. It occurred once we went over to his house, and my wife and he went off. I'd had a couple of drinks. I went upstairs and my wife and he came out of the bathroom together. She said, 'Oh, he was showing me the bathroom', but it didn't seem quite right to me, and I said so, and she said, 'Oh don't be stupid, getting silly ideas like that.' Well this carried on and then she refused to come down to the club any more.

I didn't think there was anything going on. It didn't occur to me. I never thought it would happen to me. So, I didn't see a thing. Well, by that time, there we were, working hard, arguing and she wasn't coming to the club. She said she didn't enjoy it as much. I said okay. She came around occasionally. But then, I noticed she suddenly started going out much more with her friends, or so she said. One night I came home around two o'clock. Club closed at eleven o'clock but I'd stayed to finish work and I'd got back around one or two o'clock. She was out, as she said she'd be, with some friends from the office. I didn't think much of it at the time, but then again it came to me later.

I worked over the summer holiday. And I'd come home and we'd have a lot of arguments. I'd say, 'For God's sake you're working too hard.' I said, 'Take a week off, I know a nice hotel in Southsea'. So in August she took off and went off for this week. I said, 'You don't have to work, just take the week off, get away from me and the boys.' I had the telephone number of this hotel. She'd gone on Saturday and on the Monday I decided to phone her up and see what she was doing. So I phoned this hotel, and they said, 'Oh, I'm sorry but she hasn't arrived'. And just then I knew it. I knew what was happening. And I felt sick. I said, 'Oh thank you' and put the phone down. At the time I didn't have a telephone in the house, but before she left I told her, 'You can phone me anytime at work. Phone about seven when there're fewer people there.' She phoned me on the Tuesday . . . I'm very embarrassed telling this . . . and I said, 'How is the hotel?' and she said, 'I didn't stop at the hotel, I didn't like it. I stayed there for a night, and I didn't like it.' So, not telling her I'd phoned that hotel . . . I don't know why! . . . I literally stood there and I shook and I trembled and I went sick. I made some noises . . . and anyway it's a hard thing to talk about. She didn't know then that I knew.

She phoned me again on the Wednesday night and I said, 'Where are you staying?' and she said, 'I don't know the name of the hotel, I only checked in tonight.' I said, 'Well give me the number there, I'll give you a call tomorrow night.' She said, 'No, I'll probably go to another hotel tomorrow night.' Anyway, she phoned me the next night and said, 'Alec I've got a lot of worries.' I said, 'If you're worried come on home', see. So she came back on the Friday, and came to the factory, and drove to the main gate and left a message she'd like to see me. So I came off the floor, took my towel, because I figured now she's come here, she's got something to tell me. She said, 'I'm infatuated with someone.' So I said, 'Is it Brian?' And she said, 'Yes, and I can't forget about him.' I said 'Thanks for telling me, I thought as much.' I said 'Fair enough, I'm glad you told me.'

We spent another week together and she said, 'I'll try and make up my mind.' And we spent a week together kissing and cuddling and all. And anyway, September came and went, October came and went, November . . . and I just couldn't leave it alone. I kept worrying about it and nagging her. I said, 'How are you getting along?' I was so foolish and stupid then, I can hardly believe it now. You know, saying 'Are you getting over it?' And all that crap, you know what I mean? I was worried, I wanted reassuring, you see. She said, 'Leave it alone, let me get over it on my own now, my own way.' I never wanted to lose her.

Anyway, we'd been having arguments, lots and lots of arguments. And then Christmas came – it wasn't a very happy time for me. We'd had a lot of arguments before, and I criticised her Christmas dinner. And she said, 'Listen, I'm sick and fed up with your problems.' I said, 'Whatever you do, don't leave me. Don't leave me, whatever it takes, I'll make it up to you.' I suppose I don't have a great amount of tact, and I'm a bit heavy-handed at times. I used to think you can do anything if you love someone and you belong to them, that it will all come out all right in the end, you see.

Anyway, after Christmas I wanted to speak to her one afternoon. It wasn't the usual thing to call her at work, because she was pretty busy and I was pretty busy as well. So I called her up and said, 'Can I speak to Chris please.' 'No, she's not in, she took the day off.' Bloody fuck, she didn't tell me about it. So I went home and when I came home she arrived about twenty minutes after me. So I said, 'Oh there you are, you must have lots and lots of work.' So I questioned her and said 'You haven't been to the bloody office, you've been out all day.' Anyway, when I got it out of her, it turns out she'd been out with this guy Brian and it turned out he'd been driving up from Hemel Hempstead to see her. She'd been seeing him all this time, but I had kind of figured they hadn't, that they wouldn't.

I mean, look, he lived thirty miles away, he wasn't the guy next door, he wasn't in her office, he's not quite a daily contact. So to see each other you've got to make a conscious effort. He lived thirty miles down on the M1 motorway, and that's a lot of heavy traffic, so you got to get up and do it. So they'd seen each other quite a few times, for lunch up here, or she'd go down to see him, because in her job she has to go out a bit and see people in this area. Or consider, I was talking to a girl at the Christmas party and she said to me, 'How's Chris coming along?' and I said 'fine'. And I remembered, a couple of days before she said, 'I've got to go down to St Albans tomorrow, I got to go down to Phillip's office and see how it's getting on.' But I saw Phillip at the Christmas party and he said, 'I've not seen Chris for some time.'

Looking back, she must have been using these things as excuses. Also, I'm one of those guys, when I get in my car I automatically look at the speedometer, I can't help it. I check speedometers, I check all those kinds of things. From my house to her work was about four miles, twenty or so miles a week. Well, she was coming out with something closer to fifty. So I just mentioned it – 'You do a lot of miles these weeks', and she said, 'Yeah, I'm driving around a lot.' So I assumed . . . But all these little things built up and built up. Then we had this big bust up when she'd been seeing him. And that was the only time, that I'd ever struck her; I'm not a great one for violence with women. I felt terrible.

There's a point to this, you see. When I confronted her with this, that she'd been seeing him, I said, 'Right, I'm going to go in there and sort him out, I'm going to give him a real good dusting over.' I'm just a working class male character you know . . . So anyway, she's begging me and pleading me not to go down there, and I said, 'Does his wife know about it?' And she said, 'Of course, yes his wife knows.' So I decided not to go. Now I wish I had gone, you know. We continued after for a few more days, and she was really bitter and really mean. Then my birthday came along and she gave me a present. That was the thirteenth of January and on January the fourteenth I came home and looked on my dresser and there was a note up there saying she's left me, she's gone. I wanted to try and find her. She said she'd be gone for a few days to try and sort herself out. I was really upset. I went around, tried to find her, couldn't find her, didn't know where she was staying.

And then a couple of days later on I came home, and all her clothes had gone. She took things like her clothes, she took the sewing machine, she took the cook books. She took everything she'd collected – all the presents she'd been given, everything she'd ever had, you know. At that time I found out she was staying at a friend's, at a woman's whom we all called dirty Doris – because of her personal habits, her sexual habits. My wife had struck up a close friendship with this woman from the office, this dirty Doris. I couldn't understand why my wife who was fastidious, neat and particular, why she was knocking around with this dirty Doris. She had a flat somewhere local. And I went down there to see her. My wife didn't know that I was coming, see, so I went up and knocked on the door. Doris opened the door and she said, 'Oh, it's you Alec.' I said, 'Yeah, I want to see Chris.' 'Well, you can't see her she's not here.' I said, 'She is here, I know she's here.' She walked back into the passageway and I followed her in. I walked into the kitchen and there was my wife and there was this guy Brian. I don't know why, it spread across me. I banged him, I put him on the floor. I was glad that part was over.

Then I started talking to my wife and I was weeping, I was upset, trying to get her to come back with me. And she said, 'No, now I'm never coming back with you, look at what you've done.' So I left, I came back home. I continued trying, I phoned her at work. She'd speak to me a little bit, but said 'No, I'm not coming back with you' and not to try and see her again. Anyway this went on for a couple of months, then I found out she'd left Doris's and gone to live with this Brian. His wife had left so there she is living in this guy's house, to this day.

His wife subsequently divorced him. And I divorced my wife. For a couple of years I couldn't believe this had happened. I kept trying to get her back. Two or three times she said she'd come back and one time she actually came back, and stayed for about twenty minutes . . . one snowy morning. And I remembered she said she didn't want any arguments with me, she wanted me to like her. She said, yes she still loved me, and yes she missed the boys. And she came back and she stayed for about twenty minutes and said 'I can't stay any longer', then she left. I saw her again about six months later, and she agreed she would try again. And that fell through as well. So there we are.

The legal system is a tangle of contradictions with different courts working to completely different rules – Rosemary Simon

---

First of all, my sons were very upset but they didn't show it very much. It came as a shock to them. They knew we were having problems but they didn't know it was as bad as all that. They're very quiet boys and don't show much and I was going through a very rough period myself at that time. I was disrupted in myself. I was worried about them, but I was more concerned with my own cares, my own worries, my own miseries, you know what I mean? I was drinking quite heavily then. But we – the boys and I – came to some sort of working relation, where I'd take over my wife's work and when I was on the late shift I'd cook something for 'em and leave it out – I'd cook it earlier. They used to get themselves up in the morning, I used to leave alarm clocks for them, and they became very self-reliant, which they still are now. I mean they have to be. We were not very close before mind, well not that close, but they were very helpful and they were my responsibility. And one thing – it's drawn me and the boys much closer together. We are very close now. They don't see their mother very much.

They didn't see her for the first three months. And then she used to come and visit them. This was before it was made legal by court. She used to come visiting when I was out of the house. She would come down and see them in the day, and if I was on the late shift she'd come and see them in the mornings, before she went to work. Then one day she said she couldn't come and see them any more – she'd left her flat and she'd moved down to Hemel Hempstead. Though she still travelled up here for her job. And we made arrangements, when I got custody of the boys, she asked to see them twice a week – when we got to court – Tuesdays and Thursdays. There was no question of her having custody. She left them. I said, 'There's no way you're going to have them, I mean no way at all', and she didn't press it. She could've pressed it, she might have got 'em, you know what courts are like. As I said, she made noises, but even now she doesn't really want them. That's it basically. 'Cause now, I mean, after the divorce we came to an agreement. I mean, at one time I said, 'There's no way they – I mean the boys – are going to stay at his house. He's got my wife and there's no way he's going to enjoy my boys.' So I said, 'You can see them as much as you like, but you're not to take them in his company, or I shall kill him.'

Anyway, after about a year and a half, when we were getting the divorce, I realised that they need their mother as much as I need them, you see. It was half intuition, and I was advised by my friends that it would be better if she got a life of her own and I had my life. So I gave my consent that she could have them at weekends. So when we went to court she asked if she could see them Tuesdays, I said, 'You can see them any time, from when you finish work, whenever it is. And every third weekend you can have them for a weekend.' And this is what she's done.

We've been divorced since last May. And we've been separated since . . . going on three years now. It works out now that she sees them for twenty minutes on Tuesday, she comes round at half-past five and leaves by six o'clock. She sees them about one weekend in four and she has them about every two months. She doesn't take advantage of the full access. Quite often she rings up and says, 'I can't take them this weekend because I've got company coming,' or 'I've got diarrhoea or flu', or 'We've got to go there, we've got to go here', you know. Or, in actual fact she sees them less than she could. I've been told by a lady friend of mine that it might be because her boyfriend is much younger than she is, about eight years younger. It might be the fact that she's a small attractive woman, and looks much younger than her age. It might be an embarrassment for her to be with a son much taller than her. I don't know about these things, you know, from a feminine point of view. As far as I know though, she's never taken them on weekends when any of her friends are around. And she just has them in her house. She never takes them around to their friends.

Although my wife was giving me some money for the support of the children, I wanted it fixed, I wanted it legal, so there would be no arguments, so she couldn't turn it off whenever she felt like it. So I decided to sue her for maintenance, the same way a woman sues a man for maintenance. And I did so, successfully. But I was told by my solicitor, by the way, that if the situation had been reversed she would have got much more from me than I'd got from her. I got what I got, the basic support, two pound fifty per child per week, which is nothing for teenage children, nothing you understand. I felt very strongly about that, but going on the advice of my solicitor, who I respect, if I had pushed for more, I might not have got it. I feel very strongly about it though. This is one area in which I feel men are discriminated against. We're discriminated against in the fact that if it comes to a court case on the custody of the children, it's ten to one against the man. And the man can be just as good a parent and mother, as the mother, when it comes to it they can.

However, I found that I was being taxed on this maintenance as unearned income, which is wrong. Now I knew you could challenge the Inland Revenue on this, and I did that. It took a period of time, it took about a year altogether and in the end I had to go to a judge in Chambers to get him to amend the order so the maintenance is paid to the children and not to me. I still think it is wrong, you shouldn't be taxed on this money. So I was getting a fiver a week and getting taxed on it, and she was getting a tax rebate on it because she was declaring it as a tax expense. I think it's all wrong.

About three months after our first separation I was feeling really down. I was talking with a guy from work, telling him about what happened, and he said 'Why don't you come down with me to Gingerbread?' I had never heard of Gingerbread. This guy was divorced, but I hadn't known that before. Funny, isn't it? No one knows. So the first night I went along with him to a Gingerbread party and all these people were like me and they were all happy. I talked to them and from then on I got more and more involved with Gingerbread. I joined the group and in about two or three months I was Social Secretary and about four months after that I was Chairman. I found that I had overcome loneliness by going to work and running the house but that wasn't enough. Gingerbread was the best thing for me, as far as I was concerned, they were really great. You meet all kinds of people, but they are really great. It's also like a lot of other things, I find, the more you put into it, the more you get out of it. And I put a lot into it, I did a lot of organising and I did a lot of fund-raising and I found it was the answer to all my depression. When I got into it, the group was going through a bad time, and I put a lot of energy into rebuilding it.

I've got a bigger circle of friends now, what I consider real friends, than I ever had before. One of the real disappointments to me was when you're separated or divorced, you seem to be a bit of a leper. People just do not want to know. I've got in-laws, and I've not seen them since the day I was separated. My sons get Christmas cards from them, but I don't. And like when I needed a rest – I'd been looking after the boys seven days a week, working all the time and I was going through a real depression – and I said I really needed someone to take them for a weekend, and they didn't. They wouldn't do it for me, and I mean, they're family. They've never come to say can we help you out. My mother-in-law and my father-in-law – I've never seen them at all since the day we were separated. My boys, they go to school four streets away from where their grandma and grandpa live. And they don't see them. As far as I'm concerned they can stick their Christmas cards and their money, know what I mean? What's between me and my ex-wife is our business, it's nothing to do with my boys, know what I mean? That sickened me. But these Gingerbread people, they would always help me, I could go and knock on their door at two or three o'clock in the morning and they would help me. I mean, they are real friends. They haven't got any money, but they're willing to help me out, and I want to do the same for other people in that position. They're really great.

We have been struck by the evidence of how universally the division of labour is taken for granted by which mothers and fathers in the two-parent family seek to enrich the upbringing of their children by extending their range of activities . . . Even at the level of disposing of the everyday chores, and despite the degree of merger between the traditional roles of male and female which has taken place in the last decade, many household tasks still tend to be allocated sexually. Men mend fuses and women do the ironing . . . – 'The Finer Report, 1974'

Some people regard my situation as a disaster, but I don't. It's opened my eyes to a new way of life, it's taught me a tremendous amount of self-reliance. I didn't know how much I relied on my wife. I didn't even know how to run the washing machine. I just didn't bloody know! I went upstairs to get the instructions because I just couldn't cope, I couldn't solve it. I was a soldier for a time so I thought myself competent but I just couldn't cope. I've had to learn a lot of new skills I never had before. I think I'm a better person for it. And it's taught me a lot of humility. One thing I've learned is that there is a lot more to being a housewife than I thought. The daily round of housework is completely boring, depressing and completely mind-destroying – I can appreciate that now. I didn't know it before, and now I look at the house in a completely different way. I used to sit down and relax, now I sit down and think, oh that needs doing, or that needs dusting. It's an enormous job, it's a twenty-four-hour job. I didn't know it. I know it's a funny thing to say but I'm glad I've gone through the experience I've had. I would not like to go through the bad times again, but I've learned so much.

Now, for example, nothing can frighten me at all. Unless anything happened to my boys, nothing in this world could frighten me. Because I've gone through the worst experience in my life and I've come out the other side and I feel better for it. I feel strong, self-reliant, a better person. Looking back on the person I was before – I didn't smoke or drink – I know it's very moralistic. And I used to believe she was everything a man ever wanted. But now I smoke and drink, and I lead a more complete life. My morals are shocking – why don't you enjoy it and have a good time? I said. I didn't realise it, but I was sliding into middle-aged ways. I was a typical man, used to sit back and watch television. That was my life, but now, I think I've watched television about twice in two years. Honestly, literally. I'm more aware now, like, of what's going on in the outside world. I mean, I work with a group of men and I look at them and I say to myself, you silly sods, you're knackered, you don't know nothing, know what I mean? I feel sorry for them. I mean, you've got to have a conversation about more than what's on the telly, or football. I mean their one topic of conversation is intoxication, fornication and speculation, I mean there's more to life than that, isn't that true? These are supposedly happily married men but I mean they're not really happily married men are they? I mean I've had more experience in the last two years than I'd had in a lifetime. They feel sorry for me and I feel sorry for them. They don't realise it, but I'm in touch with things, I'm having a good life. And so are my boys.

I must admit that when we first broke up my eldest boy went through a very bad time. He's a very quiet boy, or at least he used to be, and a very clever boy and I'm pleased he wants to be a dentist. He went through a bad time though and he got in trouble with the police a couple of times for some bits and pieces. Around here it's a tough area at times, and he got in with a bad crowd. I think he's out of that you know, he's gone through that. I think he was hitting out at the world, you know what I mean? However, since being in Gingerbread he's found out there's loads of kids in the same position as him, loads of them have only one parent. My younger boy took it much better. There's not the stigma that was attached to it he thought there was. He doesn't worry much about it any more. He's learnt there's a lot more kids like him, as I say. They seem quite happy with the situation as it is and seem quite happy to see her once or twice a week. She buys all this kind of crap and gives it to them but I try to tell her you can buy people things, but the most precious thing you can give is time. It doesn't matter what hour, if they've got a problem, they come and see me. I take them out – we go skating, we go swimming, though not as much as we'd like to. I like to involve the boys.

We took everything in stages. First there was the year of the separation, and then the divorce proceedings when everybody was making appearances in court about access and all that. I told them exactly what was happening at every stage. But for two years, she never told 'em she was living with another fellow. For two and a half years she never gave them her home telephone number. If you wanted to get in touch with her, you had to ring her at work. She was always a secretive type. I could never understand why. I actually think this has been a good thing for them. My boys have friends who can't do anything. I mean we've had boys around here, big boys who can't even cook a meal. I mean some of those boys can't even cook a beefburger. Both my boys can do that. They can cook, dress, and they're both in the Scouts. The older one has been abroad a lot . . . he's been to France, Germany, Copenhagen. That boy would survive anywhere. I mean he can take care of himself, and the young one is going the same way now. We have a set ration of jobs – Mondays, Wednesdays and Fridays – when we have to do certain jobs in the house. I say, 'Listen, there's three of us in this house, three of us make a mess, three of us are going to clean it up.' So I give them jobs according to their ability and if they want they can do more. One does the vacuuming, one does the washing up, they clean the bathtub after they've had a bath, we take turns with the ironing. I tell them if their clothes are left on the floor of their bedroom, they're going to bloody stay there. I'll wash their clothes if they're in the dirty clothes bin, anything else gets left. They're okay about it. You don't have to tell them these things, they know. Okay, they're kids, they forget, but basically they're good about it.

When I got married, I had a very fixed idea about how things should be done. I wouldn't go into another marriage with those ideas again. I mean there's still some jobs that are traditionally male – like mending cars and that sort of thing, which men are better at. And I still can't sew. I mean I throw things away now and buy a new one rather than mend it. I just don't like sewing, my fingers are not nimble enough. But there's no other reason, you know what I mean? I can cook, I can iron, I can clean. I can do the shopping, I can arrange the meals, I can cook the meals, know what I mean? If the woman was earning more than me, I would have no compunction about staying at home and running the house – none at all. And I would expect she could share the traditionally male things – she could do it as well as me. We could both paint, for example. I find I get turned on by intelligence. Most of my friends are teachers. Intelligent, know what I mean? Because I just get bored very quickly with women who have nothing to say. I like a good discussion, very much so, I very much enjoy that.

I think marriage is a wonderful thing and I would marry again. But I wouldn't have the same pattern of marriage at all. I've learned a lot. I've been going out for quite a while with a woman who's been divorced now for eight years. She's got her own house. And, obviously, we've discussed marriage but we keep our lives separate. She's got two children. I admire her a lot. Her husband left her and he hasn't seen his children now for about a year and a half and you know where he works? He works in a home for deprived children! But this is the thing, her husband left her, so there she was, she didn't know what she was going to do. She said, 'I've got to look after my kids', and the only thing she could think of doing was a teaching job. So she studied for three years on a student loan. Raising three kids on her own, buying clothes out of jumble sales, eating cheap meals. She showed a lot of strength of purpose. And now she's qualified and got a good teaching career. She's getting pretty good money, she's got her own house now. She's really stood on her own, she's self-reliant which I really admire. I admire her very much for what she's done. She's really strong and I've got a lot of love for her. She's got a lot of love for me and she's a great believer in Feminism. I've become a great believer in that too. Which would never have happened if my wife hadn't left. I'm a new man.

Postscript

Of all the men who tell their stories in this book, Alec comes across as one of the most truly amazing, not only in being able to analyse and articulate his experience (which the men seem to find more difficult than the women, whatever their class), but also in being able to act upon it. He was almost totally transformed by splitting up and profoundly liberated by the experience: 'I'm a new man.' He could be described in his first marriage almost as a classic male chauvinist, with fixed and rigid ideas about what a husband ought to do (work) and what a wife ought to do (housework). He described himself as 'a traditionalist in male things, traditional roles.' And he and his wife settled into a conventional marriage in which the main ethic was work and earning. He was 'happy' then with putting his feet up in front of the telly and having his food served to him.

Splitting up so much 'opened my eyes to a new way of life' that he is now planning to marry a Feminist (with the emphasis on a capital F). His views have altered radically: 'Now I would be quite happy to stay home and look after the house,' he said. Some of the potential for this transformation was apparent in his marriage in which there were obviously contradictions. Though he held traditional views, on several occasions he pushed his wife into independence, encouraging her to work when she wanted to, pushing her to take on promotion. So the later changes do not come as a total surprise, but they were remarkable and would seem to indicate that men are often as trapped as women by their male conditioning and roles.

There are two aspects to Alec's situation that are interesting and not uncommon. One was the extent to which he pulled the wool over his own eyes with regard to his wife's affair, refusing to see what was under his nose, almost a willful refusal to accept what was happening. This would seem to be more common with men than women. Another was the trauma he experienced in splitting up, quite as severe as that experienced by Eleanor and others in this book, indicating the degree of his dependence on his relationship with his wife. Finally, there was the help he received from joining Gingerbread – both practical and emotional. For Alec, as for other single parent men (more often than for women), Gingerbread proved instrumental in helping him get back on his feet and opening the doors to his new world. 'I've got a bigger circle of friends now, what I consider real friends, than I ever had before.'

3. Christine

Christine comes from a middle-class background. She married at twenty and separated at thirty with one infant and one under-five. She lives in her own house in Bristol – 'inherited' in the divorce. At the time of the interview she had been on her own for a year. She has now been separated for four years. She was in her mid-thirties and both children were finally at school. She felt she had survived the worst, raising the youngest to school age.

Her husband left her for another woman in what she describes as a traumatic experience – 'a kind of death'. But followed by a 'rebirth'. She is now involved in a serious relationship, but is still ambivalent about marriage – intimidated by the institution and its political implications. She says she would consider remarrying, but it would be for very different reasons and certainly not the need for emotional or economic dependence. She feels she has thrived on single parent independence.

Of her situation now, she says: 'I am a completely different person now than when I was married. I look almost unrecognisably different (ie. better), behave differently and feel differently. I feel I have become a person for the first time in my life and I am profoundly grateful to have had that opportunity, however painful the process. I pity a lot of married people because I feel that they have had to compromise their personal growth, or more often than not, the wife has had to compromise hers to enable her husband's. I am happy and my children are happy. We are a stable three-person family, as stable as any nuclear family. It makes me angry to read about 'problem children' from 'broken homes'. It's just not true. If anything, my children are nicer than nuclear family children. I feel that I have learned a lot and am confident of being able to give and to grow in my present relationship. My only regret is that it took me so long to "grow up", that in some ways, ten years of my life was wasted.'

'I must confess to being rather confused at the moment. Because I have met someone whom I love very deeply and whom I feel I would like to marry. I have to set this against my very positive feelings about myself in the past three years and what I suppose you could call my sexual political views about marriage. Basically, there is a conflict at the moment between what I think and what I feel. I don't know how this will be resolved. I rather look forward to finding out!'

I got married when I was twenty. Simon was twenty-one . . . only six months between us, so we were virtually the same age. And in retrospect *much* too young to get married. It's a matter of being wise after the fact, and it's impossible to tell anyone who wants to get married, at whatever young age, that it's better to wait until later. But looking back I feel that I 'matured' (ie. grew to know myself and what I wanted out of life) between the ages of twenty-five and thirty, and looking about me, I felt that this seemed to be true of a lot of people. Simon matured in the same way, and in the process of growing to know ourselves, just growing individually, we grew apart, I think, looking back. It isn't 'till after you split up that you begin to see things clearly; at the moment, at the time, you have such a vested interest in the marriage, such an investment in it (in your mutual relationship and commitment, in children, house, friends, the whole paraphernalia) that you can't afford to see things clearly. If you start questioning one thing, it calls into question the whole structure and fabric. So you bury your head, turn a blind eye . . .

We got divorced after ten years of marriage. I was thirty, with two young children. And so innocent – in every respect – at living, managing, everything – even sexually, I think. The break-up of the marriage was extremely traumatic. It was a kind of death. But it was also a rebirth. For the first time in my life I feel myself, that I can be myself. It's been like shedding weights, stripping away layers, a great burden has been removed. And I thought I had a happy marriage!

Looking back, I try to see why I married Simon. And I think it was to escape – living at home, parents, problems there, but also myself – setting off and setting up on my own. At the time I thought I was in love. And I'm sure I was in many ways. But looking back, I can see the signs and symptoms, even at that time which I ignored, which betrayed my uneasiness, how I was fooling myself. I'd had an unusually stormy adolescence – a strong, wild streak in me, unusually rebellious. And at the same time an excessive dependency on my parents. The two were in conflict. My parents never approved of my boyfriends – they worried, they worried me. There were incredible scenes, rows. I wanted them to approve, but they never did. I had a really passionate love affair between the ages of eighteen and twenty – first love – and all that implies. But my parents' disapproval of that was just about more than I could take. The relationship broke up and that left me feeling dreadfully wounded. My parents' satisfaction with that, their complete lack of understanding as I perceived it, really drove me into myself and away from them.

I left home, left university. I was a drop-out. That must have been a piece of subconscious revenge against my parents, as they valued education above everything else. I left Leicester and went to London – to be a copy-typist. I wanted to get away, to be free. Like Dylan Thomas's young man in *Portrait of an Artist as a Young Dog* I wanted to sit in my equivalent of Paddington Station and let life's winds drift me as they would. I wanted to stop doing everything I was 'supposed' to be doing – to be free and independent. And I felt I had to leave home to do it.

Given that I felt so strongly, I often wonder why I did precisely the opposite. I met Simon the first day I was in London and we immediately became inseparable. He was a very nice guy – really nice. Kind, thoughtful, gentle. Very unlike the kind of macho, tough sort of men I'd known, men whose so-called 'virility' really turned me off when I eventually discovered, as I did, that it was extremely superficial. Here was a man who didn't need all the superficial paraphernalia of virility to be a strong male personality. And he fell in love with me; and he looked after me. Which was, paradoxically, just what I needed and just what I didn't need. What I mean is that I very much needed looking after – I needed the security of my parents, that I'd left behind. That need was close to the surface and Simon responded to it. He needed someone who needed him. I was ideal. Obviously, it would have been better for me in the long run if I'd had the chance, or taken the chance then, to learn to stand on my own two feet, as they say. But we got very comfortably involved; he fell in love; he wanted to marry me (at least that's how I remember it, though I'm a bit hazy about exactly what happened during that time) and I didn't want to hurt him. And then I thought, why not? He was really nice, he was a postgraduate student, obviously destined for a career with a secure future (in fact, just like the world I'd grown up in). I didn't consciously think this guy's a 'suitable' husband – never! But I'm sure that must have coloured my feelings, and my thinking indirectly. And we decided to get married. Full stop.

I say full stop, because once the decision was taken, agreed, whatever, that was that. No further consideration was given; no second thoughts were allowed. Which is stupid when you stop to think. Because there *were* second thoughts, and a really profound uneasiness. I can see that now. But it was never allowed into conscious consideration. We got engaged and then we got married – to live happily ever after, I guess. I know I hadn't got any idea whatsoever what marriage might mean, just never gave a thought to anything.

Looking back, I think there were any number of signposts if I'd wanted to take any notice. Sex, for example. I was never passionately in love with Simon. I thought it didn't matter. I'd been passionately in love before and it had got me nowhere, except into misery. I guess something happened in my head to decide to cancel out the wilder side of myself. Settle down – ignore the parts of my nature which caused problems.

Simon and I were apart for a year before we got married, and for the first and only time in my life I suffered from acute attacks of anxiety – really severe, requiring medical treatment. At the time I put it down to overwork; in retrospect I think it was my body trying to tell me to think about what I was doing. And I had a really strange recurring dream: I'd left my car in the college car park, and I was frantically running from class to class, rush, rush, finish, finish. And then suddenly I'd remember that I'd left 'my baby' in the car. And I would be overcome with panic, rush to the car to try to feed it, nourish it before it had died from my neglect. And always the baby was Simon in miniature – in nappies. At the time, I interpreted it to mean that I was really risking my relationship with Simon during the long separation. Later, when the pattern of our marriage was established, I knew, too, that the image of Simon as a helpless baby was partly, paradoxically, how I saw and perceived him, even from the beginning.

The available information about the number, structure and needs of (one-parent) families is very inadequate – 'The Finer Report, 1974'

Anyway, we got married. Traditional white malarchy. All I can remember is being excruciatingly uncomfortable and embarrassed.

I couldn't wait for it all to be over. I felt utterly ridiculous in the white dress, veil, flowers, what all – like I was in a costume, acting a part in a play. The white wedding was for my mother.

Simon and I settled into a pattern of life to which we gave very little thought. And for that we paid the consequences in years to come. How two intelligent people could have been so stupid about their own lives I don't know. I do remember that at the end of the first year there was a big row, over money because we were seriously overdrawn. I was very upset. Before that I hadn't paid much attention to money matters and was not really interested. In my family my father had always looked after the money. I think women are brought up to let men manage money. Simon and I then worked out a budget and I made sure that we stuck to it, though Simon remained responsible for the breadwinning. It was quite a few years further on before I realised the nasty contradictions of that – of my economic dependence on him.

Anyway, I did all the usual wifely things, like cooking and cleaning and washing and ironing. I remember, occasionally, and especially at first, thinking it was all very strange and amusing and feeling like I was play-acting. Here I am, sort of thing, housewife hanging Persil white sheets on the line. And I was certainly play-acting in bed. From my point of view our sexual relationship was disappointing from the very beginning. I remember turning over frustrated time after time, crying myself to sleep. Thinking it was my fault – that I was past it (at twenty-one!) perhaps, telling myself it didn't matter. Sex was always very missionary, and we didn't talk about it. I thought it would hurt Simon's feelings if I said something was wrong, that it wasn't all wonderful.

The first four years passed pretty uneventfully. Then we decided to have a baby. A mutual, conscious decision which I think must have been a bit along the lines of – it's about time, if we're going to have children, better do it now. Before that, children had never entered my mind, either positively or negatively. They were completely irrelevant. When I thought about it, though, I rather fancied the idea, and it seemed a good time. Simon had just got a very good job as an engineer in the aerospace industry and we'd moved to Bristol. I'd got a part-time job with a publisher. It was something I could go back to.

We had the baby – with difficulty. In the end it was a forceps delivery. Our great anticipation of sharing the birth of our baby turned into a nightmare. And I remember waking up in hospital the morning after the night before, looking at the baby in its cot and being overcome with panic – there she was and she was never ever going to go away. It seemed a terrible responsibility and I felt completely inadequate. But that was a typical result of never having given the realities much thought. I know I would never have changed my mind if I'd had it to do over again – it just would have been nice to have been a bit better prepared by having given some thought to the implications. Whether that is me, or typical of human nature, I don't know.

Shortly after the baby was born, we decided we'd better move out of our small flat and into a house. So there we were, new baby, new house, and for me new work. Life got very hectic. Time got eaten up, as it had for the first four years, but now with busyness. I remember enjoying sex for the first and last time during my pregnancy. I felt uninhibited and carefree then. Maybe because of being pregnant, not having to worry about getting pregnant. After the baby, sex hit an all-time low for me. I put it down to work and tiredness. All true, but obviously, in retrospect, excuses. What sex there was was completely unsatisfactory for me. For Simon? I don't know. I never asked. He never said. But then he never asked. And I never said. By this time I'd given up, again without giving it much thought. I even gave up pretending. Never even bothered to get started, as it were, because I knew it would all end in frustration. Being passive became a protective habit.

When Allison was two years old, we were hit by a real bombshell. I had an affair. I don't know why. I loved Simon. I was just overcome, overwhelmed. Pure passion. For a few months Eric and I saw a lot of each other, we were very attracted to each other. But I was frightened by the whole business. I didn't know what had come over me. I was so taken with the guy. I was terrified what it might mean to Simon, to our marriage. Then it got to the point where I knew nothing was going to stop me. I needed to have the affair at whatever cost; and I did. It was a strange period of time. I'd get home at all hours and Simon would never ask any questions. I think he must have just been turning a blind eye out of self-protection. At the time I thought he knew and didn't care. I didn't ever really question why I was doing it. I felt incredibly guilty and hated myself for what I was doing. But I did it and about the only charitable thing I could say for myself was that the affair was a symptom of things that were seriously wrong between me and Simon.

And I got very angry with Simon. Curiously, I told him more than once in words of one syllable – usually during rows – that I was sleeping with Eric. But he never seemed to take it in, which made me angrier. Finally, I sat him down and told him. I'll never forget the look in his eyes. I'd hurt him so much I was terrified. He made me promise to end it. I promised. What else could I do? I didn't end it straight away, but gradually. Once he knew, Simon asked if I would go to see a marriage guidance counsellor with him. I agreed. It seemed unreasonable not to. My heart wasn't in it – but at the same time it was. I didn't want the marriage to break up.

It was about this time that something else snapped in me. Over a couple of years my part-time work had increased until it was nearly full-time, at least much of the time. But we were in the typical marriage rut of conventional roles. Suddenly I thought, here I am being a full-time wife and mother and a full-time worker. I got very angry. By what right should Simon have himself serviced – food, clothes, the lot. It was the first time I'd ever looked at marriage *per se* seriously, at roles, etc. During the time we saw the marriage guidance counsellor we talked through the roles. I thought it was degrading to both of us to be living the way we did. For myself I felt it was unfair, that I was effectively mothering this man (and thought more than once of the dream). For his part, I thought it must be really humiliating and degrading, if you stopped to think about it, to be a man and to be serviced, to be treated as if you were helpless in providing your basic needs.

Simon seemed to see things similarly and we radically altered the way we lived. We shared most of the 'marriage' work (ie. house, child, etc.). In retrospect I think I was still 'responsible' for the traditional female roles, and Simon remained responsible for the traditional male ones – that the changes were scratching the surface. Certainly, Simon remained the breadwinner. My earnings were not very large or regular or reliable. Simon's was the secure, larger income – mine was still pin money. In retrospect I think we had to, if we really did – as we did – want to equal out roles and responsibilities – to divide equally the responsibility for earning a living. That we never did; that was a big mistake. At that point, I think we just patched up our marriage. Though at the time, we didn't see it as patching; we saw it as totally cured. I think we both did. We got into the idea of 'open marriage' as expounded by a couple of Americans in their book of that title. For me the argument went – I loved Simon, but I needed the relationship with

Eric, that was certain. And it would have been a mistake, I thought, to say no to that. But I didn't want to break up the marriage. The O'Neills outlined a concept of marriage which said both partners should have the right to grow, that as long as you remained open about it, as long as you acknowledged, nourished and maintained a primary relationship, then secondary relationships need not threaten the primary relationship – the marriage. Each partner individually, both partners, collectively, and the marriage itself would be strengthened by allowing for outside relationships of all kinds – from friendships to and including sexual friendships.

Simon and I both thought we were launched into a new life. We used to joke about when he would meet his Eric! But our sex life was still lousy. That was what we should have been talking to the marriage guidance counsellor about, what we avoided like the plague, both talking about and doing anything about. We had sex more and more infrequently. There was a lot of under-the-surface tension. We buried ourselves, both of us, in work, in friends, in our child. Desperately trying to escape, I think, from what was wrong, whatever it was. The new life was an intellectual thing, not an emotionally experienced one. I found myself in a state of perpetual irritation with Simon – in retrospect I reckon much out of sexual frustration. Nagging. I don't know.

I'd always been a very strong personality, though very insecure underneath. Simon had to deal both with the dominating and the insecurities, which was not particularly fair. But he seemed to bring out the worst in me, and I, indeed, in him. For he became increasingly quiet, unassertive, withdrawn, timid. But we chuntered, blinkered, on. Happy, unhappy, I don't think we thought about it. I don't think we could afford to.

Combining work and motherhood is utterly exhausting. It is difficult enough when you have a husband who is willing to share the chores. When you are alone, there will be times when you will almost collapse from the strain – Rosemary Simon

---

There was a time about a year after the trauma to our marriage of my affair when I think it seemed to both of us we were going to make a transition – consciously. I decided to get a full-time, well-paid job. We talked a lot about me supporting us, and Simon taking a year, at least, off to write a book he wanted to write. I guess I felt a couple of things – that I was fairly fulfilled in my work, that Simon wasn't. I also thought, in fairness, I should earn the living. I applied for a job, and just as I was offered it, I discovered I was pregnant! The pregnancy came as a total surprise.

As I say, we had sex irregularly. I had no desire to get pregnant – though I guess I always had half in my mind, wanting another child. We were irregular about sex, and we were irregular about contraception. Who knows what goes on subconsciously? You know what people say about pregnancy never being accidental. Anyway, on one of the few occasions that we had sex, Matthew was conceived.

It was two months before I realised, with some shock, that I was pregnant. I don't know why it took me so long to realise the obvious. It wasn't until after I started getting depressed and morning sick that the real truth dawned on me. If I'd had a choice I wouldn't have got pregnant at that time – it upset plans which I think were important to me, and to the marriage. Once I knew, however, I just accepted it. Matter of factly. After all, I had, theoretically and intellectually, wanted another child. I don't know what Simon felt about it. I don't think he was too pleased – also surprised – but he too accepted it as a matter of fact. We started looking forward to it. We were particularly looking forward to sharing the birth this time, having missed it, as it were, first time round. But then we discovered that there were complications again. Everything seemed to be going wrong. I was terribly disappointed, really. I think Simon was too. The birth of Matthew was hard – and I was exhausted and depressed afterwards. But there we all were. Now a family of four.

That summer, when Matt was a couple of months old, really was the beginning of the end of the marriage, though I didn't know it until nearly a year later. That summer my mother came to see the baby and Allison. Simon had always done a lot of travelling in his work. And that summer he had to go to Australia for a month. It wasn't a very good time for him to be away. I needed him. But he had to go. I accepted it and in the end I hoped he might have a really good time. And – as I learned later – he did. You see, he seemed so dependent on me – and I still was, as I was at the beginning of the marriage, on him.

Anyway he went and came home, and we carried on through the winter. The next thing I knew – was aware of – was a letter from the wife of Simon's Australian colleague – to both of us – saying she was coming to England to visit. I naturally said we must have her to dinner, show her a good time, return their hospitality. And did so when she was here. I do know the last night she was here, Simon took her out and didn't come back until the early hours. I think I challenged him that something was going on, that he fancied her anyway, but he denied it, so I thought that was that.

Then later I just happened to be looking in his brief case – not something I ordinarily did, but I was looking for some cigarettes late one night when I was working. And I found letters. Just like in the pulp novels. A couple of letters from her, and one he'd obviously written and was going to post. I read the lot. And was, I must say, in a state of shock. They were obviously in love, in constant contact by post and phone, sharing everything from beautiful sunsets to Elvis. I was in a state of shock. I went out early, so as to avoid seeing Simon. When he came back from work I confronted him. Mind you, my mind had been racing all day. And I decided that the most important thing was for her husband to know, for all of us to get together and sort it all out. I guess this was really the logical conclusion of my ideas about open marriage. So I composed a letter to her husband. I wanted to post it, but waited for Simon. In a state of shock – in the clinical, medical sense, I would say. And I stayed in a state of shock I would say, for months. Over the next six months I lost two and a half stone – a lot of weight, quickly. No appetite. No sleep. It's very common, I'm told.

Anyway when Simon came home I confronted him. I didn't need to really, as I'd left the letters and he could see that I'd read them. He was actually indignant that I'd read them. I thought that that was relatively irrelevant in the circumstances. It wasn't something I would ordinarily do, but hardly a priority of values when your marriage is collapsing around you, I thought. Anyway, you know what people say about leaving incriminating letters about to be read? Rather like what they say about getting pregnant – that it's subconsciously deliberate.

What came as the greatest surprise when I talked to Simon, was that he and Mary hadn't slept together. It came as a surprise and it made things more difficult. It was all romantic unrequited love – and that really seemed more threatening than down to earth consummated love as far as I was concerned. It really left me feeling helpless. I really wanted him to say that he loved me most, that I was the primary relationship – as in open marriage. He wasn't willing to say that – and his reticence in that respect frightened me. I felt extremely threatened. I guess I saw all the ideas of open marriage going quickly up in smoke, though I still clung to them, albeit for a while. I more or less said that it was really imperative for him and Mary to spend some time together, get in bed, get down to earth. They had to get together, I thought. Simon was extremely angry that I wanted to write to her husband. And he refused to allow me to post the letter. He said it was none of my business. He said he was in love with Mary and she with him, that he intended to make her happy, that her husband was none of my business. He was afraid what would happen to Mary if her husband found out, I think. Simon really put pressure on me not to tell him and I didn't – for three months, but by then things got much more complicated. We were having terrible rows at the time and the arguments were becoming increasingly violent. And I thought it was pretty damned unfair that I should be worrying about that woman being hurt when I was. But that told me, too, where I stood.

The worst thing was that I felt incredibly betrayed in that the affair had been going on for a year behind my back. And I had thought that Simon and I had had an understanding based on open marriage and being direct, honest, etc. about any other relationships. I felt particularly betrayed and humiliated when I thought back to that week when Mary had visited – and when he was effectively wooing her under my very nose. All of that hurt a lot.

May, June, July was a time of really terrible trauma. Endless discussions getting nowhere – or so I thought, because where I wanted to get was back to normal. When it came to it, and I kept pushing to know, Simon said that he couldn't say that I *was* the primary relationship, and that was a terrible blow to me. It was more or less to say – that's it. But I didn't want to hear that. I didn't want that to be true. Many really violent rows. I remember one night throwing everything that would fit out of the bedroom window, trying to keep Simon out of our bed and him fighting for it. Ridiculous, you might say. But that night was particularly appalling and Allison witnessed all of it and he said to her 'It's all her fault', meaning me. I think that was very damaging to the child. But I think the raw emotion was so strong . . . and the sexual jealousy was really terrible.

I was so hurt. I remember sobbing, saying to my best friend –

'What am I going to do with the hurt?' I think I was trying desperately to hold on to Simon, to keep him, win him back. I loved him. He knew I loved him. He was extremely hurtful, I felt. Unnecessarily so, I thought. The whole process of splitting up was extremely painful. I couldn't understand why it couldn't all be resolved calmly and rationally. But I think most things in life have a cause and effect relationship, that there are consequences of one sort or another eventually for everything.

This time I asked Simon if he would go to see the marriage guidance counsellor we'd seen before. He agreed; we went; but it didn't seem to get us anywhere.

The summer centred around Simon and Mary going away together. I thought it was necessary. I encouraged it. But at the same time it was extremely difficult. He seemed . . . well he prevaricated. I don't know why. The jealousy was terrible. I had discovered a new emotion – sexual jealousy. And for the first time I really understood the meaning of the uncontrollable passions in *Othello*. It was a terrible emotion. I hope I never have to experience it again. There was also the fear of being totally replaced by another woman – the feelings of insecurity. That too was very painful. I don't know what Simon was feeling – guilt, perhaps. Really there was no sense, logic, perspective.

Anyway it was arranged that he and Mary were going to take a week's holiday in Israel. And waiting for the time for him to leave was dreadful. It was during that waiting time that things came to a head. We spent a lot of time in the pub – me anaesthetizing myself, and also because it seemed the only place and way we could talk. And I remember being in tears half the time in the local – and one night in particular when Simon made it even clearer that he was going to make a choice and the choice wasn't going to be me. So I said he should get out, and stop torturing me. He didn't come back that night and when I got home I thought, 'My life is in ruins, my marriage, my children suffering'. One of the issues still was that her husband didn't know. They were going off together without telling him. And I thought he should know. From the first day I thought he should know, from the day I wrote the letter he never got. And I phoned him up – in Australia – and told him. And I felt a great relief then. I felt it was the only right thing that had happened. I wished I'd done it earlier. Apparently after that there was a lot of trouble on their end, but at least it was out in the open. What *they* did was go out, literally the day before Simon and Mary went off

58

together, and get a divorce. And after that, there was a long battle
between them for custody of their children.

---

*But what is of general application to the one-parent situation, irrespective
of its origin, is the compulsion in some degree to cope alone with all those
circumstances which it is of the essence of the institution of the family to
cope with in partnership* – 'The Finer Report, 1974'

Anyway, they went off for a week. The night before was terrible.
Simon was acting as if everything was normal which was insulting.
I was dying. Just numb – indescribable. I didn't want to have a
row, but I was so jealous. And we had a terrible row. At one point I
had tried to arrange to go to Australia and spend the week with her
husband – I thought if we talked . . . I don't know . . . I reckon I
must have been as much round the bend during that time as Simon.
Looking back, I think it was a lunatic idea, but at the time it
seemed the only sensible thing to do. Anyway, that week I couldn't
bear to stay at home thinking about them together, so I went off
with the kids. A really weird holiday, as it turned out, but it helped
me through the week.

I guess I had in the back of my mind that Simon would come
back and we would be able to deal on some kind of open marriage
terms. In fact, he came back, walked through the door and said he
wanted a divorce. That was his first and his last word on the
subject. He specifically said he didn't want to talk about anything.
And that was that. The end.

He didn't actually move out for a couple of months. We actually
went away for the month of August – pretending to have a normal
holiday. I suppose it was a kind of final farewell. I knew there was
no going back. Back in Bristol things were very tense. We were
sleeping separately, he was going to leave but seemed unable to
actually decide when, how . . . In the end I helped him find a place
to move to. There was a great reluctance in him to actually face any
kind of reality. And I couldn't go on any longer under the same
roof, as we were. He finally moved out and we managed to discuss
and sort out all the financial arrangements, the mutual agreement
of the divorce, before he left. And we were lucky enough to have
enough resources to split more or less evenly, so we could both
manage. Once he'd gone the tension went. Things were better in
some respects, but then began a long, hard slog for me and the
kids.

What was foremost in my mind was getting Allison through it. She and Simon had been very, very close, and the first time splitting up really became clear in my mind I actually thought it would kill her. But there it was. I devoted all my emotional and mental energy to helping her. She didn't seem aware of what was happening. That made it more difficult. I felt it was vitally important not to tear him down in any way, whatever I felt. Not to be judgemental. And to help her understand by drawing her attention to other children she knew whose Dads had left. It was amazing, you know, the number of women right round you who were in the same position. You weren't aware, until it happened to you.

The first week on our own was dreadful. It was arranged that Daddy would come at the end of that week. And the week was an eternity. Every day it was, 'When would Daddy come?' Over the first month Allison went very quiet and withdrawn. I was worried, but didn't know what to do. Then a fortuitous thing happened.

As I say, I felt it was important to devote myself to Allison at first, sort of consciously ignoring Matthew who was only fourteen months and not talking then, and therefore not so well able to express what he was feeling. However, immediately Simon left, Matthew started having hysterics at bedtime, wouldn't go to sleep if I didn't stay in the room with him. Which I did, of course – it was obviously his fear of being left. One night I had to lie with him a long time. I heard Allison get out of bed and start wandering around the house. She actually looked into Matthew's room and I thought she saw me. But a few minutes later I found her in her bed sobbing. She thought I'd left, just like Daddy. And then I realised that that was what she was most afraid of – being so young. So I took the opportunity of telling her that mummies never left their children – a little white lie – but true enough to be worth saying. And that she knew I never went out without telling her. Her behaviour changed radically from the next day. She must have been really worried. She was also very good, much too good at first, obviously not secure enough to be naughty sometimes. I was really happy when she started being her normal naughty-and-nice self. That happened gradually.

Matthew, apart from being afraid of going to sleep and waking in the night (though that wasn't very new as he'd been waking two or three times in the night from the time he was born – it had been that long since I'd had an unbroken night's sleep and I was profoundly exhausted!), didn't start having real difficulties – or showing them anyway – for about four months. There was a gap when they didn't see their Dad at all – a couple of months, and then he started coming and playing good uncle, taking them to museums and the zoo on Sundays. I really resented that Daddy gave them a good time and I was left with the dirty work. The first time they returned on a Sunday, I was fully expecting Allison to make a fuss. But she bounded in full of beans. Matthew took one look at me and said, 'Go away'. And then for weeks he would be so upset when he was brought back, he would sob, those terrible, deep sobs, for hours. As time went by things got more and more stable.

I think one of the hardest things is being entirely responsible for everything, on your own, in a situation where normally things are shared. I mean being responsible for earning a living, raising children, everything, and never ever getting a break. It is very hard.

As for me, at the beginning, I wasn't looking after myself. I didn't have time and the kids were the priority. Eventually I went into a very bad depression – for the whole year of the splitting up I'd been on a kind of high. Living on my nerves, I guess the expression is. And then I went down, I went rock bottom. I was very wounded sexually – my sexual ego. That was inevitable. I couldn't really envisage the future. I felt like a vegetable – though I poured myself into work the first year, productive work and without that, God knows what I would have done. Really gone under, I think.

Things started looking up for me when I could begin to see a future – positive new developments in work, when the kids seemed, at least, to be surviving. And when I got involved for a while with a bloke. It wasn't very serious, and I was aware of that, but he was nice and he made me feel attractive again. I really needed that. It was very tempting to succumb to 'getting involved' but I knew it was silly. And I had begun to realise how much I liked being on my own. Now, I am getting to know myself. The marriage guidance counsellor was very helpful in that respect. Long after Simon had gone – nine months longer, I saw her weekly and she really helped me to sort my head out. Previously I hadn't had much time for it – marriage guidance. Now I can see it can be very helpful in helping marriages to split up as well as in keeping them together. And I discovered that they regard that as an important part of their job.

Now, after a year, we're well on our way to becoming a stable three-person, non-nuclear family. And enjoying ourselves. We live day to day. Really the only way to survive. I worry about Allison when Daddy has a new wife and two new kids who call him Daddy. That *is* going to be very hard on her. I hope I can help her through it. I feel we really are starting a new life now. We've managed a year. I've managed the money and all the 'masculine' jobs around the house. Sometimes by calling for help to neighbours. At first I found it humiliating. Now I reckon once for everything, learn and then it won't be necessary a second time. But I've certainly come to realise how ill-equipped one is to cope. All those years of learning algebra would have been better spent learning how to maintain a motor.

A number of things are very clear. I doubt very much I'll ever marry again. I think marriage can be very destructive and I find most people unhappily married hardly even aware of it, stuck in it without the will to get out. I might live with someone if I ever meet someone I want to live with. I certainly know better than ever before the sort of person it might be, or perhaps, more precisely, the sort of person it won't be. Right now I am enjoying being on my own for the first time ever. I am independent. Not through my own choice, but it's a good thing. I find I like myself, want to spend time with myself, get to know myself.

I feel there is no place in society as it is presently structured for us. Us being single-parent women. I also know we are large in numbers, larger than most people are aware of. I would like to see society properly accommodating us, instead of perpetuating the illusion of the nuclear family. When that happens – notice I don't say if – it will be after some revolutionary changes – from children's literature which assumes that the nuclear family is the norm, to tax laws, to welfare services, benefits, child care.

By comparison to most women in my situation I'm well off – with a roof over my head, with my work, with reasonable maintenance. By comparison with most single-parent women I'm lucky. Then I think how difficult it has been for me, and I think of the others – less fortunate – and I know that society has got to change.

Postcript

There are certain key similarities between the situations of Christine and. Eleanor – going straight from 'home' to husband (marrying to escape from parents), the continual and long-term lack of a satisfying sexual relationship with their husbands, the involvement of each of them in an affair as an outlet for this (as a symptom of the ailing marriage?), and the quite excessive emotional dependence they had on their husbands. And, like Eleanor, Christine struggled to keep her clearly failed marriage going (using marriage guidance counselling) rather than face the trauma of going it alone. But also, like Eleanor, once Christine had made the break or been forced to, suffered the initial terror and depression, she too thrived on being a single parent. She too 'grew up'.

Christine and her husband were slightly unusual, though, in trying to find and put into effect alternatives to their conventional marriage, including a division of roles and responsibilities in the home and outside (insofar as Christine contemplated becoming the breadwinner) and in adopting the concept of 'open marriage' to accommodate other relationships (though that in retrospect proved to be plaster over quite irremediable cracks). It is with some irony that one realises from this story that Christine ought probably to have taken the initiative in ending the marriage after the first child, at the time of her affair. But she obviously lacked the courage to take responsibility for her own life and that of her daughter. Christine's story raises some crucial questions about women and contraception. The choice of when and when not to have children is available to most women, was available to Christine before she had her second 'accidental' child. Even, to a certain extent, the choice of why to have children. And yet Christine became pregnant just before the time she was going to become the breadwinner – why? Fear? Avoidance? Copping out, however subconsciously – of the real world?

Christine was amongst the majority of those people splitting up who had great anxiety about how her children would survive and manage. She found, like the others, that the children came out of it happy and well-adjusted, as much if not more so than nuclear family children.

4. Tom

Tom describes his background as middle class – 'mixed Communist Party and Quaker.' He married in his mid-twenties, and had only recently separated, in his late thirties after spending several years with his wife and his wife's lover trying to evolve a structure which would accommodate the three of them and the two children, aged under twelve, who finally remained with their mother. Tom is now a community worker in South London.

Tom is not in another serious relationship. He says, 'I don't feel ready. I want to avoid a rebound situation if possible.' His separation was recent and he is not divorced, so remarriage is not an issue at the moment. In any case, he says, 'I dislike the cultural meaning of marriage and the effect it seems to have on people, though I wouldn't mind living with someone again at some point.'

Of his situation now, he says: 'I am anxious to stress that the interview with me was conducted fairly recently – three months – after my separation, and therefore when I was still quite "raw" about it, and hadn't had time to assume a clear attitude towards it. The thoughts and feelings belong to someone engaged in the process of making the transition from one mode of living to another and – even more than people's thoughts and feelings on such subjects usually are – they are in flux.

'I'm a bit lonely, but surviving and learning. The crucial decision at the moment for me is what sort of new living situation to embark on, my current room being temporary. Should I find a new place on my own? Or should I live with other people in some way? This problem feels more important than the problem of (sexual) relationships.

'Perhaps I should add that I miss my kids quite a bit and haven't got used to the new intermittent kind of relationship I now have with them. My relationship with my (ex) wife is also still strained – we haven't got used to the change yet.

'For the past ten years I've been heavily involved with left politics, sexual politics and cultural things and I expect these involvements will continue. At the same time, the future feels fairly wide-open at the moment.'

We met at college. She was my third girlfriend of any seriousness. I wasn't terribly sexually experienced. I considered that I had not had enough sexual experience because I went to a single-sex boarding school and I lost my virginity very late relative to most people. And I had a lot of catching up to do. That was always a block against totally committing myself to her but, in fact, I did totally commit myself to her.

I always expected I'd get married. I never questioned that, or did I? Wait a minute. I think maybe it works on two levels. This was some time ago – I left college in the summer of '63 . . . and attitudes about sexuality and so on were not the same then as they are now by any means. At a deep level I did expect to get married . . . and wanted to even as far as such radical consciousness I had at the time was concerned. At the same time I thought it was . . . sort of . . . very square to get married.

What happened was that Tanya and I graduated and almost immediately I went to Africa. I have often – and she has too – speculated on what would have happened to our relationship if I hadn't done that. Because maybe . . . if we had gone through the relationship without that separation which became this added, very intense factor, having this distance between us, it's possible that maybe if we'd gone through a process it would have ended after perhaps just a few months . . . something like that. I don't know . . . it's just a thought. I'm looking at this in the context of having finally broken up. Right? But we didn't break up for fourteen years.

We'd just started to sleep together. It was very tense. What happened was I'd just got this job in Angola and was about to go, when there were riots at the university there, so I was told I couldn't go yet, that it would have to be next week, and then the next week came along and they said, 'No, it's not going to be for another couple of weeks at least. The situation is still very dodgy out there.' And then they said, 'The university is actually closed down and isn't going to open for at least another month.' And it went on like that. I was always about to go. It's a peculiar context for a relationship to start. Very dramatic. There was a certain drama connected with it . . . even then.

Finally I thought, well I'm not going to go to Angola . . . this is ridiculous. And I moved in with Tanya. I was there four days when the phone rang and they said, 'You go tomorrow morning.' So just then, when we'd sort of finally got together – with a lot of initial shyness and not understanding each other and all the rest of it – and let all the stops out and it was very romantic, suddenly 'wow', next stop, Africa.

We pined desperately for each other for six months. And I missed her so much – also missed England so much although it was very interesting out there – that I managed to scrape the money together to come back for six weeks during the summer vacation. And we had six weeks of extremely intense happiness together in England, in Yorkshire. Wonderful six weeks, very lyrical. By which time she had finished college. At the end of it, it seemed ridiculous that I should go back on my own. We thought that she should come too.

In a sense, that's when we got 'married' rather than when we signed the bit of paper which didn't happen for quite some time afterwards. The proposal that she should come to Africa was more important than that we should get married. This was the crest of the wave of romance.

Then there were extraordinary obstacles to her coming out. I went back on my own and then for the next three or four months, we tried to get her out there. We made the terrible mistake of telling the most appalling lies, thinking it would make it easier. We were very worried, that the people there would disapprove of us living 'in sin' so I returned and announced that I *had* got married, because she was going to come and join me. It would have been fine if she'd come out and joined me the next week. But she couldn't get a visa for various reasons and I had to maintain this fiction that I'd got married in the summer and they couldn't understand why she wasn't there. Meanwhile, I was going around trying to get jobs for her so she could come but, of course, I had to get jobs for her as a single woman. Quite crazy. Meanwhile, to add to the peculiarity I was accused of being a CIA agent by the university.

Anyway, she finally did come out in December, but I'd had enough of the university by then so we travelled around in Africa together for the best part of the next year. It was a tremendously romantic year for us and also a heavy dose of certain kinds of reality. I mean it was a real test of the relationship. But again . . . in its way, I suppose . . . artificial. Not the usual settling down. It didn't prepare us for cosy domesticity. But it did create very, very deep ties between us which, really, haven't been broken.

That *is* the problem, the problem of splitting up and taking six years to do it as we have done. We were very, very close . . . still are. And that experience *was* so magical and strange and testing and challenging and awakening that, to go through it together really cemented our relationship very deeply, very deeply.

We ended up getting hepatitis and had to come back. We were in the same hospital – in separate wards, of course. We were desperate, absolutely desperate being separated from each other by those corridors and nurses. We were terrifically in love, fantastically so. In our strange circumstances, we did everything together and were quite inseparable. Unfortunately, because of the subsequent dependency, that builds up and becomes damaging.

What happened then was that we were quite obviously going to live together and the parents started to put pressure on us to get married. So we started thinking, 'Well, why not?' I was against it. By this time I really *didn't* want to get married. And she was equivocal too. But we did it to please the parents. Us and about 99.9 per cent of the world. That was the reason anyway we gave ourselves, though I'm sure there was a part of us that wanted to do it too. It was possible to look at marriage as a joke and not think of it as a serious event at all. But I think that was a bit of fiction too. That was our formal attitude towards it . . . that it was all very unimportant. But, I think the cultural importance of marriage and its significance, and everything, is massive and you're probably lying if you say that it doesn't matter. I mean, I wouldn't do it now. But even to say, I wouldn't do it is indicative of its cultural importance.

At that time our general political consciousness did not help us much with our sexual politics. I think both of us regarded ourselves as enlightened people including our attitudes towards sexuality, which was part of the reason why neither of us particularly wanted to get married. There was a certain sexual-political awareness in that by then. I think that we weren't entirely ignorant of the politics of sexuality even then. It must have been thought through in some ways. I mean, there was a notion of conventional marriage that we both felt a bit hostile towards: we felt we were a bit more liberated than that. But it's rather hard to pin down what that hostility consisted of: what its concept was, *why* one was opposed to the notion of marriage. And, in fact, we slipped into it. You see, in certain ways I never felt as though I was married, I resented that I had got married. It annoyed me. And I think that may be true of Tanya too . . . I'm not sure.

Anyway, what happened then was that we simply played out our male/female drama in a very conventional way as regards the emotional dynamics of the relationship. Up to the point when Tanya joined the Women's Liberation Movement and had the tools to start questioning. In other words, whatever sexual radicalism or enlightenment or awareness we had was no way sufficient to stop us actually playing out very traditional roles and dependencies. I slipped into the dominant person in the relationship.

Tanya was very pretty, but she wasn't my idea of my ideal woman. She was quieter and more inward than my fantasy woman would have been. In fact, there was a certain sense in which I never regarded Tanya as much a fully-formed person as I was. That's quite an admission to make. I adored her, respected her, but there was a certain way in which, I thought I suppose – and perhaps I thought this of all women – that she wasn't a total human being. Whereas I was. I knew things about the world that she didn't.

At college, and subsequently, the extent to which the blokes ran the scene was considerable. What happened was, that for two years after we got married, me and my male friends got stoned pretty well every night. It was a very male, semi-hippy, intellectual, bohemian scene that we moved in – which Tanya came to detest. And she got disillusioned with me – thought I was fucking around and not doing anything with my life. So she decided to have a baby.

We both had university degrees. I was doing a bit of Liberal Studies teaching while attempting to write stories, novels, and poems and things. And she did a secretarial course for a year, after Africa. But she just did the training . . . she never took it up as a job . . . as a profession. I was the breadwinner.

Tanya was very unhappy and demoralised by the life we were leading and felt I was wasting myself, being very irresponsible and becoming a bit of a drag. That was the period that our sex life began to tail off somewhat. I think I have to say at this point that I was a heavy character to live with and confused Tanya a lot about herself, but it's also true that she had problems of her own to do with her own psychology and her own difficulties deciding what sort of a person *she* was. When I said she decided to have a baby in order to sort our relationship out, I think it's also true that she decided to have a baby because she wasn't at all sure what else she wanted to do. In other words, the reasons why she wanted to have a baby – and it did come from her with, I must say, my immediate enthusiastic agreement – were, in a certain way, negative. It wasn't

We point to the importance to one-parent families of attacking the oc-cupational discrimination between men and women which has charac-terised the economic history of industrialism – 'The Finer Report, 1974'

simply a positive decision: 'Wouldn't it be wonderful to have babies' . . . sort of thing. How she accounts for it in retrospect is that it was partly going to sort out our relationship which she considered was going wrong, and partly that it would give her a clearer reason for living, give her a job, a purpose in life.

I was tremendously enthusiastic. And in fact it worked on both counts initially . . . as she wanted it to work. It sorted out our relationship. I, as it were, sobered up, took my responsibilities seriously, went teaching full-time rather than part-time – and we bought a house. The baby was born and we recreated, in a curious way, the sort of intense and at times, lyrical vibrations of life in Africa. We were very, very much in love with the child and through the child with each other again. And, for a time – a year or two – we were very happy again and everything seemed to be working ex-tremely well. Though at times we had very violent and fierce rows which we both found deeply upsetting and which, of course, had a content: they were about our relationship. Not in the sense, though, of questioning the institution. I suppose the roles were questioned but without any basis or critical apparatus for the questions to happen within. So it all tended to be personalized.

Tanya says she stopped enjoying sex just before we had our first child, but she also says she never enjoyed it. During the period we were splitting up one statement she made was that she never en-joyed sex with me. I think that was an historical falsification ac-tually, and I wonder if she would say that now, as a matter of fact . . . I don't know. I think in the early stages – in Africa, for example – we were very sexually happy together. Although I had a kind of restlessness. Where I was scarcely ever unfaithful to Tanya in practice in eight years or so of marriage, I was unfaithful to her in fantasy a lot. And she knew it. That was one of the tensions.

Initially the baby improved everything. The period where the relationship declined in every area was noticeably after the birth of the second child. The intervening period – when we had one baby that we adored – was quite blissful. One baby is tiring, but not actually nearly as disruptive to your life as two. And we managed that. During the period when we just had the one baby which was two-and-a-half years, the last part of which she was pregnant, we just carried on doing the things we always did, leading quite an active life. That was the period when I was involved in a lot of politics and Tanya too, to a degree. We carted little Barbara around with us. That seemed to outweigh the problems of the extra work and the responsibility and the rest of it.

The overall organisation of our relationship was quite simply that I went out to work and Tanya looked after the baby. We slipped into conventional roles. And yet I remember being more involved with Barbara as a parent than I was subsequently with Ben. I've often wondered why that was. I think partly because she was the first. There was the novelty and the fact that although I was beginning to get involved in politics, I was much, much more involved with politics later. I don't know. I seem to remember being much more involved with Barbara's daily development and, although I was working, I did a fair amount of nappie changing and stuff and didn't think it was extraordinary that I should do that. But the basic division of labour was that I worked and Tanya stayed at home.

The second child we had as a companion for the first, really. We thought it wasn't a good idea just to have the one child: she needed company. I think that was a time when the tensions were reasserting themselves, too. Tanya had a relationship with another bloke during that period. For her that would be quite a dramatic gesture of dissatisfaction with our relationship. I was very surprised, I know, when she told me about the affair. She felt she had to tell me. I was hurt. I was, by and large, faithful. I had had one or two one night things, which Tanya didn't know about. Or didn't until very much later. I think maybe it even came out at that time when she finally told me about this guy. And she said at the time that she was feeling unhappy with me and that's why she did it. She didn't feel that I was giving her enough time and attention. The affair didn't threaten our relationship. On the contrary, it brought us closer together. I mean, she had to talk about it and why she'd done it and was very contrite. I forgave her and we sort of talked about each other and what we were feeling for each other.

It was about this time we decided to have a second child. I even remember me pushing for it and her not being quite so sure, but agreeing. I think what was happening was that she was already beginning to think, 'Well, I adore Barbara, and mother love is great but there are also other things in life.' I think she didn't anticipate with a great deal of pleasure being pregnant all over again and having another very small child. But, again, I think we were slightly conventional; one didn't just have one kid . . . one had two. That's what people did . . . so that's what we did.

In fact, we did all the conventional things. We lived as a nuclear family in a house, with a couple of women renting rooms upstairs. We slipped into the situation where I was the breadwinner and she stayed at home; we had two kids – we did it all. We even had the odd secret affair which we felt guilty about. That was part and parcel of the whole thing.

As I said Tanya didn't enjoy the second pregnancy; she didn't enjoy the birth so much; she didn't feel nearly as miraculous about the second baby – didn't have that troubled, passionate, almost harrowing intensity about it. It was a much more relaxed relationship with the second baby. Incidentally, if our emotional responses towards our two children were in any way typical, the effect on the development of the children and their subsequent development as adults must be massive. I wonder if anyone has ever studied this? And, of course, from this point on, one should be including the kids in the story of the marriage, which – I'm ashamed to say – is hard to do. I adore them and get on very well with them but I find, quite often, when I think about them, when I think about what was happening, trying to think what the kids were doing and how they fit in, it's very difficult. Quite simply, the second child was a trial and a drag, for Tanya more than me. There were all the difficulties of being a parent, of being stuck at home. The massive change in one's social life, one's mobility and the rest of it, really surfaced with the second kid, and above all, Tanya's increasing resentment of the role she was being forced to play.

She was more and more trapped. I was, by this time, very involved in politics. I was working part-time still and still earning such money as came in, but I was very, very active politically at precisely the point where Tanya needed extra support and solidarity. And she got increasingly fed up. Ben was born early in 1969 and I think Tanya got involved in the women's movement about then. It seems as though we went through all that process in total ignorance. And then the questions started coming from Tanya. Initially the critique was always on the practicalities: 'Why am I feeding the child . . . why am I doing all the cooking while you go outside and do all the interesting things?' It wasn't so much, initially, to do with the actual quality of the relationship but of course that was what it was really about underneath. And that's what the rows and arguments were about which we had at that time and which were very bitter indeed. They were about the quality of our relationship.

I hope I'm not saying the wrong thing politically when I say that the unfairness, the division of labour in the home and so on is important, but it isn't the only thing that determines what is right or wrong with a relationship. For example, although we were in our early twenties when we got together, we were very unprepared at that time to have relationships that would last us the rest of our lives. We were very unformed human beings. We continued the formation of ourselves together for a short time. But what was beginning to happen, it seems to me, apart from all the dynamics of the relationship itself and how it was being played out, was that we had both reached a point where we were no longer able to grow with each other, that our further formation as people and individuals had to take place either not with each other at all, or in a very different kind of context. While – and this is the real problem about relationships – the things you do together can be very major life experiences – like having children – the fact that you do them together puts an enormous amount of significance into the relationship. Working together creates the relationship, is part of what makes the very great feelings and understandings between you; but also, it can have the contrary effect of holding you back, becoming a tie that can prevent you from seeing that the relationship has played itself out in certain ways and that you might need to move on from it.

There's another school of thought that my mother generally holds to which is that a relationship is about what you go through together and that you should always stick it out. That's the whole point, she thinks, and in old age, because you've struggled through all these obstacles, something has been achieved: the virtue is sticking out the problems. Of course, nowadays there is a tendency when the going gets rough to just chuck it in. The more that's made easy by social mobility and the fact that people's relationships break up very easily may mean the less one is *willing* to put the work in. So that the first minute there's difficulties you clear off, and that sort of thing. But I suspect, looking at my own psyche, that I still have a hell of a lot of growing to do: I suspect this is true of Tanya too. So sticking it out was no longer useful to us – our relationship had to change, probably end, for us to continue to develop as separate people.

Within that, however, there were specific problems about the relationship itself. For example, the breakdown of labour whereby I went out to work and she stayed at home was oppressive to Tanya and in general, damaging to both of us.

Tanya – it should be remembered – had determined the course of the relationship in significant ways. For example, the decision to have children came from her and all that followed from it was a pretty massive determination of the course of the relationship. Nevertheless, the way the relationship broke down was that I was the dominant partner, the one who could, at the very least, be bossy, aggressive, bullying and so on. And basically I felt that what I was doing in the world was important and Tanya's role was kind of back-up service. Obviously I now find that odious, but part of me yearns for that still.

Anyway, by 1970 when our second child was two, Tanya was bitterly unhappy, bitterly resentful, bored, angry, deeply fed up. I must say . . . I was too. I don't think men like going through these situations where, supposedly, the wife is unhappy and they feel on top of the world. The rows we were having were a real drag, a drain of energy that I thought I should have been putting into outside things. She was holding me back from the great things I was going to achieve! I certainly tended to look at it that way. At the same time, though I was unhappy because she was unhappy; the fact we weren't getting on was terrible and it was all awful.

She stepped up the critique and the home became a battleground – we fought like hell. She now had the critical apparatus – from the women's movement – with which to fight. Frequently she won the arguments and I would agree to improve myself, but it would slip back. I can't really isolate key moments, I'm afraid, but basically I was agreeing in theory but failing to put it into practice. At the same time I suppose Tanya was gaining confidence, through her women's group. Becoming active. The mere act of being active increased confidence and so on.

One key turning point for us wasn't a moment, but a kind of general social change that was growing up around us which we simply couldn't ignore. All around us people's relationships were changing visibly. Our friends were all changing in the way they were relating to each other. A lot of our friends had also all had their second babies by now and were experiencing very similar tensions in their relationships. Specifically, a number of our friends were starting to take lovers, saying that not only was the nuclear family a bad thing but being an exclusive couple was a bad thing. That it was very good and correct to have other relationships.

For many mothers part-time work offers the satisfaction of earning and mixing with other people without imposing more demands on their time and energies than they can meet. But part-time work . . . tends to be low in status and badly paid . . . Part-time workers, are, moreover, often ineligible for, or less favourably treated in relation to, not only promotion, but also such features of full-time employment as paid holidays, paid sick leave and pension schemes. Part-time jobs are also likely to be the most vulnerable to redundancy – 'The Finer Report, 1974'

Anyway, the year that everything exploded was 1972. There was one purely practical thing that was important which was that the last of the newspapers I had worked on full-time folded up and I found myself without a bread-and-butter job. And at that point it was impossible for me to hold out any longer acting as if I were the breadwinner. Because I wasn't actually making the bread. So when this paper folded up, I no longer had the basis on which to decline taking equal domestic responsibilities with Tanya. So from that point onwards, we divided the week in half and we both worked part-time. She took a secretarial job herself and I worked at a youth club and did community work. We had the kids half a week each and shared looking after the house. On the surface a good sounding thing and I felt quite gracious about it. I did enjoy being with the kids more. It wasn't such an immense sacrifice. But I felt I wasn't completing myself as a male person in certain ways, and resented what at times appeared to be interference with my life's larger projects – whatever they may have been, because they had become rather vague by then. But . . . it was a good arrangement. It was a pity really that we hadn't done it years before. I felt that as a result of all this change, my relationship with Tanya would become a good one again. And I think it did improve a bit, but the deeper tensions remained. And, in the end, I don't think they were about divisions of domestic life at all – which is what I was trying to get at before.

We also, during that summer, turned our house into a commune . . . not a proper one, because I remained a landlord which

Tanya demanded. But we ceased to have tenants living separately from us. Coincidentally, the two women who lived upstairs moved out at that time and the next people who came in shared the house with us. They had their own rooms, but we cooked together, ate together, shopping and cleaning and the rest of it which was an attempt to break down the nuclear family. I identified the problems between us as being problems of being a nuclear family. I think Tanya agreed too, actually although she was clearer that there were also specific problems between us as two people. I felt if we could stop being a nuclear family then everything would be all right.

Also, at this time, I was coming around to realise in a deep sense, that some women's liberation ideas were right. I had sort of intellectually acknowledged them as being right before, but now I was beginning to take the notion seriously that a person's life was a political question. I actually did want us to change our lives: it wasn't just something that came from Tanya by now. But all of this was mixed up with the question of having lovers, of having other relationships. This was posed as part of the same process, which made it difficult for me to sort out.

Other relationships were a way to get away from nuclear families, to open things out, to break down the negative pattern of habits that had developed between us, to establish ourselves as individuals in the world, and then to relate to each other on a different basis (rather than as two very interdependent people which we had become) and to continue our personal development in new ways that didn't rely so totally on each other. I have to say I was the one who pushed for this. I had my eye on other women quite a lot, always had done or had done for a good while. There was a certain amount of self interest then. Here self-interest and political enlightenment seemed to coincide. All our friends were doing it. It was the fashion. So I pushed for this too, little realising the consequences.

We agreed that because of the balance of power in the relationship that if I were to be the one that went off with someone else, this would simply confirm and reinforce the power structure as it was. It wouldn't be all that different than it had been in the past. And it would damage the relationship. It would reinforce all the negative things about the relationship, rather than the other way around. So we decided that Tanya should be the first. And she came round. She started to agree that this would be a good idea. What you have to envisage is a picture where there were deep psychic tensions in our relationship between us as people, for a start, which I had completely misunderstood, or understood only very partially. Also, within each of us as individuals I think we both had reached an explosive point in our lives where things were going to happen to each of us. In a sense, we were both looking blindly around for a way out.

There was this political and ideological framework of women's liberation and associated ideas that appeared to coincide very neatly with a lot of what we were feeling. I feel, retrospectively, though that it didn't explain it enough. I think that deep down we knew that we had to get out of the relationship. And that's what we were doing. We were ending the relationship, in fact, without knowing it. In ways that looked constructive.

What happened then was that she, first of all, got off with a friend of mine. In the most extraordinarily supervised way. Me and my friend had a chat and agreed that it would be all right. You may have my wife, sort of thing. Thanks very much. He also had a girlfriend and that was a bit more complicated. She was less enthusiastic about the idea. And what happened was that the four of us got weirdly involved with each other, and without sleeping together became a foursome for a while. The four of us went around together, and it was all very intense and weird. And then this guy went to bed once with Tanya. It didn't do very much for either of them. This guy said subsequently that he realised that Tanya was after one hell of a lot more than he was able to provide for her. Which is true. I think that Tanya was looking around for another man and I was encouraging her to do so. For different reasons. Though neither of us knew consciously what was going on. Meanwhile, a group of our friends moved to a commune in Ireland. And there was one couple up there – Mike and Alice and their three children. We went up for a visit in the autumn of 1972 and these two fell in love with each other – Tanya and Mike.

Again the same thing happened. Tanya saying 'Is it all right?' and me saying, 'Yes . . . have a jolly good time.' Which she did during this week, and we went back home and everything appeared to be the same. But this guy left Ireland and Tanya met up with him again. He had split up with his wife and kids. He came to London. And it became apparent what was going to happen – that she was getting very involved with this man. At which point I was up against it in terms of dealing with a situation which I wasn't in the least bit enjoying. By and large, up to that point the changes had happened – in some cases against my will initially, but in the end with my involvement and with the feeling that I was more or less in control. Which is a feeling I had always had – that I was the one that was in control. Not totally true, of course. But at least, I was allowed to feel that I was in control. But it was no longer possible to feel like that. And so I had to confront the violent jealousy that then came up.

It turned out that non-exclusive relationships were quite different from how I imagined them to be. With the most extraordinary naïvety, I had this idea of going off for romps with someone else and coming back to have even more exciting romps at home. I thought it would improve our sexual relationship and everything else, and of course it didn't. The thing is that it then took six years for us to finally split up. It was a period of extraordinary tensions and difficulties for the three of us.

What happened for the next six years was that Tanya and I continued to live with each other while she had the relationship with Mike. What that six years actually constituted was the ending of my relationship with Tanya as a couple, and the beginning of her relationship with Mike as a couple. But it was extremely confused and it was a long time before it was clear to all of us that that was what was happening. Although, it does seem to me, paradoxically, we all knew, emotionally, from the very first day. It is extraordinary that we could manage to deceive ourselves all that time.

But the reasons why we didn't realise it all that quickly are very interesting. They relate very much to children firstly, and secondly, to the very deep bond between Tanya and me. What was going on was that we were trying to question and work through and arrive at some kind of understanding of what a couple relationship is as distinct from a love relationship – when they love you and you love them but you're not a couple. And of how you come out of a couple relationship, which basically means a social relationship whether it's exclusive or not, and still keep a kind of friendship that can continue rather than just ending. Tanya continued to love me and I continued to love her, at times passionately, although not sexually passionately. Neither of us wanted to split up. She didn't want to stop having relations with me, but she wanted a relationship with Mike too. And neither of us wanted to stop living with each other and the children. So basically the three of us stayed together for six years.

We've only stopped living together in the last three months; so I can't say with any confidence how things are going to be from now on. We're only just learning how to handle that. We didn't write off the past, and we still haven't written off the past. I'm very glad about that. We *did* continue to live with our children for another six years, which I'm also very glad about. We went through a process – which in many respects was a nightmare for all of us – but, during the course of which, we learned a very great deal about human nature and about ourselves and sexuality and the meaning of sexuality and love and friendship and domestic arrangements and the rest of it which was fascinating and wouldn't, I don't think, have been learned any other way. Part of me very profoundly wishes that I hadn't had to learn it and don't in a sense, see it as being particularly useful and would rather not have had all the agony with the scars it's left. But, in another way it was a very intense period in my life and I don't think I really regret it. It's a very unusual experience to go through and it taught me a very great deal. I guess I'm an extremist really. I believe in living dangerously – up to a point. There are times when I like a little peace, of which we had precious little during that time. But it was worth it, it didn't destroy us. It very nearly did destroy us, but it didn't.

What happened was that during that autumn of 1972 it became apparent that Tanya's relationship with Mike was serious, and while I was very jealous, I was totally committed to not preventing her from having the relationship. I felt I ought to be able to come to terms with it and stand it and work through the period of jealousy. I was committed to that. That's one level. On another level I knew that we had to get out of being a couple and this seemed a way of doing it. It was necessary for both of us to develop away from each other; we were very tied together, and it was very difficult for us to get apart. This was about the only way we could do it, although we tended to cling together at the same time which was an added confusion.

I also think I looked forward very much to having other relationships myself. It took me a very long time to discover that I wanted to have my cake and eat it – to maintain my relationship with Tanya and fool around with other women. My relations with other women – some quite nice ones too – were always on my terms because I continued to have my relationship with Tanya. I was still married, therefore, I was always, basically, in control of the relationships with other people. In other words, I set myself up in a situation where I didn't have to make myself vulnerable to other people. At the same time, I was very vulnerable to Tanya.

Anyway, Mike came and lived in London and it didn't change anything really. They were lovers and Tanya and I were basically old friends with complications. He lived half a mile away for a few months and then the idea was put that he should move into the house. Once again we discussed it. By this time Tanya – in order to defend her position – had developed a very heavy anti-couple ideology and said that she didn't want Mike to be her lover . . . she didn't want to be my wife and she didn't want to be Mike's mistress. She wanted equal relationships. That seemed to be ideologically right on, but it terrified me, totally threatened me. But I agreed. Oddly, I was interested to see just what would happen actually. I had a real curiosity as to how this kind of experiment would work out even though I was going to be scared out of my wits. I was also very confused about what was going on, and I tended to be rather passive about it, just drifting along. I think a more decisive person, or a person a bit more in touch with their own feelings, might have said, 'This is silly . . . if Mike moves in, I move out.' That might have been the sensible thing to do looking back, but for good or bad reasons, I didn't. Mike moved in and we lived together for a year, the three of us. We had rotas about when we slept with each other. Tanya and I still had a sexual relationship of sorts, very difficult but we did.

Basically it was awful, but very interesting. Finally a year later, I couldn't stand it any longer. I moved out for three months and Mike also moved out. I did think at the time that Tanya would say, 'I want you to come back . . . I want you . . . You come first . . .', which she didn't do. And then I thought, 'Well . . . that's it . . . that's the end of it'. And for a while that's how it appeared it was.

In fact, I then moved back to the house quite some time before Mike did. And Tanya and I said we'd reconstruct our relationship on a different basis . . . we'd try to work out ways to be independent of each other, and all that stuff that we'd been talking about for years. During this period we talked about and analysed our relationship a great deal. Still, the thing I'm still confused about from that period and, indeed, in my life generally, is the exact place of sexuality in the scheme of things. Part of me thinks, as a result of this experience as much as anything else, of sexuality as having an almost autonomous, determinate, independent sort of ruling force which, in the end you can't understand or analyse. No matter how much Tanya and I loved each other with deep, caring concern, the fact was that we couldn't fuck any more. I couldn't admit this, whereas Tanya had known and accepted it for a long time. And she and Mike had a good sexual relationship. In the end – it seemed to me – it all boiled down to that – to sex – and everything else was just words really. Part of me still thinks that.

For a while Tanya and I were back living together without Mike actually living in the house, and with our relationship very much changed. We were much more relaxed, but we no longer thought of ourselves as a couple. Then Mike finally moved back in again, just to stay for a bit because he had no other place to go and he was about to go away and travel. But he never did. And we lived together for another two years, the three of us. By this time Tanya and I weren't sleeping together any more so the movement from one couple to another had taken place.

I suppose from then on, it was only a matter of time before we would actually split up, although what we all wanted, at that time, was to find a place where we could all live with other people in the country. In the end, they got a place on their own in the country.

In the end it was me who actually precipitated the split. They often went off looking for country places and I kind of went along with it and said, 'I'll see what happens'. I was a passive participant to these various schemes for living situations. We looked at a big farm in Yorkshire and we looked at a village in the Lake District, but by that time it was much more *them* looking and when they found something, me going to take a look. At that stage we thought it was possible I'd keep the house on in London, but participate in setting up this other thing and sort of go from one to the other or something. Various ideas and schemes got elaborated.

If your marriage is not working out, you can separate tomorrow and no one can stop you. In practice, however, this is not always so easy. It is one thing to part company because you have reached the end of your tether. Quite another to support yourself and possibly a couple of children if you have no money – Rosmary Simon

Meanwhile, I had an intense and long-lasting relationship myself, with someone else. It didn't work out in the end and throughout had enormous strains on it, no doubt partly because of my continuing relationship with Tanya. Even though Tanya and I were no longer sleeping together we were living together and bringing up the kids together, and ours was quite clearly a substantial relationship from the point of view of other people. One of the fictions throughout those six years was that I'd find a relationship the way Tanya had and then everything would be all right. But, in fact, I don't think I could have done. It does seem to me that women, when it comes to the crunch, are so much more decisive emotionally than men. It seems to me that Tanya made a decisive emotional decision about Mike which took the rest of us, including her, six years to work through. I was incapable of being so emotionally decisive, you know, deciding on someone else with all the risks and consequences that were to follow from that. In the end I stayed tied to Tanya and of course, in spite of Mike, she stayed tied to me – otherwise she would have left. But I was incapable of having other relationships of the same seriousness and depth and decisiveness as long as I lived with her. That became apparent particularly during this last relationship I had. It became clear that I wasn't in control of the situation.

So what the fuck was going on? Why were we all still living together?

What emerged very quickly – in a sudden psychological insight – was what a threesome really was. The three of us were refusing to accept certain responsibilities for our own lives. And through therapy, it became even more clear to me that I had to get out of it, that it was damaging by this time and that it had outlived its usefulness. We had struggled hard, in certain ways, and honourably so. But also, a lot of the time we didn't know what we were doing. Therapy made it a bit clearer, so I said to Tanya, 'You've got to go'. I said she'd got to go because she said she wanted to live in the country. So I said, 'Go live in the country . . . do it. Find somewhere . . . do it . . . or I leave. One or the other now. Or within the next three months, if you haven't found somewhere . . . I simply go.' And they found a place and got it.

There is no doubt whatever that there is an urgent need for a considerable expansion in day care facilities for children under five provided or supported by public authorities – 'The Finer Report, 1974'

I should say that living in the country is a very important thing going right back to the early tensions between us. I said that in the beginning we had grown together during the early part of our relationship and very productively so, to the extent of forming these very deep ties that even now haven't been broken. But the time had come, before she got off with Mike, when it became apparent in very key respects that we were becoming different people, that we had different interests, different rhythms of life and so on. Yes, part of the tension was about divisions of domestic labour and the fact that she was bored at home and fed up with me going out to work. Yes, we were sexually frustrated. Yes, we had fallen into a lot of the negative male/female patterns (dominance, submission and the rest of it). But we were also both becoming different people in key life-style ways. We needed to pursue those directions and couldn't do it together. Mike was into the country-side and health food and vegetarianism. I was much more urban, restless, rock-and-roll and sex, drugs-oriented. And ambitious. Mike met Tanya's new emerging requirements, while mine became completely different. When I said, 'You've got to go', it sounds as though I was kicking her out. But that's not what it was. It was an acknowledgement of the change that had happened.

I have mentioned that the children were a key reason why we lived together and that's true. On the many occasions we discussed separating, even if we could envisage living separately from each other, we couldn't envisage not living with the kids. Either of us. And I think, on balance, it was good for the children that we stayed together. I worried particularly about Ben, the younger one, who, on looking around for models for his identity has had half a father really. There were two blokes around which some people might think was good – two models. But, I think in this situation, it was a source of confusion for him. And he not only had to compete for Tanya with me and with Barbara, but with Mike too. There were three other people in the house who had relationships with his mother. And he was at the bottom end of the pecking order. With the effect that he has suffered a certain kind of insecurity, making him a little bit defensive and aggressive. He's eight now and I think he's okay basically. Barbara is extraordinarily strong and in-dependent.

It seems to be the case with a lot of splitting that, contrary to the myth of delinquent children from broken homes, they often seem to be incredibly independent, personally secure and confident as people. Often more so than nuclear family children. It's my observation that there's a case to be argued for children in this kind of situation.

82

As I've said, there are ways that Ben is more insecure than he might be, but by and large, comparing my kids with a lot of other kids, they seem to be pretty strong and tough characters and not disturbed children at all. Barbara absolutely, definitely not. Ben went through a difficult period, but I think he's coming out of that. They certainly don't have that claustrophobic dependent relationship you find in nuclear families. I think someone ought to study it scientifically.

One last thing. Ours was an extremely unusual way of splitting up. And where I'm at the moment is pretty frightened with massive feelings of rejection still, and lonely in a particular kind of way. That is, very aware of being alone, which is not the same as loneliness. But I also feel a new person, that I'm able to become me now, and am becoming me which, in a way, wasn't possible before when I was in my relationship with Tanya. Men in our society do have opportunities to be 'people' in ways which women don't have. But I also think it's true that the negative kinds of dependencies that build up in a relationship can hold a man back from being a 'person'. Tanya became a substitute mother for me and I had to leave home in this case, as in the previous one.

Postscript

Of the men, Tom is unusual in being politically conscious (and having applied this to his marriage), aware through most of his marriage of sexual politics and the politics of marriage, but still, despite a monumental effort of will and struggle, trapped by it. He would regard himself as progressive, and the fact that he and his wife and her lover lived together as a triangle for six years indicates the progressive alternatives to marriage that he was prepared to explore. Like Christine and Simon, he and his wife analysed many of their problems in terms of roles and the subtle pressures of the institution of marriage. And one of the similar things they tried to do was accommodate other sexual relationships within marriage.

Tom's final separation was not, therefore, just a personal defeat, a personal failure, as it were, but a 'political' defeat in that it called into question the possibilities of change that he had believed in, and made him wonder whether individual psychology was not perhaps a stronger force than he had previously believed.

Very much to his credit was the extent that he was aware of his wife's frustrations as a wife and mother – with the kitchen sink – and the degree to which he attempted to alleviate those frustrations – sharing the bread-winning and house-keeping, for example. At the same time, Tom is honest enough in the interview to confess that he couldn't completely rid himself of the feeling that his (male) life was more important than her (female) life, indicating just how deep conditioning can run. Significantly, it was after they had their first child that they 'slipped into conventional roles' and after the second child that tensions became intolerable. There was, in fact, a tendency with all the people in this book, for problems to start surfacing after the birth of children, and the constraints they imposed, and for the marriages to flounder and break down after the birth of the second child. Somebody suggested coining 'the second child syndrome' in splitting up.

When Tom was interviewed, it was still early days in his life as a single parent, but he felt strongly that he was embarking on a new life as a new person.

5. Ann

Ann comes from a working-class background and married young, at the age of seventeen. When she and her husband separated two years later, she had two children, one infant and one under two. Their relationship broke down completely before they split up, in part, says Ann, because of their age and the pressures of two infants. The second child was the straw that broke the camel's back. Her husband came into the hospital and she said, "Don't you want to look at the baby?" And he said, "She looks the same as the last one to me." He didn't seem to accept her at all. If she cired in the night, he'd say, "Get that baby out of here, I've got to go to work in the morning."'

At the time of the interview, Ann had been on her own for four years. She was twenty-four, and both children were at school. She thought she'd gone through the worst, and could go a bit further: 'I thought that if I got through the first five years, then I knew I'd be able to do the rest.' Ann still lives in the same flat in Liverpool, but now with her new common law husband with whom she's been living for three years. And she recently had a baby boy: 'My husband (common law) is delighted with his son and gets on very well with my two daughters and they with him.' She described the relationship as very different than that with her last husband: 'We get on very well together, we are very happy.' She didn't plan to remarry – 'Easy to get into, hard to get out of.' She was working as a playgroup leader: 'I hold down a good job and am financially much better off than ever before.'

She feels very strongly that she married too young: 'People used to say to me "You're only a baby", and I'd say "No I'm not." When I think back now . . . at seventeen, you know, it's ridiculous. I wouldn't like a daughter of mine to get married at seventeen, let alone have a baby at seventeen.'

I was sixteen and he was fifteen and we met at a dance, you know . . . classical organ and everything. I was living then with this friend and her mum and dad – my mum lives in Yorkshire and I was in Liverpool – and it was getting me down a bit. So we decided to get married. It was just the obvious thing to do. I couldn't stand living with the people I was living with, so we just got married and that was it. I was seventeen when I got married and sixteen when I met him. He was sixteen when we got married. Mind you, I was pregnant when we got married. But we intended getting married anyway, partly because he didn't enjoy living at home and partly because I didn't like living there either. So, you know, we thought it was great. If I'd waited until later on, well . . . a friend I was living with went to Australia, and I couldn't because I was married, and I was tied down with a baby, and expecting another one. That was when I realised what I'd done, *really*. But, you know, then it's too late to get out of.

People used to say to me, 'You're only a baby', and I'd say, 'No I'm not.' When I think back now . . . at seventeen, you know, it's ridiculous. I wouldn't like a daughter of mine to get married at seventeen, let alone have a baby at seventeen.

I'd left school at fifteen, and he'd left school. He went to work at sixteen. We were both working, and I had to give up work, which started the problems. Because the pay was about £12 a week, and getting the flat and baby clothes and things like that, you know, he didn't have money to go out. So we were locked in, sort of twenty-four hours a day, with each other, which drove us potty. We were lucky at first to get a flat. Only a one-roomed flat, just furnished with things, like out of Noah's Ark. It was quite basic really, holey lino, and things like that. But to me it was a flat and I loved it, you know. But you still get disillusioned when you see other people getting married, when they have done it right, and they have planned and got everything, you know.

I think what really brought it to a head was when I was expecting the second one so soon after the first one. I had Jennie when Susan was only just going on two. And that was it. I wanted another, but he didn't. And that's what done it. I wanted another one, I don't know why. You know, I really didn't think about anything logically then, you know. I was . . . I don't know . . . I thought marriage was all rosy, and having babies, and all that sort of thing.

We went to the registry office, but all the rest was the same, the reception and everything else. We were happy to begin with . . .the novelty of living with someone, you know. I suppose now, if I had had the guts, I would have lived with him then, and we would have

saved all this, but . . . at the time it was . . . well . . . I don't
know. I don't know what happened really. I suppose my husband
must have thought of being tied down with two children, when one
was bad enough . . . I don't know.

While I was in hospital and just before I had the second baby, he
started going out an awful lot . . .just his friends and things like
that. They were all single still. If it had been now, when they were
all married, it wouldn't have mattered so much, but they were all
single. And I think he got a taste of what he missed. Mind you, by
this time he was still only eighteen, something like that, maybe
seventeen perhaps . . . I can't remember. But still too young to be
tied down to two young children.

I was tied down anyway. I couldn't go out, and he used to say to
me, 'You can go out if you like.' But you know, you can't trail two
children into the pictures, or something like that. We were having
terrible rows. At the time I was just as aggressive . . . But, well, I
wouldn't let anyone hit me without hitting back. So, you know, it
went on, and we treated each other terribly . . . and you know the
usual sort of thing. Everything changed.

I couldn't understand it, because, you know, I always wanted
answers to everything and he wasn't prepared to give them to me.
He used to shut himself off completely. I used to want to know
where he had been and things like that. And he said, 'Nothing to do
with you, mind your own business', and so, in the end, I
thought . . . we had a fight one day and it was in front of the
children. And I thought, it's no good and . . .this was when the
youngest was about one month old . . . He wasn't so interested in
that one. He just didn't seem to accept her. If she cried in the night
he'd say, 'Get that baby out of here, I've got to go to work in the
morning', and things like that. And he would hardly look at her.
He came into the hospital and I said, 'Don't you want to look at the
baby?' And he said, 'She looks the same as the last one to me.'
Mainly because he wanted a boy. That's if he had to have anything
at all . . . he would rather it had been a boy. Though it still
wouldn't have made any difference. He still would have done the
same things. But, I can see now that it was both our fault . . .
though at the time I thought it was all his fault.

And it really was bad. But, I don't blame him now. I mean, for
what he done afterwards. For the way he grumbled about looking
after the children, I still blame him for that. But he is still only
twenty-four, and you know, there's not many twenty-four-year-

olds walking about the streets now, I think, imagine tying a father like him down with two kids! You can see, looking at it from the outside . . . and we were talking so grown up!

The evidence suggests that supplementary benefit is the main support of a significant number of fatherless families for lengthy periods of time. It demonstrates that the problem is not one of a short-term nature and it would be a mistake to view it as such. On the contrary, considerable numbers of children are spending their formative years at the basic level of resources provided by the supplementary benefit scheme – 'The Finer Report, 1974'

All the way through the second pregnancy . . . that was when it really started. He was going out again, and I thought, if he goes out he's going to get drunk and come back and start again. I thought I'd go to my mother's for the night. So I went to my mother and took both the children, and when I came back the next day he said, 'You're not coming back.' And he was angry about it, and I thought, 'Well, I'll stay away from him altogether.' And I found I was much happier . . . away from him, you know.

I needed someone, but I couldn't give in again, because he was tying me down more than anything else. He was allowed to go out and everything else, while I was still tied down with two children. Then I did start thinking a bit clearer, even though it was a bit too late. But I thought if I was going to do anything, I've got to do it now. He wouldn't let me back anyway. I mean, at first I did fight to get back, but then he wouldn't let me back. So I said I wanted the flat back. And he said I wasn't going to have it, and started one long fight. I could see his point of view, not having anywhere to live. But I had two children and I couldn't keep living with my mother. She had the other children as well. So we went to Court, but there was nothing they could do . . . private flat and all that. In the end he just gave up, because what the Court done. They made him pay me so much money at the time that he couldn't afford to pay me and keep the flat. They couldn't legally tell him to get out, but they could tell him he had to pay £9. Which is not a great deal now, but then it was a lot of money. He was only earning about £16 per week. And so when he worked it out, he couldn't afford to keep the flat anyway. So he did give it back to me. Well, he could have given it away, but he wasn't that bad. So in the end he gave the flat back to me, and ever since then we've got on more or less, you know, not too badly. We can talk to each other, but not get too deeply involved with anything about the children or anything like that, because it ends up in a row.

He wasn't at all good about paying the money. In Court, you know, when the man said, 'You'll have to pay her £9', he said, 'There's no way you're going to get that.' *I* thought it was a tremendous amount . . . but when I thought about it, well, it's not really a lot of money for two children. He did pay it, because he was under the impression that if he didn't pay it, he'd go to gaol. He still is, and I hope no one tells him otherwise. He still thinks it, but that is all he gives me. He never says, 'How much, or what do the children need?' He never asks. He'll give them money for their birthday, and say, 'Buy them a pair of shoes', but that's it, finished. Nothing else.

And he always treats the eldest one a lot better than the younger one. I don't know why, really, except I suppose he knows her and he doesn't really know the second one. She was only a month when he went away, and she's a stranger really. Now that he's grown up a bit, he's started to accept her, but it's still the oldest one is his, and the other one . . . just someone to be polite to.

I had a lot of trouble with the eldest one. She used to keep waking up in the middle of the night, crying . . . and nightmares. Sometimes I'd find her screaming, really screaming. She'd be standing by the curtains and holding like this . . . and it frightened me. I thought she'd go through the window one of these nights . . . And when I said, 'Why are you crying?' she would say she wasn't. And she was *really* crying. In the end I had to go to the doctor. She wouldn't sleep. She could stay awake all night. I had to get medicine from the doctor to make her sleep, 'cos she never ate, never done nothing. And the doctor said to me, 'She must eat.' And I said, 'Well she doesn't eat', and he said, 'Well if she didn't eat she wouldn't have any energy.' I said 'She doesn't eat and she sits up all night.' I said, 'With a one-month old baby waking up during the night', I said, 'I'm practically dead.' And the doctor said, 'Well stop giving her snacks in between.'

But if I stopped giving her snacks she'd eat nothing at all. She's growing up now and she's not too bad. But she's still a very miserable child compared to the younger one . . . very. I don't know how you would explain it. They're two totally different children altogether. I mean those two years seem to have imprinted a lot on her.

He wouldn't believe me, the doctor. He said, 'When I see her, she seems all right.' I said, 'Well you don't expect children to come out and tell you things.' It was only when she was asleep, or if something happened . . . if she fell over . . . or if she got upset . . . she'd get exceptionally upset. More so than she would normally. And he just didn't believe me. I said, 'Well, she always seems to be ill to me, all the time. She's always getting ever so hot and temperatures and all this.'

First of all I didn't go to work. I thought about it. I tried to get them into the nursery . . . which you know what it's like . . . and in the end they said they'd put both of them in nursery from 9 o'clock till 12 o'clock and I said, 'Well, it's not much use to me', I said, 'because I'd have to find a job between half past nine and half past eleven.' I think the Social Security were giving me £4 or something to make up the difference, but they would have taken that away if I'd gone to work.

Mind you, I had problems with the Social Security too because . . . well it was fine in the summer. I could just about manage. When the winter boots and winter coats started coming in and things like that . . . I found it difficult. Lucky enough my mum and dad were quite good. I mean, they didn't have a lot of money, but they'd help where they could . . . buying clothes for birthday presents and things like that . . . instead of the usual toys. But from the Social Security I found the help very poor. You know, I think I had a Health Visitor to come up and see me once, and she didn't even ask to see the children. That's the only time I seen anyone. I would have liked someone to sort of ask . . . I don't know . . . how you felt about it and things like that. Not just come and look and say 'Oh, yes, they've got beds and they've got gas, and they've got electricity.' Someone to actually talk to. Because I didn't know anyone, and you feel more lost than anything. Especially sort of 9 o'clock when the children have gone to bed and you're sitting there . . . you know, night after night after night. It's terrible. I think if I had known some other people who were in the same position at the time, I would have been better.

In the first six months I was completely lost, but then I moved round to the flats where I originally lived and I started to talk to people and things like that. I mean, some of them were older people and some of them were in their forties and things like that, but . . . before when I lived in the flats for two years, I didn't know anyone, I was just sort of locked away. But then when I started to talk to people I found it much better. There was always someone willing to have the children, even if it was only while I went to the shops, and things like that. It helped an awful lot. I didn't feel I had to trail the children everywhere I went. I was beginning to take it out on the kids. Because they were there all the time, whining and miserable and things like this. I was thinking of lots of desperate things like leaving them with my mum and going away . . . I wouldn't actually have done any of them but . . . I felt ever so bitter, you know. He's out every night and I am here. Why should he do this? Why should he do that? They're his kids as well. I felt like taking them down to him and leaving them and going . . . You know I never done it, because I was too scared that he would put them in care or something like that. I felt it was really unfair.

The overall low earning capacity and low status of women in employment needs to be tackled if women are to achieve the economic equality and independence which will help lift the lone parent out of poverty – 'The Finer Report, 1974'

He bluffed me into leaving him. I left the first night because I was frightened. I was frightened to stay there. And then, I suppose he took it as an opportunity to get rid of me. I always used to say to my friends, when the children are old enough to go to school and they don't need babysitters or anything like that, he'd want to come back. And he did! I knew it would happen. He came up one day and the bloke I was going out with was there, and he went absolutely potty. It was all right for him, but it wasn't all right for me.

I'd got a divorce. At the beginning I got a separation and then I got a divorce, but he still thought we were married. He lived with this girl, but he came up to me and he went potty. He said, 'I knew I'd catch you some day.' And I said 'What? I can't see that I'm doing anything wrong.' I said, 'I'm not married to you. You don't expect me to live like a nun for the rest of my life?' And he said, 'Come back', and things like this, and I said, 'Well, you're just too late.' I said, 'Perhaps any time before now I would have done it', I said, 'but not now.' Jennie was just about going to school and I suppose he thought I would be going to work soon . . . two incomes, and he would be just as well off. I had all the hard times and he could come back. But I said, 'Well, no, you're just too late.'

And he accepted it in the end. But he thought I would be sitting there pining and waiting for him just to ask. I think it came as a shock to him, because I think he thought he only had to snap his fingers and I would go running. While the children were babies, I think I would have done. I just wanted someone to back me up and be there. But I'd gone through the worst, so I thought . . . I've gone this far, I can go a bit further.

I thought the first five years is the worst, because, I mean, you don't really look after them once they go to school. It's someone else's responsibility. I mean, besides bringing them home and things like that. I thought that if I got through the first five years, then I know I'd be able to do the rest. But I really couldn't do that again. It seemed the longest five years I'd ever known, but lucky enough I had a lot of friends and things like that. In the end I built up a number of friends. Because when I got married I had dropped people out. There was just me and my husband and I didn't know anyone. It was ever so hard. I got ever so shy and I didn't want to mix with people and I had to force myself to go out and talk to people. I had a younger brother and he stayed with me. He was working, but he used to stay in in the evenings. And I had a part-time job as a barmaid and I got to know one of the barmaids. We used to go out once a week. And then I got to know her friends, and things like that.

And then I got a boyfriend. I remember my brother-in-law said to me, 'What a rotten thing to do to you. With one child you'd have a chance. With two children you've got no chance'. I thought . . . well . . . if that's a man's point of view . . . and that really depressed me. That thought stayed with me and stayed with me all the time, that no one would want to know. No one wanted two children. As soon as they know you've got two children, they'd be away. It was true up to a point, I suppose. Lucky enough I go out with someone who is ever so good. He treats the children as if they were his own. But, I had been all right until my brother-in-law said that, and it hit me. I thought, if that's coming from a man, that must be all men's point of view, and it really depressed me. I used to think about it all the time.

I thought that's it, I'm finished. I'll end up thirty-seven – and things like that. Going to work, coming home watching television and going to bed and things like that. But then, after a while, I used to see people. I used to think, 'How old would I be when the youngest is sixteen?' and things like this, and 'Will I be too old then?' And then I used to see people of thirty-five and thirty-six, and I used to think, 'Well you're still young at that age', but it seemed very old to me, you know. It seemed ever so old to me when I was only eighteen. When I stopped thinking about it so much, I wasn't so bad. And then when I did meet people and talked to them, the children didn't matter. If they thought enough about you, the children didn't come into it.

Cohabitation Rule: 'This is a nasty! But it is as well to know about it, so that you can take steps to protect yourself. The rule is that a woman cannot claim Supplementary Benefit, widow's benefit or child's special allowance if she is living with a man as 'man and wife'. The rule is based on the assumption that just because a man and woman are living together, the man is willing and able to support his girlfriend not to mention any children she might have. In many cases the man is neither willing nor able. Often, too, a woman does not wish a man to accept financial responsibility simply because they are living together (perhaps on a temporary basis). She either loses her independence because her benefits are stopped (she may be able to continue claiming benefits for the children for four weeks) or she is faced with the choice of breaking off a relationship that gives her emotional pleasure. Benefits are sometimes stopped because a woman is thought to be cohabiting – although in reality she is not receiving any money from the man and is not actually living with him but only sleeping with him several times a week. The procedure for trying to discover whether a woman in receipt of benefits is cohabiting is very distasteful. If the Commission's officers are suspicious, special investigators will be sent to check up on the situation. They may question you, your neighbours – even your children – Rosemary Simon

---

Someone said to me, the lady downstairs she said, 'I've seen lots of people just let themselves go when something like that happens, but you didn't.' I didn't think about it like that. I didn't think I was doing it – just doing it. I'd get all made-up and things like that. I don't know if it was just to reassure myself, I wasn't getting so old . . . and nobody would want me or what. But I used to wash my hair and set it, and cut my eyebrows. I wasn't going anywhere or anything like that. I think it was just a boost really, because I never went anywhere . . . anyway very, very seldom. I don't think I particularly wanted a boyfriend, or anyone to live with, or anything like that. But I wanted to know that I could . . . if I . . . wanted. You know, if I did really want to. The children weren't going to stand in the way.

It was very difficult at first when the children were babies. Because, people, men especially, will accept children, but not a baby, especially one about one or two months old. Because people will talk and say, 'Is it yours?' and things like that. I don't think I went out with anyone until I'd been separated about two years, and even then I don't think I particularly liked him. I think I just clung to him because he accepted the children, and he took me out. I thought perhaps if I don't stay with him, perhaps no one else will want me. But I really didn't like him very much at all. We used to argue. He really was a pompous pig. He was worse than my husband. But I just used to think . . . well, better him than no one. Someone to turn to, someone to talk to and tell your problems to, and things like that. Because you can't always say things to women, you know. Some things you just want to tell a man. In the end, when I got a bit more confident in myself, I got rid of him.

I had a lot of trouble myself at first. I think about two months after, I didn't eat, or anything like that. And my periods stopped and I couldn't understand it. It wasn't until . . . later I realised it was nervosa . . . anorexia nervosa. It was brought on by the shock of everything that was happening and being so depressed. I went right down to six stone and they couldn't understand it. They took me to hospital for tests and they said, 'There's nothing wrong with you physically. Nothing we can find wrong with you at all.' My periods still haven't come back . . . and that was from five years ago. They said, 'When you settle down in your mind, you'll be all right. When you haven't got problems.'

Everyone just used to keep saying to me 'You'd better eat.' I just didn't want food. I didn't need food. I ate when I was particularly hungry . . .which might have been once a week. You know, at first my Mum used to make me meals and she used to say, 'Eat it', and I used to pick at it, but I didn't want it. Food didn't mean a thing to me. When I was six stone I realised. I just used to think I was slim, and then when I really looked in the mirror, I thought 'You're not getting slim, you're skinny.' I was like a skeleton. And then they took me into hospital for tests. But I still don't eat a great deal. I think it's a habit, you know. I've never eaten a lot.

I've often wanted to take tranquillisers and sleeping tablets, better not if I could help taking them. Mind you . . . those Valium . . . those ones . . . the first time I took my driving test, I took some of those. He gave me quite a lot, and I started doubling up. I thought they would make me feel much better then I came to my senses. I thought, well you're on your way . . . to . . . you know, going on stronger things if you're not careful. I mean, I used to cry a lot, and things like that, and feel sorry for myself. But really, what stopped it all was when I met the bloke I go out with now, and that was when I decided I wouldn't go back to my husband and I was quite happy the way I was. In the end, what really made the difference was somebody else that really mattered.

My husband . . . he doesn't come to see the children . . . very, very rarely. Occasionally he may come up here and see the children. He only lives two minutes down the road, but it's more or less a chance meeting if he sees the children. Or if I go to get my money, then he'll see them. But he never goes out of his way to see them. He could, he's only two minutes down the bottom of this road, but he would never dream of walking up here. I've said to him often enough, 'If you like to come up, you can bring your girl with you, I don't mind. Come up and see the children.' But he never done it. I think twice since we've been living here he's actually gone out of his way to come up and see them. He hasn't been up to see them now for about a month. He never comes up.

I go and fetch my money from him. He would bring it at a push, but he wouldn't put himself out. I don't really mind, I've got used to it now. I don't like any aggravation at all. I can't be bothered fighting with him any more. I'd do anything for a peaceful life, and now I don't accept money for me, only for the children. I didn't want it to begin with, but I needed it, and I hated having to take it . . . but I needed it. He'd say, 'I don't mind the £5 for the children, but why should I pay for you?' I said to him, 'If I had a job,' I said, 'and had money,' I said, 'do you think that I want your money?' I said, 'It's the last thing I want.' So I said, 'As soon as the children are old enough and I can go to work, I won't take your money.' And as soon as I went to work, I didn't take his money. Because he still seemed to have a hold over me. I mean, it was only £4, that's all he was paying me. But it was still something for him to niggle about. I think I was right not to go to work when the children were tiny, even though I hated having to take money from him.

I was determined not to leave the children, because I'd seen it so many times. I'd done lots of different things. I'd looked after children to bring money in, and I looked after this little boy. His mother went to work right from the start, right from the time he was quite small. He was a nice little boy. His mother was separated, but he was missing something . . . not having a mother. He was very clingy and he went to anyone, and I thought . . . I wouldn't like my children to be like that. If that's what having a little bit extra better furniture means, I'd rather wait. I thought, well, they've only got five years with their parents, and if they've only got one, it's even worse. So I thought, I may as well give them the five years and live on Social Security.

Mind you, I had lots of problems with Social Security as well, 'cos I used to hate taking their money as much as my husband's. I thought I was asking them for something for nothing. In the end things got so bad . . . I had so many bills, and it was winter, so I wrote them a nice letter saying I hear I'm entitled to a grant for children's clothing. I said that I didn't find it bad in the summer, but in the winter, buying coats and things like that, I found it very hard to manage. And they wrote back a letter to me saying that the money they gave me every week should cover the children's clothing and things like that. Which annoyed me because I'd heard that other people had got it. I'd seen other people getting it. They were going to work and still claiming it. And it made me ever so bitter, you know. I did go up there once. They called me up there and asked all sorts of personal questions. And said you'd better take your husband to Court, and you'd better do this to your husband, and you'd better do that. I thought it's all right for you talking, you don't know what my husband's like. Things had got so bad between us that I was really scared about going to Court. But they badgered me so much I thought I had to, and then I decided that we would be better off if we stayed out of each other's way because I was afraid of the consequences.

But I took him to Court about the money, because they said, 'We can't keep paying you the money, you must take your husband to Court.' That was another thing why I wanted to go to work. I was glad to be able to give Social Security back their money, because they kept sending people up and spying on me.

Where I lived there was a paper shop downstairs, and I used to talk to the gentleman there, and he said to me, 'Would you keep an eye on the shop for a couple of days and I'll give you a couple of pounds, I can't afford a lot more than a couple of pounds.' And I thought . . . Great! I can take the kids down there a couple of evenings . . . Lovely! He paid me and he gave me a couple of packets of cigarettes, things like that. Someone told, and the Social Security were spying on me – night and day. They were coming up.

They were pestering me. First of all they would ask my neighbours questions, and one of the neighbours told me. She said they came and asked if I was working and how much money I was getting and if I had anyone living with me and all things like that. And then the man eventually came up to see me. I was ever so annoyed. I said, 'Up till now my neighbours didn't know my business, but they do now because you told the wrong person, you know, the biggest gossip in the street.' And by that time every single person in Winchester Street knew, you know. Which I thought was wrong. I didn't think they had any right to do it. I was trying to lead as normal a life as is possible without anyone else knowing there was anything different about me.

You do not require a specialist knowledge to be aware that housing is one of the worst problems in Britain to-day. Equally, you need not be on the breadline to run into difficulties finding suitable accommodation at a price you can afford – though it is understandable that the less money you have, the greater the obstacles – Rosemary Simon

---

But within one week everyone knew I was on my own, where my income was coming from and what have you. He talked to this woman in the block and luckily enough she told me. Mind you, she answered his questions pretty straightforward. She told him everything, and from that time on they were standing outside my house in the morning, waiting to see if there were people coming out, and things like that. And I thought . . . I've had it all before from my husband. I didn't want it any more. So I phoned them up and said, 'Look if you're watching me you're wasting your time and your money, because,' I said, 'I'm not doing anything.' And they said, 'Oh, we're not watching you.' But they were. After that they sort of left me alone, but I kept getting letters from the Social Security and they wanted to talk to me, and things like that. In the end, as soon as Jennie went to school, I went out and got a job. And the greatest pleasure was giving them back their book, you know. They don't annoy me any more.

Then I moved out and into here. I got away from all of them, the whole thing, because I had people gossiping about me and everything, you know. It was like making a fresh start when we moved in here. It was really lovely. It was a whole new life. It was the best thing we'd ever done for all of us. The children had a garden, where they'd been living on a main road, and things like that. This was the best thing I'd ever done moving into here away from everyone.

I left all the furniture to my husband. Everything that was in his flat. It wasn't very much, mind you. He'd kept on about *his* furniture, *his* flat, *his* this, *his* that, so, in the end I just gave him back everything. The whole lot. Everything that was in the flat, and said, 'Now . . . you've got no claim on me whatsoever.'

I don't think I'll marry again. I more or less live with this bloke I'm going out with now, and we're fine. Marriage doesn't come into it really. I think I'd be too scared that just that piece of paper can make so much difference. Maybe it's that you don't try hard enough once you're married. You think, 'Why should I bother now? I've got him now. He's got me', or whatever. I don't know what differnce it is really, but it does seem to make an awful lot of difference. I think at a push that I would get married . . . but I prefer not to. If I was pregnant I suppose I would, but I've got no intentions of having another baby if I can possibly help it. It's got to the point where we've got most of the material things that we want, even though they don't mean such a lot when you've gone without them.

We've just started going out places, and we can probably afford a holiday, and things like that, so it's just started to look a bit better now. I don't think I'd ruin it by getting married. I don't know what that piece of paper means but I know I don't want it.

Postscript

Ann is a classic example of the problems of marrying too young, something she came very quickly to realise, but 'too late' as she said. And she found herself in perhaps the most difficult of circumstances – young, with two infants on her own. She does not play down the problems, particularly with the children and the Social Security, and is extremely honest, analytical and self-critical in assessing what happened, so much so that she was able to cope with her anger at an early stage and to evenly apportion the blame for the failed marriage.

Ann comes across as a woman of great stamina, strength and intelligence, who quite literally grabbed her life by the horns of its dilemma in the darkest hours and consciously steered it on to a happy and productive and independent course. Hers must be one of the most 'educative' experiences in this book, a shining example of a woman now thriving as a single parent, taking control of her life and deliberately choosing an alternative to marriage.

6. James

James comes from a middle-class background: he works as an accountant with a big company. He married at the age of thirty: his wife was quite a bit older. They separated after fifteen years of marriage, with four children between the ages of five and fourteen. The circumstances were complicated by the fact that James' wife was suffering from mental illness and in and out of hospital during the period of splitting up. But James had decided to separate and went about it in a determined, but also very responsible manner. He had, as he describes, worked very hard at keeping the marriage going. In the process of separating and then looking after his children, James thought a lot about the meaning of marriage, sex and roles. When he married, he started climbing the 'commuter' ladder: the higher he went, the unhappier he was. Men are usually regarded as more fortunate than women, being the breadwinners and outside the home: James very clearly calls into question *those* values.

At the time of the interview James had been separated for several years, was nearing fifty and his children were all in their teens. They lived in a flat in Bromley.

Of his situation now, he says: 'I think my views are full of contradictions at the moment. I think my attitude to marriage has changed. On the one hand I think marriage is largely unimportant in the relationship between two people. On the other hand I think the status of being married is important – I was going to say to women, but equally to men. I think it is important to recognise that there is a particular person in the world to whom one is attached. That is a measure of commitment. And I do want my children to marry. Because it's the normal way of life.' He had finally decided on a divorce (despite the Catholic background) and was awaiting this in order to remarry a woman he had met sometime after the separation.

'I have been on my own with the kids for two years and am amazed how well we manage. We all pull together and I think we are happier and better adjusted – all of us – than we ever have been.'

It happened very suddenly. I was pretty well set for a gay bachelor life . . . not gay in the modern sense, I should say. I was twenty-eight, twenty-nine . . . working in an ordinary sort of job . . . drifting rather. I hadn't really made up my mind what I wanted to do. I was in the sales office of a small company. I had only taken the job because it was handy to my home. I was living with my parents. I got in with a crowd who used a club in the West End. And we usually met in there regularly Saturday nights, Sunday lunchtimes. One day a woman friend of mine brought in a friend of hers and it was just quite sudden: I thought, 'I'm going to marry that woman'. Just like that.

I think, to be absolutely honest, I had decided that I needed to get married. I had been, up to then, rather 'anti' the whole idea of marriage. An all-male boarding school isn't a good place to grow up. And I was brought up as a Roman Catholic; it has its compensations, but it is an awkward thing to live with. And I think I have to be a bit candid here. Active homosexuals often mistook me for a passive homosexual. I wasn't, but I wasn't actively heterosexual either. I knew two or three women in a casual sort of way. And then there was a grand affair. That was it. And that broke up. But I had decided that I wanted a permanent relationship. In simple words, I wanted to be married. Now what did I want out of it? I think I wanted to get away from my parents for a start. I'd been there too long, so it was time to do something about that. I think I needed some kind of motivation. I think I was getting worried about my lack of direction. In these drinking clubs you always get some fifty- to sixty-year-old men who have never married, who have got nothing to do, so they are there every night. I could see that, and I didn't want it for myself. I was thinking of marriage as a settling down.

Which now I consider to be the worst mistake. If people tell me they are settling down to marry, I try to tell them not to. Because if they regard marriage as a settling down, then it's not going to work. Marriage is a development, and it must continue as a development. I see so many youngsters, especially working where I do, who tie themselves up in mortgages, furniture, houses, car, dog, and perhaps children. And that is it. They are fixed for forty years; it's going to take them that long to pay, you know. And I don't like it. I don't think it's a bearable way of life in the long run. I think it's got a lot to do with the divorce rate. We need a much more decisive sort of marital education. People have got to be made much more aware of what they are getting into.

There is a pressure on people to get married, I think. Social pressure. Girls, I think, find this particularly, about the age of eighteen or nineteen. Their friends are getting married and they're not and it's almost like a rat race to find a man. But I think it works on men as well. A lot of career openings are available to men who are pretty well tied up, and not to men who are footloose. That sort of pressure exists. Apart from that there is pressure from the media to 'be in love'. If you know what I mean. The implication is there is something wrong with you if you are not in love with somebody. People seem in these days to succumb to these pressures a lot earlier than they used to.

Anyway, I met my wife. She was several years older than me. She was a Catholic as well. I hadn't been to mass that day, so we went across to evening mass at Westminster Cathedral. We were very wrapped up in each other at the beginning. The rest of the world stopped existing for a while, you know. It's a nice feeling. It's not always the absolute basis on which to marry but it's probably one of the things which make it easier to get married.

Now it gets complicated. We didn't live together in the accepted sense, before we married. I'd moved out from my parents because I thought it was about time I did, and if we were going to get married I didn't want to be straight from home, you see. So I moved out. But at the same time we were trying to save money, the pair of us, and in the end, my parents having two empty rooms on their hands, we moved back in. We each had a room. Quite separate. We didn't sleep together. No sexual relationship. I think she was a virgin but I don't know. She wasn't experienced certainly.

My father's attitude about it all was mixed. He was a convert to Catholicism – in his youth, at about the age of eighteen. He was quite knowledgeable about it. He used to speak at Hyde Park Corner and places like that. My two sisters had married non-Catholics, so he was pleased to see somebody marry a Catholic. So he was reasonably happy with the developments. My mother had her doubts, but she never expressed them much. My mother suspected even then that my wife was not well but she didn't say anything. And I certainly didn't notice anything at the time. I was very much in love.

Anyway, we were saving money with the intention of getting married. We were formally engaged. We were getting ready to get married. We wanted to stay in London and we were a bit doubtful about having children. We talked about that. But not properly. If I had to do it again, it would be different. Again, Catholicism came into it. Contraception was an issue. And I think, to be honest, we failed to communicate properly on this one. It just wasn't a subject that one easily talked about. Anyway, we found a room which we could just about afford, and we got married about a month after we'd found it. We had a big wedding – at Westminster Cathedral. I enjoyed that. I thought it was a good way of doing it. Now, looking back of course, it was one of the first signs. Claire didn't really enjoy it. She wanted a quiet, local affair.

So we married and moved into this room after a fortnight's honeymoon in Spain. Back home, and Claire was pregnant. So we left the room and found a flat down in Greenwich. I decided that I wasn't getting enough money where I was, and I got a job with a big international company. And of course that led into everything – the mortgage, the season ticket, all the draining of one's resources.

The pregnancy came as a shock. We were using the rhythm method, but we didn't talk about it sufficiently to make it work. But it didn't worry me, you know. I thought, 'All right, that's it. It's what marriage is for, in one respect anyway.' I was very happy. And so was she, I think. Perhaps she was a bit worried on the money side of things, but I said 'We'll just have to manage, millions of people do. We'll just have to get through it as best we can.' She was working, but she stopped in the sixth month. Then a fortnight before they were born, we found out it was twins. But I wasn't worried. We had everything we needed. I hadn't been at this firm long enough then to get a mortgage, but as soon as the twelve months were up, they agreed to it. However, we had to buy what we could afford to buy, where we could afford to buy it. And what we bought, in fact, was just a patch of mud at that time. It wasn't built until about twenty months later. Down in a little village in Hampshire. And I became a commuter. I wasn't worried, you know. I was still of the attitude that this is what lots of people do. Nothing unusual, you know. And I think if we had had a basically sound home life, it would have still been going on now.

In those days I wasn't a very demanding sort of person. Perhaps I took things a bit casually, I don't know. But I thought we were getting on all right. If I want something done, I tend to do it myself. So the fact that I was doing things around the house which would normally be done by a wife didn't strike me. For example, at the furnished flat in Greenwich, I took the curtains to be dry cleaned, to brighten the place up a bit. I did that. Or I came home from work one night, when the twins were about three months old and she hadn't got out to buy a tin of feed mix. So off I went up to Boots at Piccadilly. Just bad organisation as far as I could make out. I didn't really worry about it at the time. I did think it a nuisance but I'd do it.

I was the breadwinner and she was the housewife and mother. That's the way I looked at it. I was going out to work and she was running the home, but she didn't seem able to cope with that. This is difficult, because looking back I can see a lot more than I could at the time. At the time I took it pretty well as it came. The fact that when we moved down to this new house, it had these plastic tiles on the floors that *I* could get really bright and clean. *She* couldn't, so I did it. I like things clean. So I just mucked on. There wasn't anything else to do, as far as I was concerned. And I'm still very much that way. If there's something to be done, I'll do it. It doesn't matter to me.

One parent families are the subject of three systems of law: those administered by the divorce courts, the magistrates' courts and the supplementary benefit authorities. The reasons for this are historical; the three systems emerged from the ecclesiastical courts, the criminal jurisdiction of the magistrates and the poor law respectively. It is not possible to convey more than a hint of the complexity and ill-effects of this tangled web of law and administration – 'The Finer Report, 1974'

I was satisfied. I thought I was happy and we rubbed along. Then we decided, quite deliberately, to have another child, that would be Charles. Now the twins would have been about four when we decided to have Charles. Having had him, we reckoned there was too big a gap between him and the other two, so we needed yet another one – for him. So we had Nancy. This was also deliberate. It was what we thought was the best thing to do. Well, when I say we, I don't know. I like having babies around, they're fun. They're hard work, but they pay off. We'd got the rhythm method sorted out eventually. We had to talk in the end, and we did. It was as simple as that. Of course, it's not a good method psychologically. Our sexual relationship wasn't satisfactory, ever. I think Claire just didn't like sex, quite honestly. I know that sounds ridiculous with four children around, but I don't think she did. I suppose I had hang-ups as well, which would go back to that grand affair. That was the only time that sex had been fulfilling for me. I don't know . . . but I suppose one makes comparisons. There was no attraction. I wasn't sexually attracted by Claire after a while. I was . . . I was going to say ignorant, but it wasn't exactly ignorance. Clumsy probably . . . I don't know. Yes, clumsy is probably the best word – and impatient too. It was probably largely my fault, but it cooled. From the day the twins were born until literally today, I've been dead. And this is a bigger thing than one takes into account. It's a worry. I don't think sex interested her at all. I don't think it really ever did.

When we had two more children we needed a bigger house. And we got the most beautiful house you've ever seen. It was superb. And that was the real beginning of the rot. Because for some reason or other Claire took against this house, before we even moved into it. And I loved it. I still regret losing it. It was just what we needed – four big bedrooms, big lounge, separate dining room, entrance hall 17 feet by 9 feet – bigger than some people's living room, kitchen, wash-house, drying house, everything you could possibly think of. And a big garden which I was quite prepared to look after. It was superb.

But she wouldn't look after this house. And it was an easy house to look after because you had the room to do it. There was a lot of floor, but I bought a £700 carpet. It only had to be hoovered. There were all the usual things – washing machine, new electric cooker, only material things, but they help. But I think by this time – and I've got to be really fair – she was a sick woman. It wasn't her fault. But I didn't know at the time. And I wasn't all that upset then. I think I had the attitude that well, your marriage does settle down eventually. I never went out with other women. I suppose in about fifteen years I had two late nights with the lads. I was very much a home bird. But it became obvious that she was really seriously ill.

First of all, there were quite ridiculous arguments with the neighbours. I can't remember what they were, they were so unimportant. Eventually I got into thinking, 'What the hell have I got to sort out tonight?' I can remember I used to get off the train – it was two minutes walk from the station – and be looking forward to seeing the kids. I'd get to the front gate, and between the front gate and the front door I'd lose my temper. I hadn't met anyone. I'd be just in a bad mood. It became a habit. I noticed it. This feeling was becoming so strong in the end that I started doing something about it. You know, controlled it. So I suppose even in a very trivial way, I'd begun to feel that things were not satisfactory. I used to bottle things up. Anyway, I thought I'd better do something about it to keep things going. So I started being a bit more physically attentive. There's one thing I did expect of a wife when I got married which was to greet her husband with a kiss. And this wasn't happening. That was a disappointment at least. It never did happen. However, I started a little more caressing and embracing. But it wasn't acceptable by that time. I wanted some evidence of affection. I now regard physical contact as one of the most important means of communication between a man and a woman. But at the time I suppose I was just ignorant of that sort of thing.

I think the average married person tends to try to keep their marriage going. I'd always recognised that marriage was something that had to be worked at. There's no magic about it. That you have to have this intention of keeping it going in order to be able to keep it going. It was part of the agreement of being married, that one would remain married. I have known people who have gone into marriage with the idea that if it doesn't work, they can get divorced. But very few people do.

There is a need . . . not merely to revise the summary jurisdiction (of the magistrates' courts) by abolishing its inefficiencies and anachronisms, but to create a thoroughly unified system of matrimonial law applied through an institutional structure which reflects that unity – 'The Finer Report, 1974'

Eventually it became obvious in various ways that Claire was sick. The telephone had to be covered up and the radio. I couldn't make it out at first. Gradually she got this complex that the whole world was looking at her, persecuting her in some way or other. That the house was full of TV cameras and microphones. Not only was I the head of BBC (so that people knew all about her) but also of ITV; I was the man behind Mr Wilson and behind Mr Heath. You name it, I was it. I wasn't going to work in London, I was going to Aldershot to have breakfast with a blonde and then driving up to London in a big Rolls Royce. And there was another woman who wore a rose patterned headscarf whom I met at mass every Sunday. There was no limit to it. It was impossible. What mattered to me at first was that my work was going to pieces. This goes back to the old breadwinner caper. But it was important because there was nothing else to keep things together. I'd moved on to a different company. And I'd made what was considered to be a very big move – everyone thought I was taking a chance. But, I was rather proud of having done it in a way.

I told my manager what was going on and he went straight across to the personnel department and fixed up an interview with the firm's doctors. I saw them the next day and described it. And they said it was classic schizophrenia. Not only that, it was very dangerous, and I'd got to do something about it. So I went to my own doctor that evening and he came around. He said we'd have to leave it overnight, but he'd be back with the papers in the morning and I'd have to sign. It was just as simple as that. She was extremely ill.

I hadn't realised. Honestly, you don't see it. It builds up so gradually. And it's only when really crazy things like covering the radio start . . . it's just an atmosphere before that. Looking back, yes, you can see all sorts of things. Anyway, the National Health attitude to this kind of illness seems to be tranquillise them and send them home. And keep them tranquillised. Well, that's fine, if you can ensure that the tranquillisers are taken. So, three tablets disappear from the bottle every day, you're out at work twelve hours, more or less – where have they gone? They've been taken or they haven't? And it very quickly becomes apparent that they haven't. And then they don't even go out of the bottle, because she just doesn't care any more. And you are back where you started, with Mr Wilson, Mr Heath and everybody else. While she was in hospital – she was in for six weeks – they made sure she took the tablets – and they worked there, so they sent her home. She looked twenty years younger. But that was short lived. The first thing you have to accept is that you are ill. And schizophrenics don't.

Anyway, it went on like that. She went back into hospital again about a year later, but voluntarily this time, because the doctor said if she didn't volunteer then I'd sign the papers again. So it was voluntarily, technically. Then I came around to the feeling that she never liked this house, so I decided to move. I was hoping that she'd get better in a new environment, and I wanted to keep my marriage going. Because I was still a practising Catholic. No question of divorce or anything like that. We managed to sell the house eventually, not for anything like I wanted for it. But you had to take what you could get. I was sorry to leave that house. It was irreplaceable on my income by then, because obviously I hadn't made the progress I ought to have made. I just didn't have the energy at work. In fact, the firm had been very good – they'd deliberately not given me responsibility, so that I could cope with the home situation.

I fixed up to buy a fairly sizeable house again. Because one of the things which children need as they grow older – and mine were now twelve, eight and six – is a room of their own. So I found a house which I could afford, at a scrape, but we'd manage. Now, I did all this off my own bat, because Claire was in hospital again. And as far as I was concerned she was going to stay there until she was well. But the hospital authorities when they heard that I was moving, rather took the attitude that if I didn't take her with me I'd leave her there for ever. Anyway, I decided I was going to move and she was going to stay in hospital a little longer. But they just didn't want to know, so she came out the day we moved. The house wasn't quite ready. I had all the contracts but I hadn't signed them. I don't know why – I just hadn't got around to it. Anyway, she took one look at the new house and she said, 'No, can't do that, too big, can't run it.' I wasn't really bothered on that score because she hadn't been able to run any of her houses, and I knew that by then. But she persisted, so I said all right. So we looked around the town and found a little bungalow – which was just what I didn't want. I suppose this was another nail in the coffin. Again, it was on a new estate: I won't ever live on one of those estates again. It was only three bedrooms, smallish rooms, so we were worse off than we were before. However, it was a size that she thought she could manage. I thought if she can manage anything she can manage this. But she couldn't. Quite honestly, I don't think she was with us really.

Things just dragged on and on. She took to lying in bed all day. I had been fed up for a long time, with having to do the shopping on a Saturday, when I wanted the weekend to myself – to get on with the garden and things like that. So I called in the new doctor we had down there. And he put her into hospital again. But, after eight weeks, home she came.

Now something did happen that made a difference. We took on summer staff at the office because we were starting a computer development. I was told I was going to get a chap from Exeter to help me out for a few months. And my 'chap' turned out to be a very beautiful girl from Cambridge. A friend of mine in the office made a big play for her, and I thought – 'No, you're not going to win that.' And sure enough, he didn't. But he must have got her going, because she went for me. And I suppose I was ready for it. This was about two years ago. I must have been in a hell of a state, because I could do nothing about this girl – sexually, I mean. It just wasn't there. I liked her, and we shared a lot of time together, I took her out to dinner, I even slept in her house. But I wasn't going to get involved. I didn't want to know. I suppose I was impotent, actually. What with nerves and all the confusion, I literally hadn't looked at another woman for fifteen years or so. And then suddenly . . . well, it was very flattering. She was about twenty and a nice girl. I could go through the motions, I liked being with her, I liked going out with her, and escorting her around. But, I think I was scared stiff, quite honestly. It ended disastrously, in fact. Just because I wouldn't do anything. But it did make me aware that there was a hell of a lot going on that I wasn't involved in. It gave me a new perspective. I saw that I was wasting my life. And I decided to do something about it.

One of the main personal problems in one-parent families is the parents' social isolation. They suffer from loneliness – not only of surroundings, but also of unshared difficulties. They are lonely in their responsibility for the physical care of the children – a responsibility which often robs them of sleep and makes demands on them beyond their physical stamina. They carry the entire burden of responsibility for the social, emotional and moral upbringing of the children, and for that part of their education which has to take place outside school. They suffer all the strains of being compelled, as one parent, to play the part of two, in order to create within the home a microcosm of the society in which the children will become adults – 'The Finer Report, 1974'

The rail fare had jumped from about £470 to £600 a year. It's one of those things, the farther out you are the faster the train, so you pay the money and save the time. I used that as an excuse – I said I'm going to live in London, you stay down here with the kids and I'll come down at weekends. For about two months that worked. Then I found that I didn't want to go down at the weekends either. Then I was working seven days a week, I had no reason to go down. But, of course, things went from bad to worse down there. So I used to go down there once a month, clean the place up, see that the kids were pretty well provided for, and get out of it. I suppose after about six months of that I said – 'I'm going to divorce you.' I think even then I was only saying it to try to wake her up. Because it is a wrench, when you don't believe in it and it's forced on you. Then I thought, 'I'm not just saying this, I'm going to do it.'

The doctors had warned me you can't really ever keep this going, and eventually things got to such a pass that I saw that she'd got to go into hospital again. This time we found a private hospital, because part of my work contract includes medical insurance. I moved back down with the kids and started travelling back up again. But I could only do that for a short time, because the work was calling me up. So I said to the children, 'I'll send you money every week and I'll get down as often as I can, but you're going to have to look after yourselves'. So for about nine months that's how it went. It was a desperate measure, leaving the children but I think it did them good in fact. And I just had to do it. I did have the local children's welfare people on to me one afternoon when I was at work and they were a bit anxious about it. But I said they were coping with it and I was getting down there as often as I could, which was usually once in two weeks.

I wasn't happy with the situation. On the other hand I couldn't find anywhere to live in London. Until this place turned up. And then the situation was complicated because the older ones were due to take their 'O' Levels. But the schools round here were very good, they managed to sort out a syllabus which would match the exam they were going to take. And now we've been up here sixteen months. Claire is still in the hospital and I'm still intending to divorce her.

I haven't yet, because I've had other things to do. And her family are being awkward about it, so I'm sitting back and letting it stew. I think if it comes to the push and I have to sue for divorce, I'll get one. All I want now is a financial settlement and a divorce. I don't want to know what happens to her or where she goes or what she does.

I think my attitude to marriage has changed. I think marriage is largely unimportant in the relationship between two people. Because it is the settling down thing that is almost certainly going to be a disaster. Men and women settle back and say – I'm married, I've got a wife or a husband, I don't need to bother, I don't need to keep myself smart. You know, people slack off. I was so wrapped up in my own problems that I wasn't taking much notice of what was going on around me. I'm much more outward going now. And now I couldn't care less about what anyone thinks of me any more.

At work, for example. Now I take time off any time I feel like it. I think perhaps it's just a reflection of the realisation that there is no security in marriage, nor anywhere else really. Whatever happens to you, your life just goes on and you've got to get on with it. It's really no good worrying about things. If there's something you want to do, then do it. If other people have to do without your time, then let them do without it. I've done what I've done because I had to. And I think I still take that attitude; if problems crop up, they have to be dealt with. The main problem for all people in this situation is the financial one. You have extra costs, no matter how you work it out. And there is the ordinary wear and tear of trying to do two jobs. Though, personally, I think I work better under pressure. One difficulty with a single-parent father is that it is very much a woman's function to . . . well . . . train her daughters to run a house and that sort of thing. Though I think all children should be trained to look after themselves from A–Z – men and women.

I think I would marry again. I think so. But I'd have to be careful. I think I'd be prepared to live with someone if they didn't want to get married. But if they wanted to get married then I might have to . . . I think I'd have to be very careful. It's a little academic, though until I'm divorced. I'd be looking for companionship, I think. A very deep, very affectionate companionship. And I want someone to be . . . I want someone to look decorative on my arm in a way. More than that, but that's important. I wouldn't want to start another family. I want an intelligent woman. And I don't think a man can have a respectful attitude towards a woman – and I think he should – without being prepared to marry her. Marriage is under attack in all sorts of ways, largely because I think people haven't been left alone to get on with it. You get involved with religion, politics, all sorts of things – and it *is* different if you are married or single. Take a perfectly simple thing like tax. There are advantages in being married under our system of tax, but it shouldn't matter. I think there's been too much meddling, too much interference, too much laying down what are the laws of marriage and what aren't. I would like to see a system whereby two people could go to a solicitor and draw up a contract between themselves and say, 'this is our marriage law'.

But I think the status of being married is important. I was going to say to women, equally to men. And I think it is important to recognise that there is a particular person in the world to whom one is attached – and nobody else. That is a measure of commitment. I also think some marriages could probably be saved by sex education. A lot of husbands would benefit from a course from a first class prostitute. They would learn how to treat a woman. How sexually to be loving instead of aggressive. Maybe that's a bit extreme but there's certainly a need for a school of love-making. For men and women. I *do* want my children to marry. Because it's the normal way of life.

I don't want to give the impression that all this was my wife's fault. She was sick and that was it. It is impossible to live with her. I don't feel guilty. I think I did my best. It might not have been enough, but it was as good as I could do. I don't worry. In any case, I'm too busy now – I've got four children on my hands. But that's what I've learnt, not to worry.

Postscript

At first glance, James may not seem an entirely sympathetic person. He had outrageous expectations from his wife, perhaps epitomised by his expectation that she should be waiting for him at the door of their suburban home with a kiss when he arrived home from work. And he had very strong and demanding 'ladder-climbing' ambitions to which he expected his wife to conform – keeping an impressive home, just so, raising a large family with some perfection. And one cannot help but wonder how much the pressure of such expectations might have contributed over the long-term to his wife's mental illness.

At the same time, James behaved throughout his marriage with caring (trying to do what he thought would make his wife happy, however wrong he might have been at judging what that would be), consideration (in helping around the house from the early days of their marriage) and responsibility (in looking after his wife when she was ill, his children after the separation). The point obviously came when he could take no more and decided that he wanted a life of his own. Selfish? Perhaps. But perhaps, too he had a right to this life. It is probably unfair to be judgemental. He was certainly at pains to continue to support his wife, and to care properly for the children. And James attempted, to some extent, to isolate the reason for the failure of his marriage and to apportion some of the blame at his own feet. He embarked upon single-parent life with considerable determination to make it work for all involved, and at the time of the interview was succeeding. Certainly he and his children seemed happy and stable.

7. Doreen

Doreen comes from a working-class background. She married at twenty and separated at thirty with three children under the age of eight. At the time of the interview she had been on her own for eight years. She was in her late thirties, her oldest child sixteen, her youngest ten. She was living in the same flat she'd lived in with her husband in Leeds, and was living on Social Security. Subsequent to the interview she had got her first job and was thriving on the independence it offered her.

She describes her courtship as stormy and her husband as 'a wild sort of man'. And most of her marriage was fraught with trouble. Certainly when it came to a divorce her husband couldn't be found: he was in prison. And it took her a long time to finally break a destructive attachment. Says Doreen: 'Reading back through the interview, I just burst into tears, because I sounded so pathetic. But I was, and I also deserved a lot of what I got because I stood for it and let him get away with murder. I think I have been presented pretty well, because that's just how I was – completely hooked on him and love sick. I have often wondered if, out of hurt, bitterness and humiliation, I had painted an unfair picture in the interview, but reading it objectively, it was all very true and precise. I've learned a lot over the years, and my "down with all men" attitude has gone: I'm sure there is good and bad in both sexes.'

Doreen has no serious relationship at the moment, but says she would be prepared to remarry the right person in the right circumstances. She describes her situation now as 'better than it was when I was married and first split up. It hasn't been easy, to say the least, bringing up three kids, emotionally and financially, but it is still much better than if we would have stayed together. I would like to remarry or have a relationship, but feel very wary about it. I don't think I would plunge in for the sake of loneliness – though I am lonely. I would rather be on my own than live with someone for the wrong reasons and have to go through the whole miserable bit again.'

'Since the interview, my husband has contacted me – just a year ago – I think out of curiosity: to see if I was managing or to see if I'd turned into some kind of slut. Anyway he was very impressed with what he saw, a nice well kept home, three nice kids all grown up and me looking pretty good.

As I said, he remarried and has two kids, but the punch line is he wanted to come back to me, realised he'd made a mistake (so he said), was more than willing to leave his family and start afresh with me (sounds familiar). This man never fails to amaze me! When I declined his offer, he was very put out and I've not heard another word.

'Anyway, to round things off, I am coping and I am not unhappy with my situation.'

I had just turned eighteen when I met Alf. Ever so young. We were both shop assistants, and I went to work in the same shop where he was. He tried to date me for weeks and weeks, but I didn't want to know. He was a different type of fellow than I'd ever gone out with, and he just didn't turn me on, appeal to me. Then it just happened that one night we were at the same party and he said, 'I'll take you home?' And it progressed from there.

I was very sexually attracted to him. Like I'd never been to any of the other fellows that I'd gone out with. We slept together a couple of weeks later. I was a virgin when I met Alf. I lost my virginity with him. I was extremely sexually attracted to him. That was really the basis of our relationship.

We got married, then, about sixteen months later. After a very stormy courtship. He was a very wild sort of man, you see. Wild in just about every way you could think of. He'd got no respect for the law and was always getting into trouble one way or another. He'd had a very rebellious adolescence. I knew he'd been in trouble. I didn't mind. I met him when I was eighteen and we got married when I was twenty.

We were madly in love and I was terribly jealous – the whole bit. I knew that after we'd see each other every night, he would go on to other places after he'd left me. I assumed he was with other women. Looking back, there must have been other women, even then. At the time I suspected, but I tried to think it wasn't true. And there were rows and arguments. He was very selfish.

We actually broke up for about three months. We planned the wedding and everything, and then it all broke off. He said he wanted to be free, he'd made a mistake. He went to Scotland and he kept phoning me up from Scotland saying he had to have this breathing space and he would be back. Of course, that was marvellous. I was very young and very much in love with him and he *did* come back. I thought, okay, he's had his breathing space and it'll be all right now. He definitely wanted to come back and get married. He'd had his last fling.

He went off in the August and we got married in the December, Christmas Eve. We'd planned a very big wedding. We'd booked a hall and everything. It was going to be quite a lavish . . . well, a typical Jewish wedding, I suppose. Anyway he came back. The family said we should wait, postpone the wedding till the spring. But we were both twenty by then and knew it all. We wanted to be together and we thought marriage would solve everything. We never even considered living together. That wasn't really ever a consideration. Alf said it was marriage – so we never ever talked about us living together. The wedding went ahead the date we had planned. It was a much smaller affair, though, because it had to be rearranged so quickly.

I never really had any doubts about Alf. I mean, I knew about his past, but it didn't matter. He could've robbed banks and killed – it just didn't matter. I just wanted to be with him. I found it exciting – the fact that he was so wild. I'd always gone out with 'nice' boys. I think every woman loves a bastard, that's the problem. It was a ball, the things Alf and I did. And I enjoyed every minute of it. We used to do really crazy things – getting in a car and going for a coffee down to London from Leeds. Just things like that. Free things, things that really made me feel free. I'd been so stifled with those nice boys that just held your hand in the pictures and were polite to you. Somehow the worse Alf was to me, the more I was turned on by it. It was so alien from my upbringing you see, which was a very sheltered Jewish background.

Anyway we got married. We were still both working for the same shopkeeper and I remember the first week we got our wages after we were married. Our boss gave him the wage packets for him to give mine to me. But he opened it and took the money out and gave me spending money. He only did it once though. I'll never forget that. It was in the High Street and we had the most terrible row, with him going one way and me going in the other. He did apologise later on, but I think if he could have got away with it again, he would have.

We didn't stay long in those jobs anyway. Alf was in various jobs. He wasn't consistent in anything he did. He would mainly walk into a job in the morning and leave by lunchtime. And I got pregnant after being married six weeks. I got pregnant with Steven.

It seemed a good thing at the time. And we were both pleased. But we'd never really thought about children. Looking back on it, it wasn't right. 'Let's have children,' we said. You know. We never thought it all out. It was just something we hadn't done. It was another experience to go through. So I decided to try and get pregnant, and I did quickly. As I said, six weeks after we got married I fell straightaway for Steven. And when Steven was born, Alf seemed overjoyed. It was all okay. It wasn't till David was born two-and-a-half years later that trouble started.

As I said, Alf was never in steady jobs. We settled down in the flat I still live in. A self-contained three-room flat. I stopped work after I got married and never really worked again. Because there was always the babies.

We always had a lot of problems with money. Alf paid the rent – at least he said the rent was paid. Quite honestly, it really didn't matter to me. I was so green that I never thought of the outcome of *not* paying the rent. He said he was doing it. I just assumed he would do it. Fair enough. I'd always had responsibility taken from me, for me. If Alf was doing it, okay, so long as I didn't have to. I was just as irresponsible as he was in those days. Even if I would have tried to knuckle him down, it wouldn't have made any difference. He would've still done just what he wanted to do.

After our second child, David, was born, Alf started going out more and more. I don't know what he actually did – but he went on holidays. And at that time he went into business with his father.

We regard it as most important that men should not be allowed to escape their financial obligations to their families to the extent that these have been fairly assessed and fall within a genuine capacity to pay. This raises the entire subject of enforcement procedures and the possibility of extending or improving on them – 'The Finer Report, 1974'

The first two-and-a-half years were the best years of my life. Alf, for the first time in his life, was in a job the longest he ever had been. He had prospects. His father had a print factory and Alf went to work there and he seemed to be getting on okay. I thought, 'This is going to carry on and get better and better.' We weren't in any money trouble, and it was just okay. We were both happily married, still in love, with a nice child. It was all roses, and lovely. I actually felt the feeling of contentment. We did lots of things together. We had friends – friends came over and we went out to the cinema, out for meals. My mother was always good with baby-sitting, things like that. Alf was a tremendous gambler. We spent a lot of our evenings at gambling clubs. It was all part of the excitement. I loved it just as much as he did – the dressing up, going to nice places. I enjoyed it as well.

Then we decided to have the second child. Sort of together, said, 'Let's have another baby.' And I fell pregnant again when Steven was about sixteen months. Then the trouble really started after, I think, David must have been about a year.

The first trouble was that Alf had the most tremendous row with his father and stormed out of the business. This meant that Alf wasn't working again, so we were back to square one with money problems and the future no longer seemed so secure.

You see, when Alfred was in trouble, he would just close up completely and look elsewhere for a shoulder to cry on. He never came to me. I imagine he must have gone to other women. Of course, I never thought along the lines of women in those days. I just thought that I was at the end of it – it never occurred to me at the time that there were other women. I probably should have known, perhaps deep down I did, but I would bury my head in the sand. Perhaps that's typical, but if you want to make something go, well, you just slide over it and say it doesn't exist.

The first awareness I had of other women was when he did actually leave home to go and live with another woman. And it seems, looking back on it, he must have been doing it before. He would just come home late. And once the second child was born that put the block on my days of going out. He would make excuses for my mother not to come and babysit. So he could be by himself, and it was always a business thing, of course. But I knew damned well. He'd been acting strangely towards me. Like there had been no sexual relations for a couple of weeks. And Alf was going out more, and mentioning friends that I'd never heard of. And coming home with too much to drink. And he was just acting very, very strange.

So I just confronted him one evening. I said 'There's somebody else,' and he said, 'Yes.' He looked very flabbergasted. I'll never forget that evening. I don't think he meant to be found out somehow. I threw it at him. I had worked myself up to it, because he was acting so strange towards me. As I said, I didn't know there were any relationships, or anything. That was the only thing I could think of. But when I said it to him, I said it because I wanted him to deny it. You know, to ease my own mind that there wasn't anybody. And then I would find out what was troubling him. Another woman was the one thing that I dreaded.

We weren't having sexual relations and he didn't talk to me. There was no communication whatsoever. And he wasn't seeing the kids much. By the time he came home, they were fast asleep. And he was still sleeping in the morning when they woke up. There was really no communication with the kids at all. They could have been there or they couldn't have been there, for all he knew or cared. He was always what I suppose you'd call a conventional father. He didn't change nappies or help around the house or anything. I was the mum and the wife and he was the father and the breadwinner. But that's what I wanted – or rather I'd never really thought about it. It didn't matter to me. That was my role – to do the nappies and things. It didn't bother me at all.

Anyway, when I found out about this other girl, I was shattered. I was speechless. When he actually said it, it wasn't what I wanted to hear, or what I thought he was going to say. I just went blank, like a zombie. Then I just slung him out. And he promptly went, that evening.

I still loved him, but I was really hurt and shattered. And my immediate reaction was to chuck him out – not to try and grab him back. Because there wasn't any point. I didn't feel that I wanted him there, if he had another woman. There was no way I was going to take second place to this other woman. That would have been even more humiliating. Of course, I tried to find out who it was, what she was like, was she prettier than me? The whole degrading bit – the grovelling.

He didn't say anything. He just didn't say *anything*. I remember he washed himself, changed his clothes and went. I then promptly picked myself up. I didn't know what to do. I called a cab and went over to my mother-in-law.

You see, I was very close to Alf's parents in those days. I stayed with them for a week. I remember, the same evening I went over there he did phone back to see if I was all right. He was phoning from the girl's place. I did speak to him on the phone. I can't remember what I said. I stayed away a week, and then I thought I'd better go back and . . . try and resume. I went back a week later. It was terrible, because I knew he'd been back during the course of the week, and just walking in and seeing his clothes there, and everything – it was like a hell hole.

Then he started phoning. He kept on phoning. After the week I'd been away. Actually there was about a week when I didn't hear anything. Then about the third week he started phoning me, sounding very down in the dumps and miserable. But I never once asked him to come back. All in all he was away about three months. *That* time.

Pretty quickly I realised I'd have to do something for money. I thought, 'Oh my God, what am I going to do?' And I had to straight away go to Social Security. Alf never sent a penny. Nothing. I did ask him. Oh, as he left he did give me a five-pound note. That was supposed to tide me over!

He didn't visit me in those three months – or the kids. He did ask how the kids were when he phoned up. That was all. You know, thinking back, I've wondered what the kids made of it all. I really can't remember telling them anything. I don't think I told them anything. That's all a complete blank to me. And I don't remember how they took it. Steven's always been a very closed up child. I think he gathered at that tender age – he was three then – that something was wrong. But he never said anything and I never pushed him. I let it ride.

Anyway, towards the end of the three months, Alf said he would like to come back, that he felt ashamed of what he'd done. Would I meet him? he asked. Which I did. And he came back. But I could see things were still not all right. And a couple of days later he wanted to go again. I didn't know whether he wanted to go back to the same girl or just leave. He said he didn't know himself if he wanted to be free or go to this girl. At that time he used the expression 'I want to be free. I don't know what I want . . . if you're included in my life, or what?' he said. This went on for about a week. This coming and going. I eventually called the doctor about Alf and the doctor said that Alf had had a breakdown.

He was admitted to hospital. He was in there for seven months. He had been in there about a month when I found that I was pregnant again, with my third baby! This had happened in the week he came back. I didn't take any precautions. I was completely and utterly irresponsible. And I was completely shattered when I found out I was pregnant. It was the last straw, the noose around my neck. So I went to my doctor. He'd known me since I was nineteen. He knew the circumstances of my whole life history – of Alfred and everything. And I said, 'You've got to help me. I can't have this baby. I've got two children. I've got a husband in a mental home. I don't know what's going to happen to my marriage.' And all he did was he wrote me a letter to the hospital.

At that time, the 1967 Abortion Act hadn't come in. It was just before then, and you could only get an abortion on mental grounds, or if it was going to be dangerous to your life. Only the privileged few could get an abortion, or you paid through the nose which was completely impossible for me.

I was sat before a board of doctors – there was a psychiatrist, a gynaecologist and everything. It was the most horrific experience I've ever been through. I was hysterical. And I threatened all the usual things – to slit my throat, and I told them how desperate my whole circumstances were. But I was told that I couldn't have an abortion. What I could do, they said, was go ahead with my pregnancy and if I still felt the same I could have the child adopted. I don't know what I was sickened more by – the thought of being refused or the thought of having to have the baby. I just couldn't understand it. It wasn't the child I didn't want. I just didn't want to be pregnant. It was just something else to cope with.

Anyway, I went through with this pregnancy and I had Sarah which . . . you see the thing is had I not been pregnant, I don't think that the marriage would have gone on. Because when Alf came out of hospital, he came back. And I think he really did stay just because of the baby. He came home about six weeks before she was born – he came out at the end of February and she was born in April. He came home and he still was very, very depressed. They said that his affair with this girl was due to his breakdown. Which gave me hope. That made me feel a lot better. I thought it was all because he was ill, that there was no physical attraction. That he had been kind of screwed up and now he was better.

Anyway he came back and he found it hard to get a job. He hadn't worked ever, really, not steadily. I don't know if he was on Social Security or if this girl had been keeping him. Anyway he didn't work. It must have been a year or more before he resumed work. He came out of hospital and got into trouble straight away again. It was something really silly, not very serious but he got caught. And that was just another little something to cope with. Anyway, just before Sarah was born he met some guy – I think it was an advert in the paper for a job. It was second hand cars, which was the absolute ruin of him because this guy was the same type of person as Alfred. He was just going through a bad marriage, a very weak character, and Alfred just got swept up into his social whirl. For that whole year, the year after Sarah was born, it was just terrible.

When Sarah was nine months old, I became pregnant yet again. Fortunately, this time it was after the Abortion Act, or I would have had to pay through the nose for an abortion. There were no two ways about it. And fortunately the gynaecologist was an absolute sweetie of a man. I knew him as I'd been under him when I was pregnant with Sarah. He was a Harley Street specialist and he was the only one I knew that I could go to and get help. So I went to see him and he said to me, 'Do you want to have it National or privately? Because that's your prerogative.' 'Well,' I said, 'National Health obviously.' He said, 'Well, that's fine.' He said if it was up to him he wouldn't make anybody pay for an abortion. He was so nice about it I couldn't believe it. Especially compared to my first horrendous experience.

Anyway I knew I couldn't cope with a fourth child – not then! I often think of how old it would have been now. I can't tell you the relief I felt when I came to from that anaesthetic. You know, Alfred had to sign for the damned thing! His attitude was – do what you want. Have it or don't have it. He said, 'I suppose it would be nice to have another one!' And I thought, 'Yeah, another link in the ball and chain around my feet.' It didn't matter to Alfred – four, five, six. It made no difference to his social life. The more I had, the better, the more tied I was. I think he got pleasure out of the fact that I was so completely tied, whereas he was free. But then I must admit that he never seemed to *feel* free.

I think Alfred's upbringing, his family, had a lot to do with the way he was. He came from an up and coming middle-class family, and they put priorities on material things. They gave him everything he wanted. Alfred wanted to play the piano, they went out and bought him a grand piano. He was an only child, and I don't think his parents really showed feeling, love towards him. Though he was never denied anything. So all he knew was what he wanted he went out and got. It just got steadily worse as he got older. He never really had an understanding father. His father used to say to him, 'I can read you like a book. I know that everything you're going to do is going to be a failure.' They took all his confidence away. He was very insecure.

Anyway, the year after Sarah was born, Alfred would stay out even more. I would see less and less of him. He drank more, gambled more – and exactly a year later he disappeared yet again, literally walked off. Leading up to this, there was complete and utter silence at home for about three weeks. He didn't say a word to me. Nothing. And there was no sexual relationship. Absolutely nothing. I would phone him up at the office and it was just blank at the end of the line. I just had to hang up. Still, to this day, I don't know what was going on in his head. He said he was leaving, but there was no woman. The business that he was in – the second-hand cars – was folding up. Perhaps it was the pressure of that. You see, at the least sign of trouble, Alfred just couldn't cope. He would retreat to the least line of resistance. Perhaps he thought that by moving out and moving away from home . . . I don't know. He wasn't getting paid regularly and couldn't meet the bills at home, so he just ran away.

I went back on Social Security again. And he started the same routine of phoning and saying he'd made a mistake and he was sorry and it wasn't the answer, running away. But I really didn't want him back. It had been ten years, ten terrible years, and I was nearly thirty. The funny thing was, I was still in love with him. But I didn't want him back. I was beginning to listen a bit more to my head instead of just my heart or guts or whatever. And I thought, 'This is what my life is going to be like. He's going to keep coming and going, all the time.' He was never there, and I was lonely, of course. I never had boy friends or sexual relationships or anything. I had too much to contend with at home. And to start getting involved with anyone would have added to my burden.

My family were just sick of it by this stage. My mother knew what was going on, but I never really went to cry on anybody's shoulder. Anyway, my mother's not the type of person to communicate with very well. You can't tell her the nitty-gritty and everything. Alf had been really awful to my mother. All our life he was always borrowing. And he drained my mother dry of everything she had. Alf would borrow from everybody he knew had a few pennies. I had two aunts, they were my father's sisters, who Alf didn't really know all that well. But he borrowed £700 off of them. He wanted to start his own motorbike business – with the promise of paying them back. I think he paid back about £50. That was the last they ever saw of him. This was the story of his life.

My mother had three insurance policies – her life savings – which he got rid of for her. My mother, who's about sixty, works from eight in the morning until half-past five at night. She's a dressmaker in a big factory and works very, very hard – they take their pound of flesh – and she was really leaving herself short. She was always substituting our money, paying bills. She was giving me towards food. I mean, my kids never had shoes on their feet, literally. David . . . well, my mother looked down one day and said, 'He's got holes in his shoes.' And I said, 'I can't help it.' Alf never bothered to ask do the children need a new pair of pants, do they need shoes? Nothing. But he'd go out to the best men's shop and dress himself up. He was always beautifully dressed. *We* never got a thing. My mother used to have to buy *my* shoes for me. I never had a pair of knickers to put on sometimes.

My mother and my aunts gave Alf the money, I think, because of me and the children. Thinking that it would make things easier for me. They really had no love for him at all or trusted him, but they tried to do everything that would help me. It wasn't for his benefit at all. And he just got rid of all the money, including my mother's.

Anyway, Alf came back after this second . . . desertion. I didn't want him back. But I took him back because I was frightened of being by myself. I was scared of loneliness, and I was just frightened. I didn't want to be by myself. So I thought he would be better than nothing. Anyway that final year was the most disastrous and worst year of my whole life. It was just terrible.

Alf started his own business. He borrowed a couple of hundred pounds from an uncle of his to start his own motorbike business. And I think if it had started out all right, it would have been a success. He was a good mechanic. He was very talented. He was a very clever person. The thing is, he had no patience to see anything through. We all said to him, 'You can't start a business on two hundred pounds. Wait, accumulate some money and then go into it.' No. It had got to be now or never. He was a man of the moment. If the idea came into his mind, there and then it had to be. The business was starting off and he was getting good orders – it was going okay. Then there was a strike that just about finished him off. But instead of picking himself up and starting again, he got disillusioned.

I had no cash of my own. Whatever I had he'd spent a long time ago. And there was nobody else to go to for money. So he just started drinking more, staying out more. He would phone me and say, 'I'm up to my eyes in work. I'm going to spend the night in the office.' And maybe three days later he would appear, change his clothes and go out again. He was desperate for money.

I had a diamond engagement ring, a beautiful ring. It was the very last thing that I had left and I was hanging on to it. Not because it was a beautiful ring, but for material purposes. It was my only bit of security left in life. But he wanted it and he was determined he was going to get it. Towards the end, the marriage became terribly fraught, really terrible. In the very early years I got pushed about, but I shoved back and we stopped after that. Now we were in debt to the bank. That's why he wanted the ring. I got so frightened that the police would come or something. He wanted the ring as collateral for the bank and I gave it to him. Because I couldn't stand it any more. He said, 'You'll get it back in a couple of weeks. Don't worry.' But I knew as I took it off my finger that I'd never see it again. That was the end.

The old tariff of blame which pitied widows but attached varying degrees of moral delinquency to divorced or separated women or to unmarried mothers is becoming irrelevant in the face of the imperative recognition that what chiefly matters in such situations is to assist and protect dependent children, all of whom ought to be treated alike irrespective of the mother's circumstances – 'The Finer Report, 1974'

At this stage the children were completely non-existent to him. Absolutely. He used to go away. It was a regular thing every weekend. And I would say to him, 'Well I don't give a damn any more where you're going but just leave a phone number in case I need you in an emergency.' And one weekend I did. Sarah was rushed into hospital. There I was with all the kids and I didn't know what to do. He rolled home about eleven that Sunday night, and I said, 'Where have you been? Sarah's been taken to hospital and I needed you.' He just went round to the hospital to see if she was okay, and that was it. He was really irresponsible about the kids. He would promise to play football with them or take them to a match, and when it came to the day he would just ignore them and say he had things of his own to do. Steven's face would just crumple. And there was nothing I could say or do. I would just say something insignificant to them – like never mind. What can you do? I couldn't do a lot of the things with Steven that Alf should have been doing. I had babies.

There were rows every day. And the children must have been

aware of it all. They were very heavy fights. I would wait up all night for him, and I would say to myself, 'I'm not going to say anything to him. I'm going to let him see that I don't care.' But by the time he came in at two or three in the morning I'd be worked up into a state, so that it was impossible not to say anything. He would make the most ridiculous excuses for not coming home. They were classic, really classic. In the end he would have *me* apologising to *him* for rowing and for questioning him! How dare I question him! You disgusting person for losing your temper! I'm much too superior to lose my temper. Look at you, you hysterical, horrible woman! He would laugh. He wouldn't even have a proper row with me. He would laugh at me. He would goad me something terrible. I would get madder and I did sometimes pick up a knife to him with the wish to kill him. I really felt murder for him, because he couldn't even have the decency to have a dignified row with me. He would accuse *me* of having affairs! I put that down to his guilty conscience. And I would end up trying to convince him that I wasn't having these affairs – these imaginary affairs!

By this time I really felt immense anger and hatred, but I'm afraid I was still in love with him. Sexually I still loved him . . . and I was still having sexual relations with him. I must admit I hated it, because I knew at the back of my mind he'd been with some other girl and that he was coming home to me to finish the evening off. I knew he'd been with women. I mean, it was so silly. He'd come home reeking of perfume, and I'd confront him with it and he'd say, 'Oh, well, I was just in a pub and the atmosphere and the perfume wafted on to me.' I would say to him, 'It's better for you to admit it to me. How dare you insult my intelligence! Okay, you've been found out. I don't care. But why lie about it?' And he'd just walk out of the room. 'Believe what you want to believe, I don't care,' he'd say. By this time it was just a matter of biding my time. I knew he was eventually going to leave. In fact it turned out *I* finally said, 'Get the hell out of it.'

It was just before Christmas, four years ago this Christmas. He was gradually taking his clothes out. It wasn't just one fell swoop, of packing and going. He was gradually easing his way out. And it was Christmas Eve. He came and spent Christmas Eve with us and then he went. We'd been invited to a Christmas party and I was all prepared to go by myself, but he appeared and came with me. We didn't speak the whole evening and he brought me home, dropped me at the flat and went off. And then he actually went. He took all his things and went. Then about three weeks later there was a knock on the door one Sunday night – I'd just put the kids to bed – and he knocked at the door and he said, 'I'm back. Here I am. Let's carry on.'

And I just said 'No! This really is the finish. You go. I don't want you here any more.' Unfortunately my children heard all this. Heard me telling him to go. And *that* made things very difficult. Alf was so flabbergasted, because all our life together I'd given in to him completely, taking him back when he wanted to come, having sex when he wanted to. He was just so flayed that I could have refused him. I think he walked out more in anger that I refused him because he had such a high opinion of himself, than because I didn't actually want *him*, if you can see what I mean.

Anyway I had terrible trouble. David was hysterical, absolutely hysterical. He was six. I went to Steven and explained to him. And he said, 'You don't have to say anything. I understand more than you give me credit for.' But the other one, David . . . to him I was the witch, the villain. And I had a terrible time with him for about a year. He started wetting the bed. And he wouldn't let me come near him. Even now if I go to touch him, he pushes me aside. You can't get close to him. All men were absolutely taboo. At that time, he had a male teacher, and he wouldn't go to school. I was pushing him in the morning and they were pulling him the other end. And he cried all day at school. He used to say he had stomachache – which was just tension. This went on for about a year. He was petrified of his teacher. He rejected me and he was frightened of men. He was very confused. I think five to six is an incredibly vulnerable age, because they know everything and they can't understand anything. Steven was at the age when he knew and understood, at the age of nine. Sarah was too young, really, to know anything. But David . . . well he thought all the years of our life together, though very bad . . . well . . . that's all he knew. That's what he thought everyone's life was like, and I'd ruined it for him as far as he was concerned.

Then when it came to the crunch, when Alf was actually going, when we separated and there wasn't going to be anybody there . . . well I was the villain of the piece. I had made the situation. And I had ruined his world completely. David couldn't look on it that I did it because I was in an impossible situation, that I was doing it for his good. Because the rows and slanging matches that they had to listen to were just terrible, horrific.

Even my mother had trouble understanding that I'd kicked Alf out once and for all. She would be there sometimes and had to listen to all the rows, but she couldn't say anything because Alf would tell her to mind her own business. And she didn't want to say anything that would upset the applecart even more than it was. She has a sacrosanct attitude towards marriage. So the whole divorce and separation bit was a terrible thing to her. She was brought up, I suppose, to endure. All my family had always had happy relationships. We were a happy family. I don't think they could understand. This was completely alien to them.

But the time finally came when I decided it was better to end it. Even through all the difficulties that that would entail. I had lost all respect for Alf. Still, though, if he had knocked at my door and said, 'Come to bed,' I think I would have. But for my own self-respect, even that had to stop. As I said, I didn't like him any more – his character, his attitude towards the children most of all. Whatever he felt towards me shouldn't have made any difference to the kids.

Anyway, we parted, after a final terrible Sunday night scene. But he still kept phoning. This was about once every couple of weeks. 'Are you sure you're doing the right thing?' he'd ask. And at this particular point he'd got into trouble with the police. We had already been separated, and I didn't know anything about it. I could murder my mother for this. He came crying to her one Sunday morning that he was in terrible trouble with the police over drugs. He'd got caught. I don't know if it was possessing or passing drugs, but he had to have a couple of hundred pounds. My mother gave it to him to get him out of trouble. And the terrible thing was, he got caught again. There was a very big case at the Old Bailey that went on for several months. But he kept phoning me during this time asking, 'Are you doing the right thing?' And he even sent me a birthday card: 'Dear Doreen, I wish you a happy birthday. I hope you are happy in the decision you've made.' Silly things like that. And the very last I heard of him he phoned to say that his case was coming up in a couple of days time. Then the next thing I heard was a letter from Wakefield Prison. He used to write beautiful letters – very sugary. He really know how to stick the knife in and turn it. And that was the last I heard of him.

He got fifteen months and did a year. And then the Social Security sent for me to tell me that he was being released on the Wednesday and he was getting married on the Saturday. And he had a baby. All the time he was phoning me trying to come back home, he was obviously living with this woman who was pregnant.

Looking back, it seems like he really needed me in some way, even though he abused me terribly. He did once tell me that he was jealous of me. He was jealous that I could be happy and contented just to sit at home of an evening, that I could find roots. He was jealous of the way that I could cope with a crisis. I don't know why he kept coming back and back and back and back, or why he kept putting off ending the marriage, even though he'd destroyed it. I don't know whether he loved me. He never said it. I don't know what his feeling for me was. I think I was his anchor. I was his roots. And he was envious that he couldn't have those roots. Perhaps he was trying to pull me down to his level – 'If I'm down here you're going to come down with me.' But right until the end, I think had I said come back, he would have. That would have been my life. The comings and goings. He would always have come back to me. As it was, it took me about a year to work myself up to finally say, 'No – never again.'

When I married him everybody said don't, but I didn't marry him because they said don't. I married him because I wanted to. So nobody could turn around and say to me, 'I told you so.' And saying go away was a decision that I had thought about. I weighed all the pros and cons – of the children and things like that.

Since the separation, which has been four years now, there hasn't been any contact between me and Alfred or him and the children. He did ask to see them and I said no, knowing what he was. I didn't see any point in it, and I felt that if he desperately wanted to see them, he would have broken the door down, got a court order, gone to extremes to actually see them. Which he didn't do.

After he left I did keep up my relationship with Alfred's parents because I was genuinely fond of them. My mother-in-law, during the time when Alfred was actually going, was very ill indeed. With heart trouble. She had major surgery. I visited her in hospital and I kept up the relationship with her despite the fact that Alfred had gone. She came out of hospital and suffered a stroke. And I would always say to them, 'Can I come over and help or anything?' And she would say, 'No, you've got the children. You live too far. I've got all the help I need.' They would come and visit me every couple of weeks and it was a pretty good relationship . . . well as far as I thought. Up to a year ago . . . when they just cut us dead. I'm not entirely sure why, whether they had taken Alfred back into the fold . . . I don't know. I know he had started phoning her, and had said some stupid thing about hearing that I was going out with somebody, and that he'd heard I was getting married again. That must have bothered them. I don't know for what reason. Alfred's mother used to come on a Sunday, and she'd say, 'Oh, Alfred phoned and he asked how you were.' And I'd say, 'Big deal.' And she said, 'Well, he *did* ask how you were.' What can one say to a thing like that?

The Supplementary Benefit scheme is intended to act as a safety net for those in the population who have fallen on hard times, cannot support themselves by working and are unable to manage on national insurance benefits and any other resources they might have – 'The Finer Report, 1974'

I never had a penny from him. The kids never had a birthday card. One of the times he phoned, it was one of the children's birthday, Sarah's I think. I said, 'Why didn't you send a card?' He said, 'Well if I'd sent a card, you wouldn't have given it to her.' He was always trying to put on to me, what he did. He just didn't care.

There was the time I had a letter saying . . . it was a statement from the landlord . . . that we were £300 in arrears with the rent. I'd asked him, 'Are you paying the rent?' It came as a shock to me. I was not aware of any arrears. And I didn't know what to do. After this letter, I had two lots of bailiffs coming in one week – for the rates – which were over £100, plus the £300 in rent. My phone had been cut off because the bill wasn't paid. And there were various other bits and pieces which I got sorted out. I borrowed £50 off my mother and sent it to the rates people. I explained to them my circumstances and that they would just have to be tolerant. The poor man from the rates was nearly in tears, because I was in tears. He had just appeared and said I had a week to get sorted out. I gave him £50, and he said, 'Don't worry, we'll work something out where you can pay gradually.'

And then a letter came from the landlord for both of us to appear in court. I was able to get in touch with Alf at this time, and he said, 'Oh, don't worry. I'll go to court. I'll sort it all out. You don't have to bother.' Anyway it was niggling in the back of my mind, so I went down to the Citizen's Advice Bureau and showed them the letter. This was two days before the court case and they said, 'You've got to move very fast, because you have got to appear in court as well.' And they made an appointment for me to see one of their legal advisers who laid it on the line to me that he didn't hold out much hope. He thought I was going to lose the flat, because they wouldn't consider a woman in my situation on Social Security able to pay off such a vast amount. Anyway, I went to court. Alf never appeared, so I was there by myself! And it turned out the judge was very nice.

I explained my whole circumstances and from the case that the landlord put forward, they obviously just wanted their flat back. They didn't want it paid off, or anything. I was obviously a bad risk. But the judge wouldn't hear of this. There was, in fact, a judge who didn't want to see a woman with three kids on the street! The Citizen's Advice Bureau told me this is a situation in which judges do sometimes come down very strongly. They hate a situation where a wife is left to carry the brunt of her husband's debts through no fault of her own. So I was given a certain amount to pay off each month. It was arranged through the court that I could pay back the rent arrears gradually, every month, plus my normal rent. It was a vast amount to me that I had to pay back each month. And the judge did apologise – he was sorry to make it such a steep amount, but otherwise I would be paying for the rest of my life. It took me two years, as it was, to straighten out my financial situation.

Alfred's still in debt. I still have letters coming for things he owes. But these aren't my responsibility. My father-in-law helped me through things a bit, like giving me a fiver when he came every fortnight, which I put towards debts. But my mother has borne the brunt of all my financial worries, and my family – they've been very good to me. I would never have been able to pay it back on Social Security. And, of course, there were points, more than once, when I wondered 'How can I go on?' There are still days now, yesterday, the day before, when I feel I could kill Alfred. I really feel terrible anger towards him, that he should be here, not so much for the financial things, because I'm managing financially okay now . . . but just for the emotional things. I've got a teenage son going through puberty, and I can't always cope. I don't always know if I'm doing the right things. I get very, very bitter about it.

I *do* have friends. My social life is much better than it ever was in the latter years. I've got nice friends, and I go out. My mother babysits. I have boyfriends, but there's never anybody in particular. I do go out with fellows, but I don't want to get hung up about anybody. I don't think I'm able to cope with an emotional situation *and* cope with emotional things at home. Just coping with life every day is enough. I have sexual relationships with fellows, but I've never . . . they're nice blokes and I like them because I couldn't have sex with just anybody – but I don't want to get involved.

It's four years now and I still feel very down on men. I've really come to the conclusion that they're not nice people, not just because of Alfred. But when you're outside a marriage, you can really look in and see how they conduct themselves. And I think they're appalling creatures, really. I suppose there are the nice ones here and there, but they're very selfish, self-centred people. I feel very angry sometimes, that a man can literally decide that he wants to be free, free of responsibilities that *somebody* must take. Somebody needs to, when children are involved. But men can just walk off. I think because they know that the woman is going to be the strong one, that *she* will not . . . walk away.

I sometimes feel very angry towards a system which assumes that the woman will just take over. I feel angry that Alf is getting away without paying me any money. If the man is taken to court all he's got to say is he's not working. What do they do? Nothing. In fact, I'm glad Alf doesn't have to pay me maintenance, because if I had to depend on him I'd starve. At least with Social Security I'm getting regular money every week. Somebody is caring for me. Mind you, I couldn't manage without my family. Social Security isn't bad, what I get, but I just couldn't do everything on it. I went on holiday last year. My family paid for it. Things like that. My family are always sending over . . . treat the kids to this, and so on.

I would like to be completely independent. I would like to finish with Social Security. I feel as if I'm beholden to them. I can't do this and I can't do that, because they won't allow it. So I'm not really independent. On Social Security you're not supposed to have any savings. And when I went on holiday last year, I really shouldn't have gone. I worried dreadfully whether Social Security would find out and my income would be stopped. You see, I explained to them that I was going to Spain with relatives, which was true, and asked if I could cash my money before I went. And I was told that I would have to hand my books back, because if I was going out of the country I was no longer their responsibility. So I would have to forego three weeks money. Anyway I didn't tell them, but it worried me for months after in case I'd get found out. Otherwise Social Security has been very kind to me. They come from time to time to see me and tell me certain rights I'm entitled to which I didn't even know about. But I always feel that they're still looking round, eyeing my flat up.

So I feel angry that Alfred has landed me in this sitation. These men get off scot free. He's made a new life for himself and he's started a new chapter. How can he just break off relationships with me and with his children like that? As if he'd put down a book and started something else. At the moment, I don't think I *could* start a new life. I just take each day as it comes and get through it. I can't make any long-term plans at all. At times I am very lonely and tearful and hurt and bitter at what life – or Alfred, has done to me. I can't deny that. The old thing, 'Why me?' Why do all these things happen to me? Why should my children suffer? Be without a father? I would like to do so much more with them. I get mentally exhausted at times. As for Alf himself, I don't feel anything towards him any more. Anger, yes, when days are bad, perhaps. That he should be here sorting things out, and why should it be on my shoulders? But I feel no love for him. He's like a stranger to me now, somebody I could pass in the street. I really feel that I've finally achieved complete freedom from him. Finally, I've got him off my back, the hang-ups and everything. I don't feel anything, just the anger that he got off scot free.

And I'm not free. I can't go off with someone, not even for a night. You've got to make complicated arrangements even if you want to spend a night with someone. In fact, it was really a matter of luck that I'm free of Alfred at all. I mean, that I'm divorced from him. It was two years after he left before I could get a divorce – because they couldn't find Alfred. He was of no fixed abode. He was moving around, and every time they got a lead where he was he'd moved on. The only reason I got my divorce – or I would still be married to him at this present minute – was because he was in prison. And he had a fixed address. And my solicitor went to the prison to get him to sign those blasted papers. It's hilarious, I suppose, if you think about it.

And do you know, when I first went for a divorce, I was told I had no grounds! They really had to fish for grounds, and in the end it was brought to the judge as incompatibility! When I first went to my solicitor I told him everything in intricate detail, and I was told that I had no grounds for divorce at all. This solicitor said he would have to consult a barrister to see if I even had a case. I suggested mental cruelty. They said, 'How do you prove mental cruelty? It's just on your say-so.' I was told if there was actual physical violence I'd have to be photographed to show the bruises and the cuts – and of course there was nothing. So my divorce was on incompatibility – after everything!

The actual divorce was a farce. It took ten miutes. There were three cases in front of me and the judge said exactly the same thing to each of them. I can't even remember it. All those months . . . I spent days in that solicitor's office telling him my life story . . . and nothing came out in court. Nothing. Just my name, my address, was it contested, blah, blah, blah. Divorce agreed, words to that effect. All that suffering for all those years, and that was it. I was granted complete custody, care and control of the children. And then came the real humiliation. I had to go back to the solicitor and tell him how many rooms I had in my flat, and what schools the children went to and how old they were and was I, in actual fact, able to care for them properly! After all those years!

I'd had a friend who previously went through divorce. And that nearly put me off altogether. She had a bad marriage. She was only married three years and he was a real pig. But he contested it, and this divorce took five days in court. It was the most terrible, terrible humiliating experience. I've never felt so embarrassed in all my life. I was subpoenad as a witness . . . for her. I didn't want to do it, but I had no option. It was just dreadful – the things that came out. Their whole sex life in intricate details. It was terrible what that poor, poor girl had to go through. He was such a slob, her husband, and he just contested it out of spite, sheer spite. He didn't want her or anything. She eventually got her divorce, and if anybody deserved it, it was her. It even hit the *News of the World* – and that was the final humiliating ending for her.

As for me, the whole thing was a farce. Ten farcical minutes in court, after ten terrible years.

Postscript

Here again was a marriage of violence and misery. But Doreen was sexually dependent on a husband whom she seemed completely incapable of breaking with. She was trapped and kept going back with him against her better judgement (even having another child, and then an abortion) and despite the fact that doing so only succeeded in degrading and humiliating her. Why? Was it, and for the other women in this kind of situation, that the prospect of being on her own, of being independent, seemed worse than the very bad conditions of her marriage? Yet, like the same women, once forced into the situation of being a single parent, she gained confidence in herself and came to value abilities she had never acknowledged she had, all in spite of the practical difficulties and loneliness. She acquired a new self-respect and self-image and came to look back on her earlier self as a completely different person.

Doreen was typical of so many women in marrying early to escape from home, in slipping into domestic roles, in leaving all financial matters to her husband (even though she knew he was irresponsible and she nearly lost her flat as a consequence) in lacking the self-confidence to manage on her own. Doreen comes across as the classic example of the many women who under-estimate themselves.

8. Michael

Michael comes from a middle-class background and married late, in his late thirties, a woman who was much younger than he. They had two children, one toddler, one under-five, when his wife left him for another man after six years of marriage. At the time of the interview, Michael had been on his own for four years, living in his detached home in a suburban neighbourhood in Nottingham. He was then nearing fifty and both of his children had started school. He had managed to carry on working as a salesman through the pre-school years with the help at home of a series of au pairs.

Michael left school at fourteen. He said schooling to a higher level was prevented by the low income of his parents. 'Although I should have been at school with a scholarship after fourteen years, my one pound a week wages was needed for family. My parents were not well off, but loving.' Michael said he 'worked hard at work and evening classes to achieve a better standard of living and to provide a good home.' He feels one of the handicaps of being a single parent father is how it affects work. 'Now I am not satisfied that I am doing a good job at work and expect no promotion. With no promotion and no second income, an economic deterioration in circumstances relative to others is probable.'

Of his situation now, Michael says: 'I am more comfortable as the years go by because the children are more capable and better company. The worst off single parents, from a social point of view, are those with very young children and no one to look after them in normal non-working time. Single parents with older children, or relatives or friends willing to look after children constantly are in a good social position. Grandparents at home, or a brother or sister living at home allow plenty of free time. This is why I have to get out to evening classes and stipulate that the au pair stays in a few nights. However, I also have work as an outlet and am therefore better off financially and socially, perhaps than some who are at home the whole time. Loneliness is my greatest worry. I can really not unwind or unburden my daily troubles on anyone, nor can I often relax.'

Michael is not now in a serious relationship: 'No time to meet others and possibly a fear of being hurt again. Mainly it is impracticable to meet unless she comes to your house or vice versa and children are always present.' But he would marry again – 'for the same reasons most people get married, physical and mental attraction.'

I was going round the country travelling as a sales rep. I found it very enjoyable and interesting. But you didn't settle down at all – you were a fortnight here, a fortnight there, sometimes a month. This went on for quite some time until eventually when I was about forty I got married to one of the girls I met through work. My wife was considerably younger than me – about twenty. Of course at the time that was very flattering to me. I keep the photographs . . . For various reasons I didn't think I'd enough money to set up a home properly. But then having found enough money to set up a home, which was this house, she reckoned she found life too easy and got bored with it and couldn't stand the kids, she reckoned. And wanted to see more of life and go off to work. So in the end I said all right you can go out to work.

I didn't know this at the time, but I'd already introduced her to someone else at the Christmas party in 1973 and by the middle of 1974 they'd got it all tied up. But I didn't know this. They even came to parties here, with some of the people at work, which was very hurtful. I can show you some of the burn marks from their cigarette ends here on the kitchen floor. It's a habit I don't like. She persuaded me into having these parties – I'm not particularly one for parties. Well, one of these people was carrying on with her. I'm just pointing out that he smoked – so did the others – and they were talking out here for a long time, and the marks are here to this day to prove it.

Well, in the end they planned to go off, and a couple of weeks before she did go – she'd got a job and an au pair, just as if she was going out to work – Anne, that's my daughter, turned her bag out at the bottom of the stairs and there was a letter for him. This was six in the morning . . . because it was me that got up at weekends . . . perhaps I was far too soft on her . . . So, I asked her to explain this letter and she said, 'What do you want me to do?' And, of course, I told her to go.

I didn't even open the letter . . . I just saw it was addressed to him. Even at that stage she could have explained her way out of it if she'd wanted to, because she was a good explainer out of things. But, off she went. She just said, 'Well you know now, what do you want me to do?' and I said go. She said, 'What, now?' I said, 'No, get the children sorted out first.' But nowadays so many people live on with adultery that I wonder sometimes if I did the right thing. Then a few weeks after, I said, 'How about coming back, I'll forgive you.' She said no. I asked her again maybe three weeks later and she said no again. So I said, 'Well if you want a divorce, okay, I'll give it to you so that you can get married.' Then she didn't get married for about another two to three years after, and in the interval she phoned me up once or twice or three times, making overtures. After we were divorced. I would say, 'Isn't it a bit late now?' but in a way I hoped that she would press me. Another time she would say, 'I don't think it will work', and she would give up, you know.

She did eventually remarry. And this is the most hurtful part of it, because now the kids are being brainwashed with tales about when they were babies. She is now going to have a baby in a couple of months and has been talking to them about it, so much that the children are talking to other people about it, and people say to me: 'How's the baby', thinking it's arrived. This does not make life any lighter for me – there is a sense of jealousy in my attitude towards this. The children are normal loving children and will like this baby when it comes along.

First of all she didn't see the children the first nine months, except a couple of hours every few months. Then she gradually worked up to having them on average two nights and two days a month. I find that hard; it all seems to be at her convenience. Or perhaps it's just me. But she's having a friend to stay and doesn't want them, and then she rings up and says: 'I haven't had Anne for her birthday, can I have her?' I don't like them being put out of their routine, the things we do at weekends. She's had them for two weekends in succession, she hadn't contacted me for five weeks, then suddenly, 'Can I have them for Anne's birthday', and this weekend she wanted them again for Christmas because she was going away. Yet in between, in that five weeks, she'd had her friend staying there and for various reasons could not or did not want them to stay. Usually I take myself to task for being too easy. On the other hand, she *is* their mother and I do think that both parents have a right to the children, and both should be able to look towards both parents. After all, one of them might pop off or one of them become incapable of looking after them. It is also nice for them to have some normality in school. And Anne does. She says,

'I went with my Daddy and Mummy' etc. She didn't. She went with one or other of them. But at least they can talk with some truth about their Mummy and Daddy.

If you have dependent children and literally nowhere to sleep, your council will probably shelter you. In exceptional circumstances, they may put you up in a hotel. What is far more likely is that you will be sent into what is called 'half way housing'. This is usually grim to say the least and as there is a risk in this situation of your children being taken into care, half way housing should only be considered as a last resort – Rosemary Simon

---

I think I would have got married earlier had the right person come along. They did several times really, when I look back, but probably I was looking for perfection, which of course, you never find. But I did have the idea of having children and wanted to bring the children up reasonably well. I wanted the children to have a proper upbringing. I didn't want them to live where I was from – my upbringing was fairly poor really. I wanted to move away from that area and set up and start again. At the same time I didn't set out for years and years, dedicated to this task. I enjoyed myself before, got around a bit, skiing, that sort of thing. I'd got a house near where my mother and father lived, in this area, but I didn't really want to bring anyone into it. Then when I married, I sold it and came here. Yet my wife has said it would have been better to set up in that old house and then move up. And other people have said that, but I don't think it can make any difference at all.

The children were very young when she left. Alan had just turned four and Anne was walking, but still on a bottle at night. She was still going to bed in nappies then. It happened that the first au pair that came along was absolutely marvellous, and the second one too, a French and then a Dutch girl. There might have been something else in it for them, when I look back, but I wasn't ready for any changes then. And it was a hard life. I never went out socially, or hardly, for months . . . years. Neither of them were at school and I had to pay for them to be looked after. There's no day care around here. So I was completely poverty-stricken really. This was for over four years, in other words until about six months ago. I was just scraping together a little money and managing. When they both started ordinary school it was a bit easier. But you still have to pay for something after school, and after the first two au pairs I wasn't so lucky. They change frequently and an agency fee can be £40 – £50. That's a lot of money. This is one of the biggest problems. Also, you jeopardise your own career prospects and you can't do any side jobs. You can't sit down in the evening and do anything, and you can't go out at weekends. And for people who do overtime, you can't stay and do it. So you are poorer.

The effects on my career have hurt. I was travelling around, and couldn't any more. And that's where my career prospects were, in selling. What's so hurtful is that the people she went off with did stay and two of them have got another step up, including the man she got married to. Which is hurtful, because I left the part of the company that did the travelling, because people knew about it and he was there, and I had to get away from it. I got a static job here, so I wasn't in the discipline I was accustomed to, but in a new one with less mobility and less expectation of promotion. Plus the fact of thinking – are the children wrapped up warm enough to go to school this morning? etc., instead of dismissing them completely from my mind and getting on with the work. The company begins to assess you a bit lower perhaps because your mind has family welfare as a higher priority than it should be. It must be something like for a married woman but not the same because as a man you're not used to it. You learn what are all the difficulties of bringing up children, and I now appreciate that it is difficult for a woman to live in the kitchen most of her life with a couple of kids out there. I appreciate it even more how much they tie you down. And when I hear men talking about going off on their rounds of golf, etc., I can see life is a dream world for men compared to what it is for women. It's still a man's world.

It was a big blow to readjust my working ambitions. I cannot see my ever progressing now. I should have moved up about two years ago now. Earlier no one would think of you going on to the next grade till you were fifty, but now it's gone the other way, and people look askance at you if you haven't reached this grade by the time you are thirty-five. So it's much more difficult. I can't swear, but I might have just about made it further had things gone along well now.

On a practical level I've been extremely lucky. But at weekends I have found it difficult. I took Anne down to junior church as I always have done . . . but I'd never brushed her hair before or tied ribbons, and this was actually impossible to me. So we'd got the neighbour to do that. Things like using the washing machine . . .

I'd done that before. But not cooking. And one thing I was determined to do, and forced myself to do was cook Sunday dinner as normal. And I stood here and cooked a proper Sunday lunch. I got a cookbook and did casseroles and things I'd never done in my life. I was determined not to be beaten. I was here for four hours, by the time I'd washed up etc. But now its convenience foods, cold sausages, tins, etc. I've swung right back. But I forced myself to do it at the beginning. It seemed important.

I think you are much healthier in all sorts of ways when you are married. You live a normal sex life, to begin with. You feel somehow fulfilled, it's difficult to analyse. I'm a romantic sort. Divorce is a very big blow to someone like me. I'm a very practical person, by the way, but I have this romantic streak about me, like most men probably. And it isn't there any more. I mean I could forgive a lot. There was so much that was good in the making of the marriage that it is a pity that it broke up.

To tell the truth I think she was sexually adventurous. And this was her ideal. I don't know if she's happy with the way things have turned out. But now she seems to have gone back to the norm she started with, to trying to prove to everybody how good a wife and mother she really was. She has gone round full circle. It's a funny thing, her people condemn her more than mine do. She has, in fact, married the man she went off with but it was a long road and I'm told they nearly got divorced a few months after they got married. But now she seems to have settled down. Now when I hear of various people putting up with adulterous relationships I wonder whether that might have been the best thing to do. But I'm a very orthodox person, brought up fairly strictly. On Sunday our life was based around Church activities. But I wonder now whether in the future the kids would have known about something that happened twenty years ago.

Still, it may not have worked out. There's a pile of debris in the hall – a great pile of toys – all bought by her. The children don't get these things from me. They are an embarrassment to me. In a normal marriage she would still have wanted to ply the kids with these great piles of toys. And I've never seen a woman with so many clothes as my wife. I knew she liked a lot of clothes and I supplied her with money for this. I accepted this as part of the price, sort of. Because I think I did love her really. It might have gone sour, I don't know . . . but taking it all in all I've decided to cut, and that's it. It's just that so many people do live with the

jealousy and hurt that adultery brings . . . I don't know if I would
have. I meet so many people living like this, that I think it might
have been the best thing to have done. But it's impossible to say.

I did phone her up when she went, but she said she wouldn't
come back. But she was crying. I think it was very touch and go,
actually – very touch and go. But in the beginning she was quite
implaccable that she was going to stick it out. Unfortunately,
having made her arrangements she thought she'd go along with it. I
think she'd had too much of the children. She doesn't admit this
now, even to me, and certainly not to the children. She plies them
with stories about when they were babies and how happy it was. Of
course, I felt very betrayed.

One of the things that I used to loathe after she left was
sometimes being here in the evening and finding the neighbours
chatting outside like normal couples. And going off to play bad-
minton with each other, etc. while I was stuck indoors. You feel
such an odd sort of customer in my situation. One of the biggest
practical difficulties is when your au pair goes into hospital or
leaves you for some reason, and you are several weeks without
anyone. But the neighbours will help. The funny thing is, people
start talking to you as soon as your wife has gone. But it wears thin
after a while. It's not really expected to go on for ever. And I can
understand this, because we all have our lives to lead.

---

*So many of the problems that arise when a marriage is breaking up and
after are aggravated by anomalies in the law and weaknesses in the administration of the welfare service* – Rosemary Simon

---

I didn't feel very socially inclined for the first six or seven months. I
was very lonely then, and depressed. The most buoyant people are
often the ones who crash down to the lowest point after. And I was
very emotionally down immediately afterwards. I have a friend,
best friend, and we used to have a drink and discuss it. But I never
felt drunk or happy. I couldn't get drunk and it didn't make me
happy. So that didn't really work. It was a very distressing time. I
didn't sleep properly for weeks. I'd go to the doctor and say I'm
getting a few hours now, and he'd say – well it's improving. I don't
believe in drugs, because you get too reliant. But if he'd prescribed
them at the time I think I'd have used them.

I decided to overcome my loneliness by doing things and filling my mind with all sorts of things, maybe too much. I never gave up my interest in helping the Scouts, and I went to evening classes a couple of times a week. I don't have so much direct contact with the Scouts any more because I reckoned I've had enough of kids. So it's more backroom stuff that I do with the Scouts. In evening classes I did geology and astronomy and tried to learn German and genealogy. I've always been interested in swimming and Alan has just got his swimming certificate. I'm taking a course to teach swimming.

I don't know whether I do these things just to fill my mind to blot out the other hurt. But I've found relations that I never knew I had through genealogy – found out things about the family I would never have known possible if I hadn't have been by myself. I would not have done these things if I'd had my wife here. I'd have done the things she wanted to do, stayed in while she went to evening classes, which is what I was doing before, though I don't think she was going to evening classes, if you know what I mean?

I have certainly found you can be more yourself if you are on your own. I have developed these interests, for example. If I want to go to a stranger's house in Sussex, we'll go. But if their mother was here she'd say: 'Oh no, we don't want to go there.' If I want to go along to a geologically interesting area, then I'll take the children along. Maybe I'm pushing my luck as regards the interests of the children, but if I want to go somewhere, they are coming with me. I think they enjoy some of these things.

I have a much closer relationship with the children than I did. And I try not to destroy their love for their mother. They have remained close to her. She used to be a bit envious of me sometimes, saying 'You have all the enjoyment of the children and I have to look after them.' Which was quite true, though naturally I would take them swimming or something and do the things with them that fathers normally do. But I wouldn't have been so close to them nor they to me. But this also makes it more difficult should they ever go away, or should one of them die, because you'd find it well nigh impossible to get over. Whereas if you were married, they wouldn't be quite so close to you and you'd have the support of a wife.

I was happiest when they were many months without their mother, when she didn't see them much at first. Things seemed to go on happily and normally when there was only myself and the children. Sometimes I wish it would be like that entirely. But possibly it is better that my children do relate to two parents. But if she had made a clean break they, at least Anne, would have forgotten her by now, and I wouldn't have this emotional tug-of-war. They are always a little bit fragile when they come back from seeing her. They are torn between the two of us, that's what it is. I mean Anne did ask me: 'What is Bob – [that's my wife's husband] – to me', and I couldn't help snapping out: 'He's nothing.' You can't describe it to a child, can you?

I think people make things worse by saying *ipso facto* that there are problems with single-parent children without analysing it. I mean Alan is undoubtedly almost outstanding at school for his age at the moment. But to begin with it was – oh dear, he must be held back because he comes from a split home. He was put in a lower class because of that. And I don't agree with it: it wasn't right. Though it's got to the point now when in the local paper – the *Nottingham Post* – when they are talking about vandalism for example, they will say – why are the vandals not like children from single-parent families where there are no problems of this sort. This is partly due to our local Gingerbread group which happens to be politically strong and active.

Actually lots of people say that the one that suffers is me. The wife is all right, she's off with somebody; the au pair is all right, she's got a nice home, the children are all right because they are fairly comfortable. The only one that is a bit put out is myself. But you make the choice to do this, and that's too bad. The only fear I have is when I am really physically tired and emotionally upset and all the rest of it, that I'll react violently on the children. I'm too easy on them, I feel, generally, but then when I'm really tired I feel I'm holding back a great waterfall which is going to burst and I don't want to descend on the child and start hammering him. Alan doesn't get to sleep easily and if he isn't asleep by about ten, or if he starts worrying me and is naughty, which he sometimes is, sometimes awake and talking to me till 11.30, then I'm very fragile. I manage to hold myself back normally but I sometimes wonder if I might break. Usually Alan will go to sleep if I tell him a story – anything from my life. Although I only did National Service after the war, he imagines that I was Montgomery's right hand man. So I have to make up stories from my eighteen months in North Wales, plus stories from when I was a boy at school and so forth. His bedtime story is my life story – slightly embellished. I get scared sometimes that he gets too close to me, because I don't want him to be reliant on me completely. He's young now but he's got to grow out of that hasn't he?

My attitudes to roles you expect men and women to play have changed a little, obviously. For example, I do a bit more washing up. I didn't readily volunteer to do the washing up on a Sunday previously. I might do the washing up sometimes, but I thought I was doing the wife quite proud to come out and volunteer then. On the other hand I had much more time for doing house repairs, those sort of male roles which are normally expected of you. I should probably do a bit more of that if I was married again, and probably expect her to do a bit more round the other way. But I'm not complaining about my wife about that. When you get it right down in cold logic, you think what is marriage all about anyway. But you can't change yourself completely. I was certainly put off marriage in the beginning. Now I sometimes think I'm getting so eccentric, like an old bachelor, that I wonder whether I could adapt to anybody ever again. You know, I like my tea made in a certain way, I like to come home and not eat if I don't want to, eat if I want to and eat whatever I want to eat. I've been on my own for four years now. I don't say that I would be against marriage, but I think the probability of someone coming along who could live with me is extremely unlikely. I mean, she'd have to take on two children and possibly I wouldn't want any children of hers – which is asking a lot. And then you've got to have all the other things to fall in line as well. When I go out and meet people, which sometimes I do, the women might be divorced or single, but living quite a comfortable existence, thank you, and they wouldn't dream of giving it up to be imprisoned inside a house bringing up a couple of kids. Because there is this . . . I don't know whether to call it emancipation . . . but the position of women in society has changed a lot in the last few years. Occasionally I do meet women – most of them have children – and I might be friendly with them. But when I weigh it up, they might take on my problems, but I have to take on theirs. And I usually back away from it, to tell you the truth. I appear to want to flatter myself with having these friendships, and I'm quite happy to have this sort of association. But somehow I don't think the right person is going to come along. And, I hate to think of it, but in eighteen months time I'll be fifty. And that seems very ancient. Probably when I reach fifty-five it won't seem very ancient, but by then you might as well say – well that's it, forget about it – you're not a film star or TV personality and you haven't got much money. I don't think I'm going to get the ideal person . . . that sort of girl just isn't going to come along.

Gingerbread has played an important part in my life. In supplying shoulders to cry on in the first instance. One thing I would like to say about this whole situation is that when men suddenly find themselves alone, they never expect it to happen, they don't know where to turn, and there seems to be precious little help that they can find in the beginning. When this first happened I thought I should make a book or directory about how to go about it. I found that the social services that I pay for did not help me one little bit. But the Church of England social worker, whom someone put me in touch with locally has been wonderful. Any help is wonderful and they've helped me out in a couple of tight corners in the last four years by supplying somebody when I've lost an au pair. That's what it amounts to. It's the practical side of it that is so pressing. And also occasionally coming to see me if I want them to, but not if I don't want them to. Neither do they want to know anything about whether you are a Jew, Muslim or Catholic, they'll still help out. And they've been most useful.

But I also find Gingerbread useful. For meeting people. I saw a woman last night that I knew in Gingerbread when it first happened. I just keep up the friendship, that's all. They all have their problems. It's interesting. Also, you go inside people's homes and see a kind of people that otherwise you'd never have met. Gingerbread has been most useful in the emotional support really. There is the practical side, taking the children out occasionally – Guy Fawkes parties and that sort of thing. Also it probably gives you a channel in to which to push your energies – if you want to pressure your MP or whatever. It's been very useful for that, because you can do something positive.

I know that I'm never going to get day care here, never going to get any help, even when the law says I'm supposed to have it. I've never got it. All the social services did when one of the au pairs went into hospital was say they couldn't help. After a week I said, what am I going to do, go to work and leave them in the house? So they said you can't do that, it's illegal under the age of eleven. Very quick on that but they couldn't do anything. In the meantime I was getting neighbours to help out. I have been pretty lucky with them, but as I said, they can't do it all the time. I know I wouldn't want to for a prolonged time – well otherwise you wouldn't think the chap was doing his best to help. A woman can get away with it more than a man. I must admit I don't like putting up with other people's children. Some people will help me if I help them, but I'm not very happy to put up with other people's children. Funny aren't I? I should do, but I'm not. I will do for the neighbours' children – although they barely ever ask me – because they have helped me so much, and I would gladly help them. But there are other people who want *quid pro quo*, and I don't want to do that in balanced quantities. Whereas with a woman, perhaps there is that inbuilt ability to put up with a few more kids running round the house. I might be wrong there. It could be purely psychological upbringing and nothing to do with what is inbuilt. But because you are the male you think you shouldn't have to put up with all these kids and you get annoyed about it. But the female is the reverse. Still, I'm quite sure there are many men that make better mothers than women and there are many mothers that never should have been mothers. I'm sure of that.

I do sometimes feel very sorry for myself, and this is the last thing you want to do. But you do sometimes, and you mustn't, because this snowballs back on to yourself, I think, in the end. Having said that I still can't help feeling sorry for myself. But I sometimes think, your slip is showing, you're saying something to someone, and the only reason you're saying it is because you're asking for their sympathy, so shut up. And I find myself doing that, you know. Why don't I look on the positive side and try to think how lucky I am in certain ways. The only thing is that, in spite of there being 100,000 men in my position, and 600,000 women, and that one in every ten children in the country is brought up in this way, there still isn't really the understanding of the situation that there might be. In church on Mothers' Day, it drove me berserk really. I came blazing out and said to one of my friends – 'I'm fed up with all this emphasis on "mother".' And he said, 'What's the matter with you, you've got a mum haven't you?' I was very annoyed. People just don't understand the situation. They are very insensitive. And yet we don't want any special treatment. We only want fair do's really.

I know of many married couples where perhaps the child or children are not all that wanted anyway, and the parents carry on as if they didn't exist, or the child isn't getting the real love it should Or they both live adulterous lives under the same roof, not really husband and wife at all. And when they come to analyse it, although we imagine that people live in ideal situations, in actual fact there are a very large proportion of married families who only superficially live a normal life. Often, it's cracking at the seams so much that it's worse for the children than it is in our situation, much worse. I think children can have much more harm done to them in nuclear families than in single-parent families.

Postscript

Michael is typical of a man who married later in life with very strong expectations of what a wife and marriage ought to be like. He actually thought helping with the dishes after a Sunday dinner was something quite generously out of the ordinary. And he was quite shocked when his wife failed to conform. There is such a pattern of unachieved expectations, and such unsuccessful struggle to conform to things which would seem to be so impossible to most people, that one wonders if it is the people involved who fail at marriage or whether marriage fails them.

Michael comes across as fastidious and as a perfectionist, characteristics still apparent after the separation in his concern about the cigarette burns on the lino which had been there for years, and the clutter of toys in the lounge. In the interview, even after a period of years, he comes across as still quite bewildered and angry about what happened to him. There is a certain element of – 'She'd got me, a nice house, nice children – everything she could have wanted, what more could she want?' He was managing well as a single parent, but nervously, without a lot of confidence, somewhat insecure in trying to function as both mother and father to his children. Michael's case illustrates the particular practical problems of single-parent fathers attempting to carry on working with pre-school children, trying to maintain a precarious stability with an endless series of au pairs. Michael still missed the 'comforts' of marriage and did not seem to have analysed what might have gone wrong, or his part of the responsibility for the marriage ending. At the same time he comes across as quite rightly proud to have managed to raise his family single-handed. He had found a lot of help from Gingerbread, and precious little from social services.

9. Jane

Jane comes from a middle-class background. She married at twenty-four and separated ten years later, with two children under the age of two. She lives in a large house in Manchester with her elderly mother, her two children who are now at school and her lodgers. At the time of the interview she had been separated for three years, she was in her late thirties, the children under five. She had worked part-time over the past four years helping in a pub in the evenings. When her children started school she took on additional work as a waitress and was effectively working full-time in a variety of part-time jobs that allowed her to be home-based.

Jane says she is not in another serious relationship because she has neither the inclination or the time; she would not remarry, 'because it's so much trouble splitting up.'

Her husband left her and their two young children and their very conventional marriage to live with another woman by whom he subsequently had another child. Says Jane: 'The girls' father, after spending two years abroad with his woman, has now returned to England. She left him to go back to America with the child. It was the old story of it turning sour when they lived together. He now comes and puts the girls to bed about once a week and might even be with them on a Saturday if I want to go out.'

Jane describes her situation as 'one of progression. In the last four years I have become much more involved with the community. I've become active in the local Liberal Party. There are lots of meetings and I'm on a number of committees. I would never be doing this if I were married. With both girls at school I have started to do some more waitress work, and have also become active in a local community project. Because I do not have to concern myself with the needs of a male, I find I can spend time with the girls taking them swimming, to the gym, theatre and that I can take part in pastimes without feeling conscious of not spending enough time with one's spouse. I feel I am a stable and mature person, although I had no father (he was killed in the war) and a disabled mother. My brother and I were brought up mainly by grandparents.

'Most of the time I feel happy and confident. My friends have changed, they are mostly local. My social life is different as a divorcee. I have been going out once a week with a married man, but we are ending the relationship by mutual agreement. I have been very energetic in making the house comfortable and easy to look after. I have made decisions, many I would have hesitated making in a married situation.'

Peter and I met in 1963 at a party, on June 15. I was twenty-two, he was twenty-one. I remember the exact date. He was nine months younger than I am. To me it was just a party at the time, but I felt for him something I've never felt for anyone else. We hit it off immediately.

I remember thinking, when I was sixteen, that I might marry when I was twenty-four. And it turned out that I *did* marry when I was twenty-four, after knowing Peter for two years. We didn't actually live together during that period, but we saw a tremendous amount of each other. For about two years we dated. Before that I'd never been out with anybody for more than about two months, so I hadn't been used to long relationships. Peter and I used to have long conversations on the phone. I think that's one criteria of being in love. And of course, sex. We slept together before we got married. It was the first time for Peter – though not for me – and I think that this was one of the factors in his case. I was the first person he slept with. And the second person he slept with was not very long after he first slept with me. That apparently was rather unpleasant. I think he suddenly realised that he'd missed a lot.

He was very quiet except that, even in those days, he showed a slightly split character, because in normal social life he was very quiet and virtually didn't speak until spoken to. But at a party or any big social event, he was quite often the man of the moment. He was a great one for small talk, and could chat superficially. In large gatherings he could switch on charm, but if you spoke to him – say – amongst a group of people talking about anything serious, he would very likely not say a word. He seemed to go into a shell. But I know for a fact that he was very intelligent, and he seemed to know something about everything. He was a scientist, and they're always a bit odd.

I had an abortion after about eighteen months with Peter. I found I was pregnant, so we decided to have an abortion because I didn't want to get married at the time. Then, about six months later, I decided we really ought to do something, so we decided to get married – on my birthday. I didn't want to *have* to get married. I wanted a white wedding. And it was a beautiful wedding. Everybody is still talking about it. It was the first marriage in my family and, in fact, the first marriage in Peter's. It was a great occasion for both in-laws. We had eighty people to church at four o'clock in the afternoon and then had a supper dance in the evening. It went on till twelve o'clock. It was great fun.

For the first two years of our married life our home was very minimal. I didn't have to demand of him to paint or mend anything, but I did most of it. Perhaps if I'd known at the beginning how useless he was . . . on the other hand, I'm a very practical person and he was very brainy – so I thought we would be compatible. He says I nagged him but I think . . . I thought as long as you'd got money to pay people to do the decorating or the mending, then it didn't really matter, how impractical the man is – so long as he's thinking. But he didn't even think in the end.

In the first two years we were both working. Peter got a good job in the Civil Service in Manchester and stayed there ever since. The head of his department died about three years after he joined. They couldn't find anybody else, so he became head of the department. He was young, about twenty-seven.

It really was a good time for both of us then. We just lived from day to day and had a great social life. We went to parties and had people in to dinner, went to dinner and to cinemas. We weren't very cultural. But we were both working, and we were quite well off, so we could afford to have a good time. Peter enjoyed gambling – he did a lot of gambling in that period. I don't know how much he lost over the time.

We sold the flat and did a grand tour of Europe. We went everywhere. We had a great time there.

We came back and bought a house in Salford, a tiny, little two-up and two-down. I felt it was the best thing to do. I'm very glad we did – at that time – because it was only about £4,250 and we weren't all that wealthy because we had spent our savings on the holiday in Europe. But we never went without. We didn't have fantastic clothes or fantastic furniture, but we enjoyed doing things we liked doing which was entertaining and seeing people. We were there until – it must have been 1972.

We both continued working, but I was never happy in my jobs and often gave up a job, did other things and joined another firm. But he was still in the Civil Service and we could afford holidays.

We travelled a lot. In Europe as I said, in 1967. Another trip in 1969. And again in 1970. We didn't have any children then. There wasn't a lot of pressure to think about.

From the very beginning we had a joint bank account. I never think much about money and I don't think he did either, because it came and went. When he gambled I think he often enjoyed losing more than he did winning. But it didn't worry me. I never brought it up because I didn't want for anything. There was one year in fact, he had a fantastic win. He won nearly a thousand pounds. We bought the refrigerator, the radio and the car. But that summer we found we couldn't afford to go anywhere, as I suppose after this big win he started losing. He played Black Jack and the horses. I went with him sometimes, but generally not, because it was boring. It amused him, but I was all for leading one's own life. He had his gambling. When he finished work in the afternoon, he would often go to the betting shop. Every Saturday afternoon he was at the betting shop or watching sports on television. I enjoyed cooking for dinner parties and I did pottery and I quite often did work shifts as a waitress.

We did some things together and some things separately. We decided we wanted children. Then I got pregnant. I finished the Pill a year before I even conceived. As far as I was concerned having children was a joint decision. But it turns out now that apparently he says it was my idea. I would never have had the children unless I had been sure he was interested as well, and he seemed to be very good with our friends' children. As it turned out he was marvellous with the children, but he wasn't able to face up to the responsibility, of the years of complete dedication to bringing up children . . . I don't know. Anyway, we were still living in Salford when I got pregnant. It must have been around Christmas time when Peter heard that *this* house where we live now – which belonged to his aunt on his mother's side – was for sale. She had been living in it as a sitting tenant, and she had bought the freehold the minute the property was put in the Council's hands. Then she wanted to sell and we were given the option to buy it. At least I heard of it and I immediately said to Peter, 'You must buy it.' I think if I hadn't worked at him, he probably would have let it go. But to me it was a progression and I couldn't really see myself bringing up children in a tiny house which you probably have to stay in for about six months of the year because of the weather. I wanted to live in a bigger house. This was one of my ambitions. As far as I'm concerned now, materially, I've got what I want, though having a roof over your head and food in your stomach, of course, isn't everything.

Our recommendations for legal reform, financial support, and improvement in the conditions of housing and employment are not the entire answer to the difficulties of one-parent families. There are more intangible consequences of their situation which material benefits and efficient and sympathetic administration can alleviate but not cure . . . the development of social and educational services has a principal part to play – 'The Finer Report, 1974'

Anyway, I had to push Peter to decide to buy this house. I don't know whether he would have done something in his own time, or whether I was just impatient . . . but even when buying the Salford house it seemed I always had to be on at him to contact the estate agents or the solicitors. I really did most of the organising and making the major decisions. But I was a little depressed because he never paid bills until the third asking and in the end I paid the bills and sent off the cheques because it used to annoy me. He said it was a good way of saving. Of course my arithmetic isn't as good as his – he used to tell me off for not knowing exactly what was spent or where it was going. I never kept books. If there is no money there, then we don't spend it, but if there *is* money, I know we can pay the bills.

In fact, all our married life – to me – was casual and nice. We got the house, but we couldn't move into it until the baby was born. The idea was that Peter was supposed to come and get the house ready for me. It was in a terrible state. But when we came here it was still a bit of a shambles.

From the beginning we had student lodgers. Originally it was quite useful, because we had two students who came before the term began and they helped with the decorating. From the beginning – I had a baby of two months old, five men to look after and a big house. It was hard work, and a bit unsettled at the beginning. But to me it was working for ourselves and our future. I didn't mind it at all. Even at the beginning I had no help in the house and I didn't even send the sheets to the laundry. I washed the sheets and ironed them. In my memory I can't ever remember Peter getting down on his hands and knees and thanking me, but now he accuses me of never thanking him for all the work he did in the house and for constantly nagging him.

It was hard work but it was what we wanted. I guess I could see the end of it. Perhaps this was it. He just couldn't see the end . . . I don't know. One always tries to think what on earth it was that made him . . . go off. We had a new house and a new baby and I felt that everything was all right, and we were both happy and doing what we wanted to.

Then we decided to have a second child. Because Alice was obviously going to be spoiled rotten and I thought it was good for her development and personality to have another child to work with, or against. She was about a year old when I got pregnant again. I said I wanted another baby – and if he wasn't happy with it he should have made more of a noise about it. I said, 'It would be nice to have another child, wouldn't it?', and he didn't object. So we had Kate.

But there was a fly in the ointment before her birth. I was pregnant and my mother was going to be on the scene imminently. She was going to come and live with us. Which *I* thought was all right. I felt it was my duty to look after her then. She wasn't going to be able to look after herself. She was living with my grandpa – my grandmother was in the process of dying. Peter didn't really object to it. I thought it was perfectly reasonable – we had a big house and she could have a bedsitter in it.

However, I think that when she came he was getting a bit unhappy, because she really got on his nerves. With all my responsibilities – all he had to do was to go to work and come back – he could have organised for her to go into a home. In fact, she could have gone into one very recently but I decided to have her still for a few more years. It only took about three months for them to have a vacancy and Peter could have done this from the beginning. He didn't object too strongly at the time. I assumed that everything was all right and that we would carry on. But we didn't. That was the beginning of the end.

There was another woman involved. Well, we've always been quite honest. It was only three weeks after Kate was born . . . in fact, he stayed out all night . . . for the first time ever. We'd always been quite honest. I'd had three affairs during our marriage, during the first five years, and I told him about them. Not each time. I think once, and then four or five years ago I confessed all to him. It seems that, since then, he decided not to love me. As soon as I was pregnant with Kate he went around a lot with women, and was really becoming quite sick with it. Apparently he used to go round telling all his men friends, and they were getting fed up with his talk. I don't know whether you've heard men talk about their . . . escapades. It gets pretty sickening after a time, because they just don't seem to put it in the right perspective.

Sex was unfortunate from the beginning. At our engagement party he wasn't very well and he went to hospital and they diagnosed chicken pox. But it turned out he was suffering from rheumatic fever. He was very seriously ill for a couple of months before we married. I remember in hospital asking if he was sure he wanted to marry me. He had a lot of opportunity for thinking in hospital. So, if he'd had any doubts, then, he could have worked it out for himself and said, 'No'. But there wasn't anything during that period.

Before we got married, our sexual relationship was great. After we got married I thought it was pretty poor. I didn't think he was interested. This is my story. Often on a Sunday morning we used to stay in bed, but nothing happened. He just wasn't interested. And I put it down to his rheumatic fever, because I had read that up to ten years after the fever, often it does affect your sexual powers, so I left it for two years. I did talk about it with him, but he was non-committal really. Whether it didn't worry him . . . I didn't think he was particularly disturbed by it. I don't think he was that worried by sexual powers or interests. His mind was on higher things.

I don't think I said in so many words that I wasn't happy or satisfied, but he must have known. To me, my extra-marital relationships were just getting rid of my excess energy, because I know that I have a lot of energy. Perhaps if I hadn't done that, I might have decided to leave him. They were mostly casual affairs, but one went on and off for about a couple of years. Another was on and off for six months. But it was once every three months or something like that – it wasn't very regular. These were people I met at parties and through friends. I think Peter knew only about the one. I think I told him and he partly guessed as well.

He didn't seem particularly upset. If he'd have got really angry and given me an ultimatum, perhaps I might have thought about it more. As far as I was concerned we were a modern couple and we could have these extra-marital relationships without harming our own development. He wasn't having any affairs himself, but I thought he should, and I think I told him that I think it would have done him a lot of good. He didn't *not* look at women, he didn't *not* go out with them, but when he was attracted to other women perhaps he didn't ask them the question or hadn't the confidence. But after I was pregnant – whether he all of a sudden woke up or something – he really had a lot of confidence with women and he didn't beat about the bush with them any longer. He had a lot of conquests from the time I was pregnant with Alice.

I didn't mind because I thought he was aware of his own mind and his own actions. I didn't think it would consume him as it did. Looking back, I think perhaps my affairs did offend him in fact, but I didn't regret doing it. As far as I was concerned I was still his friend and helper and servant – and what have you. To me it was just making me sweeter, as it were. I suppose that when I had relationships I was really so confident about the marriage with Peter that I didn't really think they would damage the marriage.

Anyway, when I was pregnant with Alice he started having lots of different women. I didn't know everything at the time, but I've heard from friends since that it was more extreme than I thought at the time. I know that when I was pregnant we didn't have sexual intercourse because he didn't fancy it. I don't know if he thought it might harm the child or something . . . but of course it doesn't, and a lot of people do.

From the time I had Alice and then Kate, I didn't have any more sexual relationships. I made up my mind that once the children had come on the scene, then especially the woman doesn't have any other relationships except perhaps when they're older. I wouldn't have had the time anyway. Having children puts a completely new perspective on one's marriage. Before, you are two single people who happen to be together, but after the children come on the scene you are a family . . . with different obligations. It is interesting, looking back, that before we had children I had the relationships, and it was from the time that I was pregnant and starting a family that Peter started having relationships. I don't know what you would make of that. All that time, though, I still felt happily married and confident about our relationship. And it was quite good.

If there is a practical argument for trying to patch up your marriage, it must be money. One of the nastier effects of divorce is that, however fairly the family wealth is divided, everyone involved is likely to suffer financially – Rosemary Simon

I don't really know what went wrong. For the last four years he'd been talking about leaving the Civil Service. But *I* thought it was just the job for him, because he's not a go-getter, he's not somebody – apparently Capricorns are ambitious, but he never seemed to be. And non-materialistic, but he always maintained he was materialistic. I've often wondered why the woman he's gone off with is different from the other ones.

I realised it was different when he started seeing her so regularly. It was three, four nights a week and he was coming back at three, four o'clock in the morning. So in the end I told him he could forget it, he might as well stay out all night and come back for breakfast, because he was disturbing me coming back at four o'clock in the morning, and, what with the girls as well, I wasn't getting much sleep. I knew it was the same woman – obviously someone becoming increasingly special. I told him, 'Think what you're doing'. But I think he really couldn't think. To me he had a heart transplant. He was one big prick and no heart. He was just thinking of sex all the time. With her. He'd got a problem for a while – one of the diseases affecting the organ. So he wasn't able to have sex, but he still saw her and it was during that period apparently that he decided he loved her.

He wanted to go with her, at one point, on holiday. In the end he very kindly didn't. But he more or less accused me of preventing him having some enjoyment. *I* was depriving *him*! He went out with her on Saturdays and Sundays. To me an intelligent human being shouldn't need to be told that he was doing something that was obviously detrimental to his family. I thought it would be a passing thing even then, because I didn't want to deprive him of having external enjoyment if that's what he wanted and if it made him happier when he came back to his family. It was Christmas Eve he went out to buy Alice her present. He went after lunch and didn't come back till about nine in the evening. He'd gone to see *her*. I told him we'd better go away for a week-end and sort this out.

As it happened it wasn't a week-end – just one night really. His parents came to look after the girls and the house. It was just a miserable week-end. We more or less decided to part then and there, but we decided to give it another month. He still went to see her three or four times a week. I wasn't jealous, because I don't think I'm a jealous person, but it just made me intensely angry. In fact, I told him he could see her once a week – once a month. What *he* wanted, in fact, was to remain in the house, have his own room, *me* still cooking for him and washing his shirts and *him* seeing this woman about five times a week. He as good as said this to me. And *I* told *him* it wasn't on. If he didn't neglect his family I couldn't have cared less, but he was neglecting us. He came of an evening, played with the girls for a couple of hours, and then left at six o'clock, and stayed out all night. He was just another lodger.

That month even – it was so ridiculous – he said, 'You won't leave me, will you?' The last month we had a lot of social engagements. He was supposed to see whether he really wanted to go to her, or whether he would stay with us. He was supposed to be making a decision – a choice. We had a lot of commitments that month, and it would have been even more difficult to say, 'I'm sorry, Peter's left me, so I've got to come to the twenty-first by myself'. Whenever we were out at a party he always had his arm around me. Terribly affectionate. And off and on we'd still have a sexual relationship.

But there were still lots of problems. Not least because of this other woman. Needless to say I didn't think much of her—she was ruining my marriage. It wasn't that I was jealous. I don't think I was. But I could see my world crumbling about me. Peter and I had worked hard for what we'd got. It meant a lot to me as I'd had such an unsettled childhood. I certainly wanted my children to have a father. But along she comes and . . . I don't know what she wanted. Peter was about ten years older than she was. She was about twenty-two. She was American. She'd only been here two weeks when Peter met her. I think perhaps she'd got a father complex, looking for a father figure. Maybe she was on the lookout for a married man, I don't know. But I don't understand how she could carry on breaking up this marriage, especially with the children. She even met Kate, because he took her up to her . . . I've not met her and I don't want to meet her. He took Kate up to her, to show her his little girl – to show this woman, I presume, what she was up against. And she could so easily have gone back to America. But she preferred to break up a happy home. I reckon she knew what she was doing.

During the last month we were together we were at a restaurant . . . we'd decided that would be the month that would make or break us . . . and he said, 'I'm so happy that we've decided to stay together', but he was still seeing the other woman. I reckon he didn't know what he *did* want. But he moved out at the end of that month. There weren't any more rows. We spent a few evenings just talking about it quietly, and it just seemed that he did not think about us any more. We were just not in his mind. One weekend I remember we were having a drink and, for conversation, I was talking to him about the education of the girls and he just didn't want to know really. He didn't want to concern himself. So he left, really, by our mutual agreement.

We decided that we were going to be divorced. It was his idea actually, because this woman, being an American, couldn't stay in this country unless she got married to an Englishman. Also, I know that the modern attitude has improved, but I think a divorced or separated woman still has a stigma about her. If you don't get divorced though – then you're nothing. At least when you've got a piece of paper, you know your social status. Even if it is as a second-class citizen.

It's been nine months now since he left, and I still don't know how I feel. I told him when he left that if he really did go – and never came back – then we could no longer be friends and I never would be able to recognise him as a person even. And this is what happened. I find that when he comes to the house – to see the girls – I can hardly look at him. And I find that if I've got a knife in my hand I might easily plunge it in him. I don't know why, but there's still this terribly angry feeling. I think because of the way he deceived me. Ten years is a terribly long time. It's a third of my life, and to me, it just seems as if he's wasted my life. I don't think I would feel so bad, in fact, if he'd been my husband and left me at fifty, instead of thirty-five. At least, then, one's prime would have been finished with, but at thirty-five one feels one's in the prime of one's life.

You're more or less a prisoner to two tiny children, and the responsibilities of bringing them up, without really much outlet. Because a woman on her own . . . well, you're not often invited out to dinner parties, or even invited out to the theatre. People just forget about you somehow. I feel very angry towards him now, because there were so many choices open to him, except leaving. A lot of people split up because they feel they have to make a choice between one woman and another. There are many marriages still, in which adultery instantaneously means the end of marriage.

I think it wouldn't be so bad if he'd had different girls. Perhaps it was the fact that it was just this one woman all the time. I guess I increasingly began to feel that I was being replaced by someone else. So it was personal. It would have been all right perhaps, if I was the first woman, and she was the second. But that wasn't the way it was. Though he would have been happy for me to continue having him in the house. I suggested, jokingly, as far as I was concerned, that he could still live here, and I'd look after him, and when we had dinner parties, he could be around. He would have been quite happy about this! I didn't mind being first woman to her second woman. But when I became second woman, that was really it. I was his drudgery, and she was his entertainment.

On top of these stresses often comes the frustration of foregoing sexual relations or conducting them clandestinely so as to avoid the notice of the children or the neighbours or arousing the suspicions of the officers of the Supplementary Benefits Commission – 'The Finer Report, 1974'

As for divorcing, I'm in a very enviable position, because we have got mother living with us and she's got money she puts into the family pool – so financially we're not destitute. The girls have got a lot of toys and a lot of books and I take them out a lot. I didn't have a father, you see, so this was the big thing to me. I would never have had children without them having a father. I had them on the assumption that they were going to have a father. And now they are going to grow up without a father. He was going to be their intellectual stimulant, and I was going to be their person to take them out and cook and look after the house and mend a blind or something. But I think, especially the younger one, is going to be scientifically minded and I'm afraid I'm not going to be able to help them in that way.

But in most ways I'm fortunate. Obviously there are a lot of women with no roof, no income. I haven't had that problem. I've been lucky in being reasonably financially secure – and I've got the house. The divorce is a fairly straightforward divorce. People tell me that thirty-five is very young and that I'm an attractive woman.

But as far as marriage again is concerned . . . Why does one get married? I mean I've got everything that one would get married for – security of the home, and children, and I have got quite a lot of friends and companions. In marriage, okay, there's always somebody around, but in this house there's always somebody around anyway – mother, the children, the students.

Probably the only thing I'd like is to have a relationship with somebody – but not get married to them. I wouldn't mind the opportunity of meeting someone that I fell in love with. It would be good for me and good for the children, because if you're happy in yourself you're a much better mother, a much better person to be with. I know at the moment, often the older one especially, wants me to do things with her, and I'm just too tired. I do devote a lot of time to them. They're both very energetic little girls, and it just seems that after doing the house, I've still got them to attend to, whereas if there were a husband, at least he could have half the burden. When you're divorced, the whole burden is on the mother.

I don't know whether it's bitterness I feel . . . I hope I'm not bitter, because I think that would turn you into rather a nasty person. I'm still . . . well, I just have this feeling of anger. It shouldn't happen. There are many people with modern ideas about marriage, and I was one of them. Now I wonder if modern ideas are possible. It certainly seems . . . perhaps you can only have extra relationships if everything is really happy – job, marriage. But then probably you wouldn't have extra relationships . . . if you were completely happy otherwise. So Peter and I must not have been. Perhaps there were ways in which we never were.

He is a quiet person, and I often used to ask him to tell me about things. He accuses me now of *not* asking him about his job, but whenever I asked him about what happened during the course of the day, it was a monologue, it was an interrogation. He never used to have conversations. Apparently this other woman is going to do everything for him. It really is a joke.

When I first met him, he didn't dress well. It was the beginning of really dressing kinkily and *I* was aware of it. I didn't have much money to spend on clothes, but I used to dress as modernly as I could. But he didn't. He used to wear the most diabolical of things. When I first met him he was in a terrible old mac. I remember having conversations about clothes with him, and he always used to say, 'What do clothes matter?' He never used to *buy* anything for himself. I used to have to go with him to buy anything like trousers or sports jackets. And *I* used to buy him the kinky shirts which he wore to every party.

Apparently this woman was going to buy his clothes, and generally look after him in the way that I did in the beginning. He is going back to square one. Back to square one – but kicking us in the mouth at the same time. *He* gets away with everything! He said to me recently – when we actually spoke to each other – he said, 'The only thing you're missing, the only thing you haven't got is me.' But unfortunately one never thinks of these things at the time. To me he was a husband, a father, a provider. Now what's he got? He's only got this woman. What has he left? He's left a very dutiful wife, two gorgeous children, a lovely home in Manchester and a country retreat. To me material and emotional happiness are the most important things.

Our life was pretty easy compared with many, many lives. I really just don't know *what* he wants. He walked to work from here – which in Manchester is a fantastic thing. We had a nice circle of friends, which, of course, when you break up must come to an end. As far as I know, this woman's not working, and so he's got to provide for her. With this woman I think it must be a hundred per cent sex, because he's forgotten what it was like with me. Because of the house, because of the children, we didn't have much time for it. He just couldn't see into the future. I mean, now, after three years, everything would have been absolutely marvellous. We could have got back to our old selves, but of course now, it's too late.

It's horrifying. Especially with young children. It's horrifying, because it is a time, when, by the very nature of things, life is most difficult and responsibilities are most time-consuming . . . when one doesn't have a lot of energy and when one can't be free to come and go. And it does require a bit of foresight, doesn't it? People say that thirty-five is young, but do men also think that thirty-five is young any more? In fact, he's still only thirty-four, and he's gone for a younger woman. Surely the whole point of getting married is to have children. But if it's just going to break up after having children, what is the point of getting married? Is it the way men are brought up or educated, or just their make-up? Mind you, I think women leave their husbands as well . . . perhaps this is what I should have done to have brought Peter to his senses . . . perhaps I should have just left him for a month or so.

When Peter left, both of the children were under two. They were too young to understand what was happening. Fortunately they were so young that they were not aware of the social structure. And we are in a house where we have men, so they are not deprived of male company. Alice is becoming more aware now but, in her mind, Daddy goes to work and takes them out on Wednesday afternoons and often to his apartment where this other woman is. So she knows he lives with this other woman. And he takes them swimming on Saturday. On Wednesday nights it takes me till about ten o'clock for them to go to bed and Thursdays are often impossible, because I think Alice, especially, is aware that her father has neglected me to live with this other woman. I'm not a believer in childhood. I think a human being is an adult from the moment they're born. A person.

She speaks to me about Ellen but I tell her I don't want to know. And I've told her that if it wasn't for Ellen she would have her Daddy. I don't think she realises the enormity of the situation. I intend, gradually, as she understands more, to make it clear to her . . . that if it wasn't for this person, she would have her Daddy still. At the moment she doesn't talk very much, and I don't talk about this. I would leave it to her to mention it. Daddy comes into the conversation and we talk about him in a third person sort of way, and obviously she speaks to them about me. When it comes up she says, Daddy said this, or Daddy does that. I just talk about it casually and let it go. I don't harp on it at all. And Kate of course, is too young to really know one way or the other, though she adores Peter in fact – it's incredible! She hardly sees him. Yet, whenever he comes, she gets all excited. Whether it's a reflection of Alice's excitement, I don't know.

I do know I think that it is all terribly unfair. And now I hear that Peter's woman is pregnant. He didn't even have the decency to wait until we were divorced. I don't think he can have any feelings at all.

Postscript

Usually it is the men who have very rigid notions about marriage and fixed ideas about men's and women's roles in it. But one of the striking characteristics of Jane's story is the extent to which she had such strong expectations of what sex, marriage and family life *ought* to be like (this perhaps because of her unsettled childhood). For example, there is her vision of the perfect wedding (though of course most popular literature puts great emphasis on *the* wedding and most women do too) and her belief that a woman can have extra-marital relationships before she has children, but not after. Indeed, Jane's ideas about extra-marital relationships and 'modern' marriage are probably not as commonly held as she would seem to think. And one feels that her husband was perhaps slightly bewildered by her expectations – her instructions, for example, to indulge in his own affairs for the good of their marriage.

Jane comes across as a formidable woman, and her husband rather intimidated. She was obviously the dominating force – making the major decisions in their marriage: the decision to have an abortion, then to marry, to buy the first house and then the second, to have the children – even to choose her husband's clothes. It would have taken an extremely strong personality to match her organising abilities.

But these strengths stood her in good stead as a single parent. She managed so well on her own with the children that even her husband commented that she lacked nothing but him, with the implication that he didn't matter. Jane thought they had everything a married couple could want: 'What has he left? He's left a very dutiful wife, two gorgeous children, a lovely home in Manchester and a country retreat. To me material and emotional happiness are the most important things.' At the time of the interview she could not understand why her husband had left, or what part she might have played in it. (There was, at the very least, the unsatisfying sexual relationship from the beginning.) She blamed her husband entirely and the other woman, to the extent that she told her children they would still have a daddy if it weren't for the other woman. She was still at the time of the interview quite consumed with anger and a sense of the unfairness of it all, confused because what she had valued had been rejected by her husband.

In the marriage and after it, Jane was determined to raise her children in a fashion she felt she herself had been deprived of. And she dedicated and devoted herself to her daughters. Her incredible strength of character and enormous energy unquestionably created a nurturing environment for her children who were thriving in an active and loving single parent family.

10.   Joe

Joe comes from a working-class background and works as a builder. He is self-employed and lives in his own house with his sons in East London. He married at twenty-one and separated twenty years later, when his wife left him for another man, leaving the boys, then under ten, with him. He and his wife made another attempt to live together two years later, but that failed. At the time of the interview, Joe was in his mid-forties, had been on his own for five years and his sons were eleven.

Joe was not divorced at the time of the interview, but said he would like to be: 'My wife won't grant me a divorce. We've been separated for two years, but she's going to hang on and screw me for whatever she can.' At the same time he still had ambivalent feelings about his wife because on another occasion he said, 'Even now, I'd go back tomorrow', and thought sometimes they could get back together 'when she's fifty-eight or sixty and calmed down a bit and can sit back and talk about it.' But he also feels he's started afresh. His wife lives in the family house and he pays the mortgage and rates. He now has a second house for himself and his sons. He thinks he might marry again if he found the right person when the boys were older. 'I know what I want, but to find it is another thing.'

I was twenty-one, met a girl, she was nineteen, knew her three months, got married. More or less my first girlfriend. It was my first sexual relationship. Got married, lived with the mother-in-law for about six months, got fed up with that because she was so petty about having the light on too long, even though we were paying the bill. Then we got a caravan, lived for six years in Ilford in the caravan. All electric and running water and everything except for an outside toilet. That was the most inconvenient thing but that didn't matter really. She wouldn't have any kids there . . . said it was too small, but all the other people . . . they all had kids, you know?

I suppose I was in love at the time. It's very hard to differentiate at that age what love is and what sex is. You think when you have sex you've got to be in love, but it's not really that way at all. We fancied each other anyway. That was basic. Love grew through the years. Even now . . . I'd go back tomorrow. I'd go back tomorrow and start all over again. I'd always planned to get married. I thought it was the right thing to do . . . that's the way I was brought up . . . you get married and when you get married you stay married through thick and thin. The moral things mattered then, not like today. You never had anything . . . you only had each other. You had your dinners and your breakfasts but you didn't have any luxury things. And that's a good thing. People had more time for each other then . . . plenty of games, walks and things, whereas now, they plunk themselves in front of the TV or play a record. There's no communication between people.

I'd always intended to have children too. If I'd had my choice I'd have had as many as would fill a bus. It gives you something to aim for. We both worked all the time, when we got married, and it was eleven years before anything came, though not from a lack of trying. I tried anyway. She didn't want children, she said. She was on the Pill anyway and she wanted to be on the Pill. I wanted her to go off it at one time. It was a rum thing really. She went to the doctor's and said she didn't want to have any children and never did want to have any children. I couldn't understand why she didn't want any children, because it didn't seem natural. He sent her to a psychiatrist and he said, 'Well, it's just there and there's nothing I can do about it.'

There was always a basic disagreement about having children. In the end I just didn't bother to talk about it. After all those years you just thought, 'Well, there's not much point.' I tried all kinds of approaches . . . good approach, angry approach, nice approach and then the horrible approach, and it just didn't work.

The sex was really good in the beginning. When we got married . . . didn't do anything else. Good for a while. Good for three or four years actually. We just had a normal, good relationship like people have . . . yuh know. Then it started falling off. Because of this thing about children. She wanted to go on the Pill and I didn't want her to go on the Pill. And so she went on the Pill and that was that. And there wasn't much one could do about it. And that's when the sex started going off.

I don't think it's right for someone to make their minds up about something like that. Something seemed to be false . . . making love if you're not going to have children. Naturally you don't want a woman to be pregnant all the time . . . I'm not that type of fellow. It would have to be a joint thing. Although I wanted kids very badly, there was no point in me saying, 'All right, I'm going to make a mistake tonight' or anything like that. It would have to be a joint thing. In the end it was, but only under duress. In the end she said, 'You might as well go, you're not going to get anything here.'

We hardly had any sex life for six or seven years. And in the end I went to the doctor and then to the psychiatrist and he said I might as well pack it in. *He* suggested that. He said, 'You've had a very good eleven years . . . or eight or nine . . . now you've got to do one of two things . . . either one gives in to the other one, or pack it in.'

But I didn't pack it in. We talked about it and then after about a year I said, 'Well, that's that. I might as well go home.' And then she said, 'Okay, I'll have children.' But even on that basis it wasn't quite right. It sounded . . . anyway, it happened. We had twins. And then it sailed on. It sailed on for the last six or seven years. She was quite pleased really – having twins. She really was. And when she had them she was a different woman . . . she really was. She was happy.

There was a lot of caring for them, a lot of looking after them. We shared that. I used to get up in the middle of the night, change nappies and feed them . . . anything to make it easier for her. And I used to have four jobs as well – Littlewoods football round, worked in a pub outside Victoria Station, plus my full-time job and I worked in a club on weekends. But I got the money to give them the things they needed. I was over the moon.

Childminding services are still woefully inadequate . . . if anything school age children are more difficult than infants. Some schools remain open after school hours and during the holidays – but comparatively few . . . Professional babysitters are expensive, especially if you live in London . . . Rosemary Simon

---

Then when they got to be five or six, things changed again. Sex was good for a couple of years after the kids came, but when they were two, that was cut dead, and I thought, 'Well, there's no sense in resuming it' and I never said anything. So it never went on any more – sex. That was that. Then, all of a sudden, the kids started to get on her nerves. They always talked back to her. All kids do this . . . all kids get naughty and you've got to correct them, because if you spare the rod you spoil the child. But it wasn't like that. It wasn't a slap, cry, get on with it . . . it was like a nag . . . like a thing that went on forever. If a kid did something, say taking sugar out of the cupboard and spilling it all over the floor, instead of getting one good hiding and a ticking off, it used to go on for days. Like saying, 'Don't you ever do that again with the sugar', and it went on and on and on for days until they did something worse than the sugar and then it was something else. That's how it went on. Then when they were seven or eight, the problems with the children just got worse and worse. She really went after the children. And there was more violence in the marriage. Everyone knows this is bad for children. It was not the sort of environment I wanted for them.

That sort of thing wasn't on. So there were a lot of rows. You see, what I used to say was . . . if you have an argument – which everybody does – you don't do it in front of the kids. I mean . . . in the end things got so awful . . . and it was often in front of the kids, so I would pluck up my courage and used to say, 'Don't do it, there's not much point in it.' And I just didn't used to bother. I used to tell my father-in-law and my mother-in-law about it and they used to say, 'Stand up for yourself.' And I used to say, 'Well no, don't worry about it.'

In the end I did hit her one night but it just wasn't any good. It didn't make me feel better. It's stupid, isn't it. There's no point in it, is there? It was clear in the beginning that there wasn't going to be any point in it. I knew in the beginning there wasn't going to be any point in it. And it just got to a pitch where I suppose I lost my cool so many times – never as a result of hitting or throwing things, just sort of getting out and around the block with the dog sort of thing. Then I'd come back and give my point of view. But it was all pointless, just pointless. Then there was all this aggression, especially in front of the kids . . . well that was it.

I mean you sacrifice your life, you'd do anything for your kids, if it had to be you or them . . . it would be you. In my case anyway . . . that's the way I think anyway. So that was it when the kids started to suffer. But the rows were always over the kids – 'David done this, Sam has done something else' – well, what does she expect kids to do? They'd have all their things –

toys and stuff – out on the floor in the living room. And they'd have to clear it all up in the morning: it had to be clear in the afternoon and in the evening. If anyone came to visit they'd never know there were any kids in the house. I mean tidiness is okay, sure. But the kids would say, 'Can we leave this out tonight Dad, because we want it in the morning and we don't want to get it out of the cupboard' and I'd say, 'Well . . . leave it out then . . . don't tidy it up, leave it for the morning.' But that wasn't allowed. They had to take it upstairs. Now, I suppose that's a good thing . . . tidiness . . . but a bit extreme. It's like a newspaper. You put a newspaper on the table and you want to know where it is in the morning, don't you?

She stopped work when she had the kids. And she hasn't worked since. It never came up. There was enough money coming in and she never really thought about going to work . . . bought a little car and all kinds of things like that . . . the word 'work' never came up.

Then suddenly she just changed . . . one week she was okay, the next not. Even the psychiatrists turned around and said, 'Well, there's not much we can do. We're putting her on Valium, this, that and the other.' Which they did, and said there was nothing wrong with her . . . just neurotic. Other than that . . . nothing.

But you never knew where you were with her. Say you had a night out with the lads or stopped off at the pub on the way home from work, you could say to yourself, 'If you're ten or fifteen minutes or half-an-hour late . . . ' or no matter how late you were . . . if you knew you were going to be late and you were getting involved and picked up the phone and said, 'Love, I won't be long, make so-and-so and I'll be home at such-and-such a time . . .' I couldn't say that. Because I'd get it right in the neck on the phone. Therefore, you knew what you were going to get when you got home . . . so what was the point of having it twice. You couldn't say anything . . . you couldn't say anything. If you weren't there on time, you was in trouble. But you could go to work Sunday mornings and Saturday afternoons and you could say to yourself, 'Right, I'm going to go out and buy myself a bottle of Scotch, and a bunch of flowers for her and go home to her saying we'll have a nice evening in.' But I couldn't do it. Because she didn't like drink. As the years went by. In the beginning, she used to drink more than I did. In the beginning she liked drinking . . . yeah. We used to go out once a week . . . then once a month at one time. Then she never wanted to go out . . . never wanted to go to parties, never wanted to go to the pictures or the theatre. Never wanted to go anywhere. I don't know . . . you just never knew what was going on.

She was a terrific woman for looking after the house though . . . not half fantastic. But you'd be so unsettled, you'd be waiting for the next thing. You'd think, 'Oh, this is lovely, this is smashing, why doesn't it stay like this all the time?' But you knew that it couldn't . . . it wouldn't go longer than two days at the most. Something happened, somebody did something, I did something or the kids did something. There wasn't anything reasonable that upset her. It could be just anything. She'd be upset by my just being there or talking in the wrong tone of voice, or having a day off, or going off on the motorbike . . . 'You going for a ride on the motorbike?' I'd say. And she said she couldn't because of the kids, but she could have got the baby-sitter in from next door . . . there were a couple of girls from there that could have done it. Or even when we didn't have the kids I'd say I was going for a little run, 'Are you coming?' And that would be the wrong thing to say. It could be anything, anything. She's a lot better now, although I haven't seen her for a couple of years.

Eventually the atmosphere became absolutely intolerable. You just didn't know what was going to happen. If you left a cup on the sideboard and went out of the room for a minute, she'd say, 'Why'd you leave that cup there?' It should have been taken out to the kitchen straight away. Like if you have a cup of coffee while you're watching telly and you're using the arm of the chair, then when you've finished it and you're still watching the telly and you go to put it on the floor . . . you're not to do that. It's not supposed to stay there . . . it's supposed to go to the kitchen.

Finally we just had one big row and she left. And went down to her mum's. Then I found afterwards that she had a fella. And that was that. She'd been having an affair and I didn't know about it until after. I really didn't get upset because . . . the point is . . . what can you do about it? Can't do anything about it. No point in running away from it. Of course I was jealous but . . . still am. Modern society treats these things casually. But . . . sure I'm jealous. But I'm not going to rant and rave . . . I didn't have much of a chance anyway because she wasn't there. She'd already gone and I'd found out through her mum and dad about the other fella. She went down there and then she went off with her fella. So, I thought after all that, it was a good excuse to get out.

But I also found out other things that upset me terribly – like she had an abortion. This was after being married for so long – finding this out. *That* really done me as well. I was more upset about that than the fella previous to the marriage. I knew she wasn't a virgin. I didn't know what type of things went on, had gone on. After all those years, finding out she'd had an abortion affected me more than the fact that she wasn't a virgin. It was the deceit . . . the fact that I'd gone so long without knowing about it. We'd talk about things. I'd tell her things I used to do with women. And I found out afterwards that there had been umpteen boyfriends before I knew her, and I'd just never known about all that. You don't sit down and say how many boyfriends have you had . . . you don't think they're going to go out and get it at the age of sixteen. And I heard about all the trouble she had with her family – arguing with them and running away at the age of fourteen. Well . . . you just don't think of those things do you?

But after she left, her mum and dad sat down and told me about it. They weren't on *her* side . . . although sides shouldn't really matter, should they? If you have your own personal nature . . . you can't change that nature. Psychiatrists would say, 'You've got to change for that woman.' But you can't. It's like somebody says to you 'Talk to me while we're making love' . . . some people like to talk while they're making love. But, if you're not the kind of person that can do that, you can't and if you are to keep your mouth shut, you can't. You can try . . . of course, you can try . . . and maybe it can work. But in the end, inside of you, you say 'Ah hell, I'm just going to be myself.' That's what I think, for whatever it's worth. You can't change your personality. I don't think you can.

I felt a bit upset when I found out all these things – I *was* a bit upset over it – *very* upset over it, I suppose. Not knowing. If I had known maybe I could have understood a bit more. It could have made a difference. All these things were locked in the cupboard for all those years. But any sensible human being would have thought, 'Well, it could have been because of that' – all these problems – instead of facing a big blank wall and thinking, 'Why?' Because there *was* a reason why . . . and all the time it was like standing right in front of a pane of glass and you couldn't see it because you didn't know about it. We'd still be together now . . . we'd have been all right if I'd known. Lives can be changed by what people say to each other – especially when you live together, are married or whatever the case may be. I think it would have helped a lot if I'd known. I think people should say what they feel. And what's happened . . . it's a terrible loss.

Not all one-parent families suffer from a housing problem, nor are the problems of those who do common to all. There is, however, an un- mistakable and pronounced incidence of hardship and disadvantage in housing to be found in the group as a whole. Its members are more than normally likely to be sharing accommodation with others. They are much less likely to be owner-occupiers, and much more likely to be living in privately rented accommodation, especially in the furnished sector, and particularly in areas of housing stress, where lone parents and their children live in low-grade accommodation at high rents – 'The Finer Report, 1974'

Anyway, it turned out that after she left, she wanted to come back. And she came back after a year. I let her come back . . . I wanted her back . . . as simple as that. In spite of everything, I wanted her back. The kids needed a mother and needed some sort of stable relationship with their mum whatever type of person she was. So she came back for six months.

The sex life was okay. I put the other fella out of my mind – although it was still there. It was *very* difficult. But if you don't overcome it – jealousy – you don't get anywhere and if you overcome it, as time goes by, it gets better. Because you say to yourself, 'Well she is with me . . . not with him.' And if you grab hold of something in which you can believe . . . it helps. Anyway, a woman may have two or three affairs, but if she chooses one man to be with all the time, that man's got to be lucky. It leaves room for jealousy and you could get riled up . . . but if he doesn't allow himself to get riled up too much, it'll be okay. I mean, you can say to yourself, 'After all, she's living with me, she comes to bed with me every night and she's *my* woman', and that's it. In that way, you do overcome it. If you don't, you could be forever rowing over it. You can sit in a room or drive down a road on your own and you can start thinking, 'I wonder what they did that night, I wonder if she did one of her little kinky things, I wonder if she was doing things she used to do to me?' and two hours later, you've got yourself into such a state you can't even do your job. You get so mad you could go through the door spoiling for a fight. It ain't worth it.

So I just put it out of my mind. As much as I could. It's still there . . . don't get me wrong, it's there . . . but you've got to put it out of your mind. You can't put it completely out of your mind . . . it's there . . . but you can't let it run like quicksand, because . . . if you let it slip . . . it builds up and builds up . . . I've done it, I've done it going down the road in a van or sitting in a cafe . . . and it's ticking in your mind all the time . . . and you're wondering to yourself all the time, but if you let it run . . . you're crucified. It did me . . . I must admit and in the end I started drinking.

I used to drink before she left. Not a lot. No more than the average fellow . . . maybe three or four gins a night . . . a drop of sherry. But then I drank more when she left. I had the kids and I used to do all the things, do the jobs, earn my money, pay the rent, have a game with the kids, take 'em out to the circus . . . whatever the case may be, then I used to sit up until two o'clock in the morning and have a drink. Though I didn't let it affect me in a way in which I couldn't go to work . . . I *got* to go to work because if I let myself down, not only do I let myself down, I let my kids down and I would in no way do that. If I woke up in the morning with a headache – and there were several times when I had too much – I've done the work . . . I've gone and done it. It's been bloody hell, but that's my fault.

The kids and I managed after she left. During the holidays, I'd put them in the van with a load of comics and sweets and wherever we stopped, there used to be somebody who'd say, 'Come in.' I always meet them from school . . . take 'em to school, meet 'em from school. In the beginning they didn't want to have school dinners, so I used to meet them and take them home, but it split up the day so badly that I couldn't get started on any work. So, in the end, I got them to take school dinners. Not that I 'got them' to take school dinners . . . we talked about it frankly at the time and there was no giving in, so I said 'Right, you're going to start school dinners.' And now they've just started to walk to school. They're ten now. Even now, I'd take them to school. But you can't go on wrapping them up in cotton wool. I take them to school when it's raining. I pick them up now and then, although I shouldn't do. I must admit that's my fault. They come out of school and I'm near there and I like to see them home . . . I like to see them at the end of the day anyway. So I do work my way down to where I live and pick them up at four o'clock. They get themselves dressed, go downstairs and get their own breakfast . . . they cook whatever they want . . . fried eggs or bacon, have a cup of tea and off they go. I think it's quite good really. It teaches them to be independent.

I think they suffered a bit after their mother left the first time. But I told them what was happening. You see, they saw so many things going on . . . the fighting and so on. They'd say 'Why has mum gone?' and I'd say, 'Oh, she's just fed up.' And that was that. I think if there hadn't been the two of them, it would have been difficult. But there being the two of them . . . they helped each other out.

Anyway, she came back for six months, and then it all started again. We started to row. About the kids . . . and also she found out I was having an affair with someone – because I told her. Maybe I shouldn't have, but I did. I'd been faithful to her all the time we were married, up to when she left. And then I had an affair. Some of my mates said, 'There's not much point in her asking you questions and you asking questions . . . the best thing to do is to leave it alone and finish with it.' I mean what's been done had been done and there's no point in getting all worked up about it. But it didn't stop. 'Was she good in bed,' she'd ask, 'was she better than me, did she have bigger tits than me?' and all that sort of thing. That's how my wife used to talk. And in the end, it got so bad that I used to go home so pissed I was just numb. And that was that. So in the end we just left. Me and the boys.

I went to the school and told the headmistress all about it and their teacher.

I couldn't stand it any more. I couldn't get rid of her. How can you throw anyone out of their own home? I wouldn't throw anyone out of their own home. She'd been there all those years and she was entitled to half of whatever there was and she was still entitled to have her own home although she did go in the first place. But, in my own mind I forgave and that was that. I went to the school and told the headmistress all about it, and their teacher. I also went to the police as well, and the welfare people and told them. The social workers . . . quite honestly . . . didn't know what to do. I shouldn't say that. Some are very good, but with some of them it was like having an unmarried woman telling a married woman what it was like . . . the pain . . . of having a child. I wanted all these people to know what was happening, so the school would know about the kids if anything happened to them . . . if anybody came to collect them that shouldn't do. I went to a solicitor and applied for a custody order. And I had to keep out of the way then, for so many days because, until I got that custody order, it was touch and go.

We got a flat for a while and in the end I got a house. I thought, 'Well, I can't live like this all the time. It'll drive them around the twist.' It was driving me around the twist worrying about them, because the flat had no garden, no place for their school friends to come. So I thought, 'I got to get another house.' I stuck my neck out and I got myself in trouble with the tax man . . . but not a lot . . . a couple of thousand pounds. If they catch me with a couple of thousand pounds, I thought, at least it's going to good use . . . it's not going on evasion or whatever people do.

I got the custody, the other house, started to fix it up . . . there were lots wrong with it. I didn't have any money or anything. But then everything was all right. All their mates came around to see the kids. My wife stayed in the other house and I paid the mortgage. It was only £5 a week by then. But then there were the rates. She says, 'I can't get rid of the rates.' So there were two sets of rates and that crucified me. I've got to take jobs on now to pay for her damned rates. I've been to court three times over her damned rates. And now she won't grant me a divorce. We've been separated for two years, but she's going to hang on and screw me for whatever she can. She's probably thinking to herself . . . or could be thinking to herself, 'Give him a little bit of time and he could hang himself, or run out of money . . . I'll screw him to the ground as much as I can and at least I'll have my husband and kids back.' But it won't ever happen again.

From 1955 to 1971 it progressively became less worthwhile for a lone woman with children to take up full time employment and cease to claim supplementary benefit unless she could earn well above the average wage for women in full-time work – 'The Finer Report, 1974'

Well, it could happen when the kids are grown up. When I say *could* . . . that's when she's fifty-eight, or sixty and calmed down a bit and can sit back and talk about it. Maybe we could have each other in older age for company, something like that. But I've basically started afresh. And I'd like to be divorced. When you've made your mind up about something . . . you've made your mind up. You give so many chances . . . and you weigh it up and when the scales overbalance the other way . . . that's it. There's no sense in going back because if you go back into the same things you've already gone through, you're only going back over the same footsteps. You're going to go through the same emotions again and this time probably a lot worse. So . . . it's best to leave it alone. And that's what I'm trying to do.

Unfortunately, every month or so the kids might have a hole in their sock, or at school they're all playing around and get a tear in their shirt, and I get a little letter from her saying, 'What are you doing now?' – trying to build up a case for custody. Therefore, it's not really ending, is it? It's just going on and on and on. Every time she sends a letter I've got to send a letter back. My solicitor says, 'You'd better answer that one.' And I say, 'No . . . no more . . . I'm finished with it.' And he says, 'You've got to . . . they'll get you.' She's definitely trying to build up a case for custody. But I say, 'Well, let them get me then.' I'm not going to pay her any more money. Anyway I answered them. Now they're sending the letters to the house. And I just write back whatever I think . . . I can't write or spell very good . . . but it's my explanation and that's it. It could go on forever . . .

I don't think I would marry again, but if I did this is what I'd like to think . . . I'd like to meet a girl . . . a young girl, not because she's young, but because she'd just want a home life and kids . . . not dashing down to the pub every night and going to parties every week. That ain't on. You've got to have stability because if you don't . . . you ain't got nothing. You want to come home and smell the dinner cooking, or come home and have your meals there – and all the back chat and small chat and what have you. No . . . I don't want to get married again. You never know . . . I might do. You never know . . . I might go right the other way when the boys get a bit older . . . I might play around. But I don't think so . . . my nature isn't inclined that way. I know what I want . . . but to find it is another thing. I have thought, to be quite honest, that when this thing is finally over, that a churchwoman . . . a woman who believes in the church . . . would most likely be the sort of woman who suits me. Or I might move somewhere and marry a country lass. But I suppose even a country lass these days, wants to move to the big city. Sex isn't the most important part of a relationship between two people . . . there's got to be more than that . . . I'm not saying sex isn't important . . . you've got to have it to get to know the other person. I know I'm going to contradict myself, but it's very important. You've got to have contact . . . you can do it with your bodies . . . you can do it with your eyes . . . you can do it by touch . . . but you must have contact. If you don't . . . you can't relate . . . you don't have a relationship.

Postscript

Joe was another person with strong views of what marriage and family life *ought* to be like. He'd always planned to get married – 'That's the way I was brought up, you get married and when you get married, you stay married.' His preconceived ideas clearly created a sense of frustration throughout his marriage – particularly his determination to have children ('a busload if possible') and his wife's wish not to have them at all. The frustrations were obvious for him, and implicit for his wife who comes across in the interview as a most unhappy woman.

Their marriage would seem to have been a recipe for disaster from the beginning – with the different views about children, the tensions (and particularly his wife's problems) after the children, and in their sexual problems (for which they sought professional help). By the end of the story it seems surprising the marriage lasted as long as it did, they seemed so fundamentally unsuited to each other.

Joe is impressive, like the other men, in his capabilities at coping as a single parent father, continuing to work and to raise his children single-handed though by the end of it he was remarkably unable to analyse many faults of his own. There's a tendency to see himself as a whited sepulchre – 'I don't know why she wanted to leave. I had three jobs, worked hard for the family – why did she do this to me?' And at the time of the interview he still seemed confused about his feelings towards his wife. In one breath he says he would have her back, in another that he only wants a divorce. But he was honest enough to acknowledge the contradictions and to try to think them through.

11. Judith

Judith comes from an Irish 'immigrant' family: her father had what she describes as a working-class occupation, but both her parents came from a middle-class background. She married at eighteen and separated at thirty-five with three children, two teenagers and a five year old. She works as a social worker in Bradford.

She chose to leave the marriage and did so two years ago, for 'feminist' as well as 'personal' reasons', it was a choice between her 'self and her marriage and she chose her self". She took all three children with her at the time. Subsequently, however, the youngest child, has returned to live with the father. 'I have very good relationships with my children (much better than ever before), even the eight-year-old who is happy to relate to me in an unconventional relationship. We see each other frequently and are happy living apart.'

Judith says she is in a serious relationship: 'We live separately, me alone and he with his wife and children, because he cannot easily detach himself from the responsibility of being a father and provider and his wife supports fully the idea of being a dependent. I'm in no hurry to push him into something for me, as it were. He has to work out his own problems himself, just as I had to.'

Judith's separation was the consequence of an increasing self and political consciousness and a growing self confidence. And she regards her new status as a single person and a single parent as a continuation of a process of self liberation. Her approach to life is positive and analytical as can be seen by her account of her situation now: 'I see myself as someone who loves life and wants to love every single minute of my life. I also want to live to be quite old and to always live a busy and active life. I intend to stay healthy and fit and am taking positive steps to ensure this. I feel very strongly that my attitude to my physical state is the vital-key.'

'I am consciously working on myself and am about to organise for myself sessions of co-counselling so that I can develop my strength as a woman and a person. I feel that many more people can see my beautiful side now (whether physically or spiritually) because I recognise it and therefore acknowledge that I am a beautiful person. A great way off the former unworthy, ugly, unloved self that I used to be.

'I am enjoying lots of new practical hobbies—although I still spend a lot of my time doing things for my kids and work. I love my work. I can develop almost any new skill with my work in mind. I write a lot, mostly about how I feel and what is happening to me when I experience pain and anger and hurt. I also write when I feel I've broken through something new.

'When I do get low and feel depressed, I know it is only the working out of former hurts and patterns laid down since my childhood. I cry when I need to and seek support where and when I need to. Occasionally I find myself alone when I need to have support and that can be difficult. My life just gets better and better each day. And other people pick up on the good feelings. It's really good to see other people deciding that it's time to make their lives work, too and I see that happening with people who relate to me. They realise they can do it, too.'

I was eighteen when I got married. The thing about marriage, coming from an Irish Catholic family, was that sexual activity wasn't permitted until you were married. So in a way I got married in order to have sexual activity. I was having a lot of hassles with it, partly because I hadn't worked out what I felt about contraception. I also wanted security, a lover's security, because I felt very isolated in a way. I had cut myself off from my family. I was working in a reference library. It wasn't a career: I hadn't worked out what I wanted as a career. I'd just left school.

I'd had a couple of boyfriends. I seemed to be attracted to Latin types. My first boyfriend was an Italian, and he was into screwing women. He was the first person I'd had a sexual experience with. I really wanted someone to love me, and I thought that was the only way to get love – for men to screw me. But it didn't work that way. It was a pretty nasty relationship because I was exploited. I had to get myself out of that in the end. I was very depressed by that for a while, I did a lot of crying. And the only support I was getting from my mother was 'I told you so' – which doesn't help much. That's when Phil came on the scene, when I was just getting on my feet, having had all the stuffing taken out of me, after that relationship. And I didn't have very much self-esteem. Phil was in a similar sort of situation really. He had come to England as an immigrant and he was very lonely. So when I met him we were both in a very vulnerable phase, really.

At the time it seemed terribly romantic. But now that I look back on it all, it wasn't really, it was a game being played. And right from the beginning he was very volatile and temperamental and difficult and that gave him a lot of power. I couldn't cope with people who had emotional outbursts; my reaction was to submit, so that gave him a lot of power from the start. Sexually it was very romantic. It was the first time in my sexual life that things were beginning to work. I was just beginning to understand how I felt sexually. But he didn't want to use any contraception. He had a Catholic background. He left all the responsibility with me. I did get pregnant once and I had an abortion. It was a back street thing with all the stigmas attached. It was frightening too, because I didn't know whether it was safe or not. I knew it would have been easier to have the baby, but I didn't want to. I wanted an abortion even though it was against everything around me: it was against my parents, it was against Phil, it was against my upbringing. It was also against my feelings, in a way, but I just didn't want a child at the time. So it was a pretty independent act. The guilt trips that were laid on me were terrible. And that's actually how I got into getting married. Also because my parents moved at that time. I was uprooted and hated it. So I went to live with Phil. But that was a stigma in my world and the only way out of this was to get married and make it a legitimate living together. That is what we did in the end. And that's how we came to get married. Not long after we got married . . . I can't work out why . . . I felt okay about having a child and I became pregnant.

I terribly wanted to be happy. I thought you got married, you had children and everything would work out. You'd be happy. And it did work out . . . partly. I was very happy being married, I was happy being a mother when I had Louise. I was very happy being pregnant. It was a good pregnancy.

I carried on working when we got married. I didn't really need to go to work. I just decided I wanted to do it. But Phil made a drastic change in his work style, which was very difficult for us, because he had to start at the bottom. And there was prejudice against foreign workers even at that time. He was earning a very low wage and it was difficult to live, with a little baby. So I got a cleaning job when Louise was about three months old. But when Louise was about eight months old, we found we didn't have enough money. We were very poor. And I thought, I'm going to have to work. So I had to get back into work to get more money. I didn't realise at the time that there were other things going on inside my head – like it was me that was deciding on my own that things should be better, me making the move and telling Phil what I was doing, rather than working things out together.

So I got myself a job in the fish market, which was horrible. I hated it but at that stage I wanted to have a job I could leave at any time if I didn't like the child-minding arrangement I'd worked out. It was a trial. It was very hard leaving Louise, because she was a very lovely baby and I was very fond of her. It was a big struggle to leave her, but eventually I found someone who was good and loving and caring and I was able to cope with the idea of going out to work and leaving Louise for the day. It was a long day – twelve hours. Then I became pregnant again about two years later. I had intended to have two children and at the time I wasn't trying not to. It wasn't a planned pregnancy but it was one I had accepted as a possibility. So I left the job.

The financial circumstances of one-parent families showed that they were, in general, much worse off than two-parent families. Two groups among them are slightly better off than the others, though still worse off than two-parent families generally: widows, who already have a State insurance benefit, and lone fathers, who can command higher earnings than lone mothers. For the rest, over half are on supplementary benefit; for most of these it is their main source of income, and some live at this level for many years. Of those not on supplementary benefit, about 15 per cent appear to be living actually below the supplementary benefit level, managing on maintenance payments and part-time earnings. Those who work full-time are better off financially than the others, but because of women's low earnings and the restrictions that having to run a home and a job are likely to put on their earning capacity, they are still much less well off than two parent families, and far below the level of those where both parents are earning. The main factors in determining whether or not a mother can work full-time, and hence achieve the higher level of income which goes with it, are the number of children, the age of the youngest child and whether or not she shares her home: mothers with several children, at least one of them under five, and living on their own, are least likely to be able to go to work – 'The Finer Report 1974'

I was hoping Phil's work prospects would get better. We were still very poor, living in pretty awful accommodation. I wasn't materialistic but I wanted to have a home I could call my own. I wanted to feel secure. Phil was learning to cope with work, and learning how to do things about the house – building cupboards and new furniture – and he began to make our place quite homely. He made the baby a cot. So, although we were poor, we were beginning to get things together. But the flat was damp and in my pregnant state I said, 'I can't live here any more, I'm just not going to live here, that's all.' I moved to my mother's house with Phil and Louise. While work was being done in the flat.

The atmosphere at home was not good. But I got myself into such a state at that time – I was panicky – I just would not live in that flat. And I remember I took control of the situation in my own way – I just refused to do things. And when I came out of hospital having had Sara, I still wouldn't go back to the flat even though the work was done. So we stayed in this one room in my mother's house and said we'd save whatever money we had and buy a house. The months went on and we lived with my mother. I was depressed, I didn't want to do anything. I lost a lot of weight. A lot of it was obviously in my head: I hadn't worked out what was going wrong. We saved some money, but the first bit of money was spent on a trip to Greece. Phil wanted to go, and I quite wanted to go too.

It did us a lot of good in a way. It got us away from the pressures of living with my mother. And when we returned I began to work again to get us out of being dependant on other people for living accommodation. By this time I had two children to be minded and I didn't have a very good child-minding arrangement to begin with. It was very difficult and I was quite unhappy. And I felt the children were emotionally unstable. It was hard on Phil too, no doubt about that. But he didn't support me in the idea of working. He just said, 'It's your decision you have to work it out.' So I had to take full responsibility for whatever arrangements I made.

Phil was the breadwinner, but not very successful financially. I don't think he ever earned much, never more than I did when I was working. But his contribution was making things. He was very good at making things. But he was basically the breadwinner, and I was the housewife and mother even though I was also working.

About a year and a half after I started work, we raised a mortgage and a loan and got ourselves a nice little house. The children had their space, we had a little garden, and things were coming together pretty well. I enjoyed my work. I think it developed into an escape, the work, though I didn't acknowledge that at the time.

These were happy times, except that there were too many hours away from the children. And Phil was difficult to deal with, I'm afraid because he didn't like to acknowledge that I was playing an equal part in the breadwinning. That was always a problem. My justification was that we needed the money. And I could earn as much money as a secretary as he could in the office work that he was doing. I was able to buy things for the family and I got into a materialistic thing – buying them good things. I didn't want any tinny little rubbish, I wanted something good. That mattered to me. My work gave me a certain freedom to make decisions over what was going to be bought. I had some power there, which I was glad to have. That mattered quite a bit to me.

It was then that I decided to change my work and life style. I decided to study to be a social worker. And once I decided to do things, I generally got on and did them. And I got it all organised. It was a fairly aggressive decision to make, given the fact that we'd just achieved a certain amount of harmony and stability. In the long term it was going to put me outside Phil's earning capacity and make me more independent. But at the time the primary motivation was to have more time with my children.

It was a considerable struggle because it meant giving up earning quite a big salary and living on a grant. It meant that Phil was going to have to support the decision, because the money wasn't going to come, and he was going to have to wait three years before I could earn money again. It was quite an investment. He accepted the idea and I went ahead and got accepted at college. While I was at college Phil took a part-time job after work in order to earn a few more pennies. Which worked for a little while, but not for very long. At least he began to work a little harder to get more, whereas I had always been the one to earn more money whenever we were short. And it took him out in the evenings, when he wasn't the type of person who went out at all. Which gave me the space to study. But it didn't last very long, and when I was at home studying, he was very resentful that I wasn't giving my time to *him*. After the children had gone to bed, he wanted my undivided attention. My studying caused him big tantrums; he used to throw books around and tore up my work and threw it around. That was difficult but I had set my mind on doing it and I was going to do it. I enjoyed going to college such a lot and, of course, he resented that. I was really beginning to find myself and I was expecting him to take care of his own needs. But he had the expectation that I would take care of his needs. Looking back, I see it all as being related to the pursuit of my independence.

When I qualified, I almost immediately got a very good job, which really knocked me out. I saw an advertisement for working in a social work unit which interested me. I didn't think I'd get it because it was a really high hat interview. It was a new unit and they were being selective. Working there the first year was really good, because I was working with people who were really thinking and stimulating. It was very child-centred, putting the good ideas I'd read at college into practice. I found it very difficult, but very challenging . . . so letting myself get pregnant again was a bit of a cop-out. But I accepted two things in getting pregnant: that I was going to have a child, that I wasn't going to have an abortion; and that I could take some time off work and then go back. When the time came, I left the unit with all good wishes from the staff who said they wanted me back as soon as possible. I thought that's what would happen.

It is abundantly clear from our evidence, from the findings of research and the conclusions of other committees in recent years that one-parent families are at special risk in becoming homeless – 'The Finer Report, 1974'

In the meantime we got a bigger house, a better house, but a house that needed an awful lot of work done to it. It was going to take years to do. I can now see very clearly that this was my way to keep Phil busy while I was doing what I wanted to do – which was to enjoy working and to enjoy my children. I can see all this clearly now. I can see that what I was up to were machinations to get all this going. I'm the one who arranged to get that house; I worked very hard to get that house.

In this bigger house, in order to earn some money while I wasn't working, we took in some students. I got a Japanese girl to look after Hannah – who was about six months old – and I went back to work. It was a nearly perfect arrangement. It gave me the freedom and the space to go back to work without feeling guilty that Hannah wasn't being cared for properly. In the early years I'd never been quite happy about this thing, but this was good. It wasn't so good from Phil's side and he became very jealous of the fact that I also had a companion in the house. He felt cut off. I didn't see it from his side at all, that he was being cut out more and more. I was not giving Phil very much time and not thinking anything of it.

Then he created problems for the Japanese girl which I found incredibly hurtful. I presumed it was his way of getting at me and letting me know that he wasn't very happy with it. What happened was we went on a holiday and she wasn't going to come. And he cut off the electricity so she didn't have any hot water or any heat. I thought it was a completely unreasonable thing to do and I let him know that I was very displeased about it. I didn't see anything I'd been doing as unreasonable. And he succeeded in ousting her. It left a lot of bad feelings. He went about it so unpleasantly that I just couldn't forgive him. This was the thing about Phil; he didn't work on principle. He always expected me to support him just because he was my husband. We always had disagreements about that, right from the early days, even before we were married.

I was enjoying work and getting a lot of satisfaction out of it – I discovered I was very good with children. I was getting stronger and stronger as a person. Getting good at my job, getting confident about working. It was growing gradually, but it was such a new thing to me to feel confident and to do things confidently, and to feel that I could do things well. And I began to get into other things, things to do with politics. I got involved with a number of anti-racist campaigns. And through these, I was meeting up with other people who were also politically motivated. This was the first critical activity I'd ever engaged in.

We were getting further and further apart and he resented more and more my friendships. He was often very awkward with people. He was trying to let me know that he didn't approve of what I was doing, and he used to cause me a lot of embarrassment. That was his way of protecting his interests. He would embarrass me socially, just by being petulant and rude. And it did embarrass me, it hurt me. And he regained whatever control he felt he had. I didn't like rows, so he could get back the balance of power, by being awkward and difficult. I would capitulate to those kinds of situations. He knew that being difficult was a good way of getting at me. That was his way.

What actually eventually made me move out was my involvement with one of the parents from the unit. He and I attended a lot of meetings together, spent a lot of time discussing political, and racial matters and we were both very much into kids. We used to spend time with each other's families too, but it was only he and I who took an active part in it. It became apparent to us both that our friendship was quite a deep one. It freaked us both out a bit when we realised, because we hadn't really thought of ourselves as being emotionally attached to each other. But although we felt very strongly about each other we both had families that we were committed to. I wanted time to sort out what was happening in my head – I was very scared about what was happening. It became clear to me that I wanted to move out just to have the freedom to have this new relationship with this man who I was relating to intellectually. I wasn't thinking of getting out just to get into another arrangement with another man. But I wanted the freedom to determine my own friendship and I could see that I wasn't having that freedom with Phil. Ron and I talked about the idea of doing things together. We couldn't see living together in the immediate future, but we didn't rule it out for a future date. He talked me into the idea that I should just go back home and carry on and we would meet later that week and talk to each other about how things were going. Phil felt trapped and he said, 'No you're not going to meet him.' And I said, 'Well I'm going to.' And he said, 'Well you can't,' and we had a big fight about this. And I thought, 'Well I'm not going to have somebody saying to me that I'm not going to do something that I want to do'. So really, what triggered the idea of leaving was that I wasn't going to have somebody telling me what I could not do, when I wanted to do something. So I decided to get out. If Phil wasn't going to allow me to meet somebody else, then that was just too much. And I left on that issue, on that principle. And I moved out with all three of my children.

'*Financial hardship is virtually synonymous with lone parenthood. The poverty trap is no idle phrase. To subsist indefinitely on Supplementary Benefit is effectively to become poorer and more dependent as every month passes. Yet, mothers who try to work and pay their passage find that the path to independence is strewn with insurmountable hurdles . . . A woman who works full-time may be even worse off*' – Rosemary Simon

---

We went to a friend's house and we didn't leave a forwarding address because things were so difficult. Phil was creating a really big scene and he had a very big tantrum, shouting and screaming:

his way of getting me to submit was to be terrifying. Not in a physically violent way, but in a very threatening way. I needed space and I needed to get away from him. The children were rather frightened and upset by all that was going on. They were not too happy now about things that were going on. Phil's power over me was now extending to Louise. She wasn't allowed to do things. I wanted her to be free to do whatever she wanted to do. Like go out dancing. Phil had a car, but was not going to collect her from places she went dancing. So, when she went dancing I'd walk down to the bottom of the road to meet her off the bus. I did that for her because I felt she ought to be able to do her dancing, if that's what she wanted to do. So Louise supported me quite a lot in moving out – she was fifteen at the time. Sara was thirteen, and her feelings were very mixed. But she came with me. We disappeared for three days and the only contact we had with Phil was telephone calls, which I maintained. He was in a terrible state. He wanted to get back what he felt he'd lost, which was a whole family.

The kids wrote cards to Phil and he wrote letters to them. His letters were very sad, and pathetic. He would send them things to try to get them to come back; he was asking them to forgive him for things that he'd done, trying to win back his family. And he was beginning to see certain errors in his ways with the children. But, I wasn't going back. Another friend found a room in a house – this house – and I jumped at the idea of a room of my own. I was going to make a go of things on my own; I was very serious about that. It was going to be very difficult, but I was going to carry through with it. One thing I'd done was, one day when Phil was out of the house, I'd got in and got some clothes and things that we were going to need to survive longer than a day or two at a time. And we – the children and I – moved into the room. Phil knew I meant business.

I liked the idea of being on my own, of living on my own and working things out on my own. And in order to get to this stage I had to rid myself of a marriage that wouldn't work, that I could feel wasn't working, though I never acknowledged why it wasn't working. I never looked at my part of why it wasn't working, until I'd left and was on my own and had the space to do so. In order to get the place to be on my own, I had to go through quite a bit of struggle and a lot of harrassment from Phil and from my family. Though friends were very supportive. I had to keep myself fairly emotionally controlled to be able to work. It was difficult living in one room, for lots of practical reasons and it was difficult getting my finances sorted out. But I was going to make it work, and I did make it work. And after two months I got this flat which is upstairs in the same house. I needed a lot of emotional support from Ron because the wearing down that Phil was doing was emotionally very draining. Ron supported me because he realised and understood. Phil had got it into his head that it was Ron who had made me, or who had told me to leave, and it was not so. Getting free from Phil emotionally was one of my problems. Very often I didn't have support in the situation and I had to work things out for myself. And although I found that difficult, when I used to work things out for myself, I would get a much bigger buzz than if I'd got emotional support from Ron. And that increased the idea that I could do things by myself, weather the storm by myself.

Practically, things began to work out. Hannah – who was six – went back to live with Phil. She wanted to, that was her home. Louise went to live with her boyfriend – and she's actually expecting a baby now herself. Which will make me a grandmother – Louise is like me in that I feel she will sort out a lot of her ideas about being a woman through motherhood. So it is just Sara and I living here now and that is working out well. We can talk to each other easily and are good friends. We began to talk much more openly with each other, not only about our relationship to each other, but about our relationships as women and about our relationship to men. I would confide in her about my friendship with Ron. I was open and honest about everything I was doing, because I'd made the space for myself to do that, which I hadn't been able to do for years and years. Growing stronger as a woman . . . well, I hadn't expected it to come about as it has. Living on my own has been so good. Having Ron as a friend was very special, but I could see myself as separate from him.

For a little while Ron got scared because he thought he was getting dependent on the friendship. That freaked him out and caused him to pull out altogether, or what seemed like altogether for a while. That was one of the biggest blows. But I had to come to terms with it and did come to terms with it pretty well, in that I decided that I'd made a stake for my own independence, and I meant it. So what was I doing grovelling about the place being emotionally hung up, just because Ron decided that he wasn't with me on this trip. So I got myself together pretty quickly about that. And then Ron came round pretty quickly too, realising that there was something in our friendship which was pretty special, that he could relate to me, while still working out things on his own. But that was good too. I got stronger by myself, seeing that I could cope with the idea of not having Ron as a friend. I broke with the idea of having emotional dependence on a man. That was a very big break for me, quite amazing and liberating.

I got very angry about the fact that a man could make me feel so bad, that I could feel emotionally down because a man might not love me as I wanted to be loved. I got very angry about that – why should a man be able to do that? And it became men, not this particular man; it became – why should men be able to do that to women? Why should men have that power over women? That's how I saw it, the man/woman thing. And I decided that I was getting strong as a woman and that I was going to be strong about this. And could be, because there was such an awful lot of love about me. I saw it as him not coping, not me being cast off, as it were. Or not being worthy, which was one of my hang-ups before – that I was not worthy of the love, or the friendship. But I was okay and it was his problems that were causing him to cut the relationship.

The evidence we have received put it beyond doubt that housing problems closely rival money problems as a cause of hardship and stress to one-parent families, and we attach the greatest importance to measures likely to improve their situation in this respect – 'The Finer Report, 1974'

Now we've gone from there: we can have a friendship but we're two separate people with an amazing bond of love that doesn't negate either of us as separate people. We're both really appreciating that very much. Ron's come a long way with his own consciousness, too, as a person. He's sorted out a lot now. So it's still an emotional attraction to a man, and a sexual attraction as well. I am able to feel myself growing and growing all the time with these new experiences. Things get better and better and I feel stronger all the time. I've become my own person for the first time in my life. This period of living on my own has been so fantastically important. I didn't know how much I'd needed it until I got it. I do see a possibility now of Ron and I being able to live together, because we are such good friends and we give such a lot to each other. But in a way that would be very different from my previous experiences of living with somebody. I know now how much space I need for myself. I would take the time I need for myself and it would be part of whatever agreement we entered into. I would be able to identify my needs, and the spaces I need for myself. Ron also understands that he has needs of this kind too. I don't think I'm ready to live with him, but if he decided to leave his marriage to live on his own, I would be ready to support him in that idea. I would like to see him make a go; I think living on his own would be as great a benefit to him as living on my own has been to me. I wouldn't go into my relationship now without the space to be alone. And I wouldn't encroach on any other person's need to be alone. I'd try to save that space away from them, and I'd understand from another person's point of view too. I've learned to like myself and I could never have done that married.

Some people put this thing on you – you ought to feel guilty, *don't* you feel guilty, walking out, you know. But it just isn't there. I don't feel it. There isn't any need for it. We all feel happy. We get what we want from it. The children are learning from me, the tools I've only recently acquired. And that's really good. I'm just following the course that I'm on, because I know it's right, for all of us, whatever people say or think.

Postscript

Judith is remarkably modest about the nature and significance of the decisions she made in her life – and also about the strength of character needed to make such choices. She made a transition from the most conventional of marriages (housewife, mother of three, part-time worker) to the most unconventional of situations – choosing to leave an unsatisfactory marriage, leaving one of her children, living alone and still functioning as a loving and nurturing mother. Hers are the sorts of decisions that society instinctively frowns upon, and her story goes some way towards showing that there *are* viable alternatives to nuclear marriage – even to 'conventional' splitting up.

Judith was convinced that her marriage was damaging to her self and to her growth as an individual, and hence to her husband and children. She had the courage of her convictions to do something about it, however difficult. She was prepared not only to live alone, but to use that experience – plus the inevitable loneliness – as an opportunity to discover herself. What comes across is the amazement and joy she has felt in her self-discoveries. Her story radiates the confidence she has achieved and signposts some of the possibilities women are often prevented from achieving.

12. Paul

Paul comes from a middle-class background and he now works as a teacher in Birmingham. He married at twenty-three (his wife was nineteen) and separated four years later. His circumstances were extremely unusual in that he and his wife had been separated for over a year when their child was conceived: so they were both, as it were, single parents before the child was born. It was a situation in which there was great pressure for both of them to come back together for the sake of their unborn child, but Paul did not feel it was right to 'ruin his life' just for the sake of the child. At the same time, he felt responsible and therefore decided to try to create an alternative structure for fathering. The child is now three years old and he says, 'It is working well for all three of us. It hasn't been easy, but better than had we gone back together. It *is* possible, but difficult.'

Paul's situation was further unusual in that as a teacher in daily contact and dealing with many single parents, he knew what the problems were in advance. 'Certainly the moment a child arrives you are in a state of crisis because society does not in any way gear itself to the single parent – male or female.'

Of his situation at the moment, Paul feels basically optimistic: 'I've created a structure that will work for me, and seems to work for my daughter and her mother. But I am not an idiot, and haven't got my head in the clouds somewhere. I know there will be problems in the future. But the way I have done it has, I think, been least harmful to my daughter.'

We met in the Far East. I was in the armed forces – a reconnaissance officer – and Karin was on holiday before finishing her teacher training. We were young: she was nineteen and I was twenty-three. We were on a romantic island.

I was very drunk one night, in quite a nice night club. And a very pretty young lady saw that I was drunk and helped me sit down. I looked in my pockets because I wanted a drink, I had no money and she bought me another one. And then I had the problem of finding my way back home, eight miles in the dark. This really beautiful, hazy lady was saying, 'Come on, I'll help you back'. So she took me back to where I was staying. That was the start of a relationship, a very quick relationship actually, a few weeks. It was very romantic. Then I fractured my leg in a fall. And the fracture was so bad that I went to hospital. But she visited. And because the fracture was pretty bad they evacuated me to England. But that six week period, the sun, the romance made me fall very much in love with her. And I promised to marry her. I'm being brutally honest actually.

I went back to England, convalesced to March, Karin flies home soon and we marry. We don't know each other very well. I was slightly a moralist then and she was a very pure, nice girl. I was the first bloke she'd slept with. In many ways this is very important as it developed. I felt obliged, because I hadn't been with someone so nice and innocent before. So emotionally, I was trapped. There was an attraction there. We had the same sort of feelings about life, a philosophy about the good will of people. I wanted to get out of the services to do something more rewarding. All those things entered into a contract of love, I think.

I think I was swept along by an unreal world. I think we both were. But there are two areas of interest to me, looking back. One is that I felt trapped within a military environment, she felt trapped within a teaching environment. We both became catalystic in enabling each other to get out. I think Karin wanted security. And she wanted a companion. I sort of required that as well, but in a different way. I've always been a loner, because of the job I was doing and something to do with my childhood. But from the very start, Karin had certain rules and regulations about marriage and how she felt. I used to be a sportsman and go away for three to four weeks at a time for tournaments. That was fine, but when we got married immediately there was a new structure: 'I don't think I want you to go' and I said, 'Fine, I don't want to play sport.' It was put to me that she would be rather lonely if I went. So I found myself becoming a different person. Even at the very beginning. I've always played sport. But I gave it up when I got married. 'I need you, please stay.' Which can sound nice to start with, but in the end can become very controlling.

To start with military pay is very low in terms of the average wage in the country. So, even when we were both working later, money was short. I still enjoyed drink. Still smoked. So there was very little opportunity to save. But both of us had ideals about what we wanted. And one of them was that I wanted to be a teacher, working with children. And I jumped from the structure of the military with lots of independence and autonomy on an individual level into a very paternalistic organisation, and found that I wasn't very happy there. So we had lots of unfulfilled bits and as I talk about the ideal of marriage I may sound cynical. Because of being let down or not fulfilled. Even at the very beginning. And that is paralleled right through my marriage with Karin. I'll go back to that.

Karin gave up college when I left the services, and went to work as a civil servant – in computers, actually. We both made radical changes. But both together, both sharing, both aware that we were influencing each other quite drastically. And my sport finished. It was quite an issue to start with. But Karin became so upset during these arguments that I usually gave in. Karin is, was then, a very introvert person. She found it very difficult to show an emotion. She'd store it in her head, it would go into her heart, she'd just hold on to it. I'm a bit more extrovert in terms of emotion, I express emotion outwardly. I think it is insecurity. You deal with insecurity in different ways: Karin dealt with it inside, I dealt with it outside. What actually happened was she went into a very unsatisfying job. And I started the teaching which was a new area for me, and an opportunity for me to extend my knowledge, grow, develop and meet new people. Exciting people. I got into a growing area, while Karin remained in rather stagnant water. She still had lots of dreams and feelings about what she wanted to be: she wouldn't mind social work, she wasn't sure, she wanted to deal with communities. But she wouldn't really commit herself to anything. Not that she couldn't. But she wouldn't. She takes a lot longer than me to come to terms with herself.

I go through two years of training, Karin then returns to college. She rejects the computers, and then she starts blaming me that she could have completed her teaching, when she was nineteen before I married her. She went to Solihull to complete her training. She gets the top student award and is very pleased about that. Karin is working hard as a student teacher, me then at a residential school, out day and night – we never got together. Till we were further and further apart. Karin on her own, growing older now, as a teacher, and me having quite good status, responsibility and enjoying it very much. So I was finding it more and more difficult to communicate with Karin, she with me. We became very separate people. During that time I'd never thought about having relationships with other people. It was still very much in my mind that the marriage would work. And I suppose I buried my head in my work. I expected everything to turn out well. Then I started doing co-therapy with a couple of female teachers – with whom I had relationships. Which was rather alien to me. There was a conflict there. You have the marriage, which you believe in – and the morals of it – and the innocence still of your wife, which you also believe in. You'll protect that, but there's all the guilt you feel. But I went ahead and did it. I was growing up more and more, I think, in terms of what is right and wrong in relationships. And then, of course, I *had* to look at the relationship with Karin. And it dawned on me that I couldn't remain in a marriage situation just for the sake of a marriage situation.

And the year Julie was born we had separated. She wasn't even conceived when we had separated completely. We were in the process of reconciling ourselves as separated people. It would have been no problem. Karin could have done her own thing, I could have done mine. There was a mutual split. And we were both in an excellent position to separate – independent, both working. But we decided to put on a front when my brother got married, and we slept together at my parents home, when we both got drunk. We put on the front to protect my parents, who were going through a very difficult time. A very practical reason. And we slept together, and had intercourse after the reception, a willing arrangement on both sides. We then separated, I dropped her off at her place, I went back to my home.

Things were looking up. Then two months later a knock on the door – 'Paul, I'm pregnant.' I said, 'Sit down,' she sat down, and we talked about it, and talked retrospectively about what we had been going through in the last five years. And I was quite frank with her and said, 'Well we are going towards separation, what do you want to do?' I feel quite strongly that a child not born into a situation can be adversely affected and I wanted her to think about termination. This was completely unacceptable to Karin. I'm not entirely sure why, but there was her very innocent naivete. And there is a great Christian drive in Karin as well, and all sorts of moralistic issues in terms of children. She had to make a decision very soon about termination, and it was out of the question.

She then finished her teacher training during pregnancy, which was very hard for her. I admired that a great deal, she kept to something and completed it and got this top award. Then, three months before Julie was due to be born she tore her placenta and was immediately hospitalised from that time on. Then of course there was a crisis for three months. If the placenta did collapse completely then the child would die anyway. So we had this fantastically emotional three months' crisis with lots of confusion on both sides. But she knew that I wouldn't drop her, that I would support her and we would try to work things out after the child was born, to make it as best for her as we could. This is very important.

I was living at that time in a bedsit in Birmingham costing me the earth. When the child was born Karin couldn't stay on in the place where she was living. So although we were separate, although I had made some protest about having this child, because I felt I had some obligation, I continued to support her. And I managed to get an unfurnished flat in Birmingham for her and the child and get it done up. Just before the child was born she was allowed out of hospital, saw her new home, liked it, and said again, 'What are you going to do?' I told her to go back to when she told me about Julie's conception, that I didn't think it would work. But I think because she had a child inside her, because she felt big and now a mother, she felt things would change. But they couldn't change. Not for me anyway. I had managed to separate a lot more, I think, than Karin had. Unconsciously I think she felt this would bring us back together. Karin didn't know what she wanted. I think she was still entrenched traditionally with: 'I have a child, this man has got a lot of respect for me still, this just might pull it through.' But I can't say whether that is what she thought or not. Perhaps it was confusing to her that I was taking such responsibility by providing a flat. But point one – I was still married to Karin; point two – she was carrying our child whether I wanted it or not, and I still had some responsibility for that; point three – when that child was born where would they live. To me it was a pretty simple responsibility. But Karin was still pretty ambivalent. I have to say this – perhaps it's chauvinistic, I've an open mind on it and I want that to be recognised – I think Karin even then was beginning to use the feministic, motherhood responsibility bit towards the man, towards me. Very unconsciously, but it was working. You know the traditional role of the helpless woman. And I think in many respects I colluded with that.

Certainly from the moment a child arrives you are in a state of crisis. Because society does not in any way gear itself to the single parent – male or female. But crises can be worked through. I say that from a professional point of view. But this particular kind of crisis isn't so easily worked through. In normal crises you have: denial, anger and then possibly rejection. Then you have depression, then you have reality. In this case reality hits you the moment that child is born. Or even as soon as you become pregnant. From that moment on there can be no denial. The denial usually comes very simply in terms of single parent families: they are single parent families, because one of the parents has denied the marriage and family and has gone. In my case I said I would accept a certain amount of responsibility for that child – because I love it. But I will not let that child destroy my life for the sake of con-vention – the convention that I should continue to be married, live with the mother and that everything would be happy. As a teacher who has some experience with marital interaction or relationships, I knew it was a very disastrous area. I had some experience in that area. So I made a decision. It hurt me that the child would never have a conventional father. But it would have a father. That's how I treated my crisis. I would not be there as husband to my wife with the child in the middle I would let my estranged wife become a single parent and my daughter would be brought up in a single parent family. But I would be there supporting as best I could. I made that decision before Julie was born. And I've continued ever since. She's now coming up to three.

Karin had to start to work within seven weeks of the child being born. She often had to work late. And I said I would babysit two nights a week. So I used to come over about eight in the evening and stay until nine the next day. For partly selfish motives. I thought it would be nice for me to feed, calm, change the baby. Because the child was there now. I'd made one effort to stop it being born. But now we had a child, let me get to know it. For perhaps fourteen months I did this. I did nothing really, just looked after the child. But it gave the child some security, because it had a male figure immediately to identify with. She got very used to me, and it has paid dividends now. Karin was working late several nights a week, then having a demanding baby to feed all through the day: then I'd come the next night she'd get back late, with huge quantities of work that had to be done at home, so she barely got any sleep and was pretty tired and irritable. And I had to – in my mind anyway – support that area too. I was also paying quite enormous maintenance. Karin got an extremely high maintenance allowance from me – to my own detriment, which she could possibly forget about now. It was a struggle for me, but I quite consciously decided to do this for a short period of time – eighteen months anyway. Because Karin wasn't earning that much money and her living wasn't that good. But Julie had quite a secure first eighteen months. Karin wasn't a typical single parent, and she doesn't realise that even now. The reason she wasn't was that there was some input through the father.

It wasn't all quite so calculated as it might sound. It was as it evolved, and the responsibility evolved. I wasn't prepared to see Karin go to the cleaners, and rent was quite high at the time. She could have lived on supplementary benefit. But I know what that is! So I did a compromise by giving good maintenance and babysitting facilities. Which was also productive to me because I had some contact with Julie. This has carried on. And I now have Julie from Friday to Monday morning every fortnight.

Let's look at security for children. Karin and I did not separate in anger with fights; it was just a dying of a relationship, with a rebirth perhaps on Karin's part when she found she was pregnant. Otherwise it just finished. I can't look back and talk about those horrible fights we used to have, how I hate that person: it was just a natural disintegration of the marriage. That has helped with Julie. Then for the first few occasions that Julie stayed with me – in her verbal stage – it was, 'Mummy, want mummy'. If I hadn't thought through about where I stood, I could have been looking at that kid and saying, 'Look here's your father, damn your mother, I'm here looking after you, don't you see I love you as well.' So with my training and thinking, I was prepared for Julie when she came to be with me. I'd say, 'Well, mummy is at work', and reinforce it by saying she was going to see her tomorrow. Now, when she comes she doesn't cry for mummy. She understands. Daddy lives with a girlfriend, Julie comes to Daddy and the girlfriend. And we have a cat and friends who come in, and they are identified now. So Julie knows where she is coming. And we think she is quite safe, emotionally.

Julie has grown up reasonably well, even though she'll never have a father like other mums and dads, not like in a nuclear family situation. But she has a father in a very consistent way. When she goes to school, there will be very simple practical things – the teacher will perhaps naively say, 'What do your mummy and daddy do?' But Julie will be able to say, even though daddy has never lived with mummy. She *is* going to have problems growing up asking her mother and me, 'Why don't you live with mummy?' And we have that whole area of truth to give to her, that daddy cares very much for mummy, but daddy wants to live somewhere else. We've started that now, very gently, helping her to cope with that. But she is in an unusual position. Her situation will only be abnormal to her when she is confronted with so-called normality, say at school. Whereas most single-parent children go through this crisis of separation, so they are acutely aware of two kinds of reality. This is where Julie is a bit more lucky. She's never had the trauma of separation and loss.

I feel tremendously involved with my daughter. And I think this child will grow up pretty well adjusted. I'm outside it really, but very gently supporting at the back. Some of the conflicts with Karin are over very small things. I am reminded that, 'I have your daughter all the week, you have her once a fortnight.' Now that is the reality. But what one can then say to Karin is, 'Look, you might have a daughter, but I do a lot of work with her when she is here, and you still get good maintenance from me, you get contact with me, you can still ring me if there is a problem in relation to this child.' In fact, what I feel happens in the process of separation, is that usually the victim is the female, that is statistically so. The female then sets up a rejection of males for anything up to two years, but often at least a year. A complete rejection of meaningful, caring relationships with males. And there's often an unconscious sharing with the children that men are 'yuk'. If the mother then doesn't come to terms with this, and starts beginning to trust men again, often the children, especially the female children, grow up with some resentment (unconsciously stored) as to what men in relationships mean.

But in terms of well-adjusted single parents, one often gets friends coming in who are not sexual partners, not involved emotionally, but male friends who come in whom the mother trusts. Usually that's enough for the girls and the boys to identify with, to start building up their own trust again. The mother has been hurt deeply by the breakdown of a marriage or relationship, but the people who have been really hurt are the children. Because they are still developing, learning what relationships are about. I think sometimes both parties – when looking at the single-parent family – are preoccupied with how they feel about it and sometimes forget the enormous damage that it can do to children.

Why are boys not asked whether they would put a career before marriage? And why, anyway, should combining a career with marriage pose problems for girls but not for boys? It is always unquestioningly assumed that whether women work or not, they will take full responsibility for housework and child care, thus sparing men, from having to make any choice between career or family – 'Wedlocked Women' by Lee Comer

---

I have a friend with two boys, of twelve and nine. She had ten years of domestic bliss. Then suddenly, Christmas Day, he said, 'I'm going, I've found another woman.' And for three years she was destroyed. What has happened is that she hasn't really worked through any trust towards men. There haven't been any men in her life for the last three years. And she is bringing up two rather effeminate boys. I'm not saying this always operates, but I've seen it happen. And the reason is that she has brought her children into her . . . 'You are the ones I care about, you are the ones I love, we can get through this together, can't we?' sort of thing. The mother's feministic feelings are transmitted to the children. Now, if she had had just a bit more contact with males – even the milkman – and could talk in a natural way to them, the boys would have had some male identity. I'm not saying it has to be someone with a deep relationship with the mother, just someone they can identify with and know is normal and acceptable.

Women's earning power is notoriously low . . . – Rosemary Simon

---

A lot of single parents feel that their children are not only well adjusted but that there are real advantages in being single-parent children. And I'd endorse that all the way. In my own experience, if I'd have lived with Karin with Julie, I think I could have finished up battering Julie. Because of the intense latent interaction between myself and a wife I could not communicate with.

When you become a single parent, you become an extremely vulnerable member of society – however much money you have, however many social contacts. Unless you deliberately go into a relationship to have children as a single parent – find yourself a stud, get yourself with child and carry on, but again I question that in terms of motive, and your needs as opposed to the child's. There are pressures for single parents whatever their circumstances. If you are pretty together as an individual in society and have some resource – which not many unsupported parents have – you still have many problems to solve. Which on a positive level will make you far more independent, and you will project this independence on to your children. I've seen lots that do work that way. But lots tend to over-identify with the children. And sometimes the children become very precocious and very controlling of the mother. There's a huge area of professional concern for any child from a single-parent family. And my child is going to have the same problems. In no way do I dismiss that. But I know that my child's future will be far more secure with me being away and doing the job I am doing with her now, than had I stayed with Karin.

Paid domestic help costs a fortune . . . – Rosemary Simon

Things that have to be worked through in the future include the possibility of Julie having a permanent stepfather. Because my role is so loosely linked with Julie at the moment, that when a new male comes in, there will be lots of competition. Perhaps he will become a new daddy. And that in many ways may be the final feeling of despair for me – being the father who cares about the child but not the marriage. I don't think it is to do with any unresolved feelings about Karin. It's to do with the very lonely job of supporting an unsupported mother with very little recognition. And really as soon as another man becomes a part of Karin's life – and I hope she will have a meaningful relationship – it's very natural and right that Julie then begin to identify with that male figure. Who would probably be fathering her more of the time than I would. I then fall back into the very traditional position of having access. Which I'll have to look at very carefully. I think I would feel very threatened, about her a great deal. But I think when another man arrives in a permanent relationship with Karin, I will have to be prepared to give in. Let go. But with a great deal of jealousy, and envy – that he has a beautiful little daughter, ready made, who is quite safe. It will leave some responsibility to Karin, to reciprocate the kind of care that I have extended to both of them.

I've created a structure that will work for me. I don't think it would work for a lot of people. I think this is the important thing about being the father. It takes a lot of patience learning things like changing nappies, sitting very gently with a small child crying for mummy, and saying, 'I know you really want your mother, but this is your father here.' And not getting angry. Because if you get angry, when you've only got her for a few days, that anger could be that much more apparent, and possibly more destructive.

I would never marry again. Perhaps going through a bad marriage has enabled me to look at traditional structures in a much more positive way. And then become quite cynical about them. If I had wanted to remain in a traditional structure, I had a very attractive wife, cooks quite well, good dress sense, and a nice child, so what more could I want? In fact, I require a lot more. And a child does not keep me within that for the sake of conforming to what society wants. I remember sitting down when Julie was born, saying, 'I will not be here as a traditional father.' I looked at her in her cot and said, 'I will not be here, I'll do my own thing with you, which I hope is not too destructive, and will perhaps give you some benefit.' And I've tried, and so far it has been reasonable. But I am not an idiot, and haven't got my head in the clouds somewhere. I know there will be problems in the future. But the way I have done it has, I think, been least harmful to her. It's not her fault that me and her mother couldn't get it together. I don't see why she should be handicapped too much. And I don't see why society should handicap her. Or indeed Karin.

I have created an alternative family structure because the one that society offers is inadequate. That is society's fault, not mine. So I resent the fact that I, or my child, or her mother should suffer unnecessarily for it.

Postscript

Paul and his wife fell very quickly into a conventional marriage patterns, with pressures from themselves to be a very 'closed' couple – he, for example, giving up 'his sport' in order to be at home with her. In the end, they both found this structure inhibiting, though Paul probably more than his wife, in that she tended to be dependent on him when he was inclined towards more independence.

What is illuminating is that it was marriage as much as the individual relationship which Paul, at least, rejected, having experienced it. Paul: 'It dawned on me that I couldn't remain in a marriage situation just for the sake of a marriage situation.' And that Paul as a teacher with experience of dealing with the problems of single-parent families, deliberately chose to raise his child as a single parent rather than within an institution of marriage, a frustrated relationship and a nuclear family. He was obviously aware of the disadvantages and the problems, but unlike most people, was also aware in advance of the advantages, and was determined to exploit these. At the time of the interview he seemed to be doing so successfully. His course of action might on the surface seem rather selfish, but he also comes across as caring, analysing his situation and acting on his analysis as best he can and in the best interests possible of all those concerned.

Directory of Useful Organisations

Abortion Law Reform Association (ALRA)
88ᴬ Islington High Street, London N1 (01-359 5209 or 359 5200)

Deals with abortion services.

Adoption Resource Exchange
40 Brunswick Square, London WC1 (01-837 0496)

Deals with adoption of children with special needs.

Advisory Centre for Education (ACE)
32 Trumptington Street, Cambridge (Cambridge 51456)

Provides information on education.

Apart Aid
Victoria Chambers, Victoria Road, Farnborough, Hants.

Offers a counselling service for the separated and divorced.

Alcoholics Anonymous
7 Moreton Street, London, SW1 (01-834 8202). General Service Office (01-352 9779)

Provides assistance for alcoholics.

Association of British Adoption and Fostering Agencies
4 Southampton Row, London WC2 (01-242 8951)

Provides advice on adoption, including agencies.

Association of Local Advice Centres
709 Antrim Road, Belfast (Belfast 777239)

Deals with supplementary benefits problems.

BIT Information and Help Service
97ᴬ Talbot Road, London W11 (01-229 8219 & 8210)

Offers a variety of help, including accommodation.

British Pregnancy Advice Service (BPAS)
Arranges inexpensive abortions – branches throughout the country. For further information, telephone:

Birmingham: Guildhall Buildings, Navigation Street, Birmingham B2 4BT (021-643 1461)
Brighton: Wistons, 138 Dyke Road, Brighton, Sussex BN1 5PA (0273-509726)
Coventry: Counden Clinic, Barker Butts Lane, Coventry CV6 1DU (0203-51663)
Leeds: Second Floor, 8 The Headrow, Leeds LS1 6PT (0532-443861)
Liverpool: 5th Floor, Harley Buildings, 11 Old Hall Street, Liverpool L2 1BB (051-227 3721)

Brook Advisory Centres
Offer family planning services to married and unmarried.

London:
223 Tottenham Court Road, W1 (01-323 1522) and (01-580 2991)
55 Dawes Street, Walworth SE17 (01-703 9660)
Kings College Hospital, Denmark Hill SE5 (01-274 6222 Ext. 2662)
Lewisham Hospital, Ante-Natal Dept, High Street, Lewisham SE13
St Bartholomew's Hospital, Women's Outpatients Dept, EC1
Birmingham:
9 York Road, Edgbaston, Birmingham 16 (021-455 0491)
City Centre, Top Floor, 8/10 Albert Street, Birmingham 4 (021-643 5341)
102 Hamstead Road, Handsworth, Birmingham 19 (021-554 7533)
Bristol:
21 Richmond Hill, Clifton, Bristol BS8 1BA (0272-36657) Telephone this number for appointments at:
   Filton Clinic, Shields Avenue, Bristol 7
   Downend Health Clinic, Buckingham Gardens, Downend, Bristol
   Granby House Health Clinic, St John's Road, Bedminster, Bristol 3
Cambridge: Advisory Centre for Young People, 33 Clarendon Street, Cambridge (0223-55003)
Coventry: Coventry & Warwickshire Hospital, Stoney Stanton Road, Coventry (0203-23369)
Edinburgh: 2 Lower Gilmore Place, Edinburgh 3 (031-229 5320)
Liverpool: 9 Gambier Terrace, Liverpool 1 (051-709 4558)

Catholic Housing Aid Society (CHAS)
189a Old Brompton Road, London SW5 (01–373 4961/2)

Assists with single parent housing problems – with regional branches.

Catholic Marriage Advisory Council
Clitherow House, 15 Lansdowne Road, London W11 3AU (01–727 0141 & 0142)

Provides marriage guidance and help with the rhythm method of birth control.

Central Bureau for Educational Visits & Exchanges
43 Dorset Street, London W1H 3FN (01–486 5101 & 5961)

Distributes booklet, "Working Holidays" about children's holidays without parents.

Cherish
c/o Maura O'Dea, 335 Lower Kimmage Road, Dublin 6.

Provides help for single women wanting to keep their babies.

Child Poverty Action Group (CPAG)
1 Macklin Street, London WC2 (01–242 3225/9149)

Provides information on welfare benefits, family poverty and related issues.

Church Army
CSC House, North Circular Road, Stonebridge Park, London NW10 (01–903 3763/9)

Offers marriage guidance and emergency accommodation for families.

Church of England Board for Social Responsibility
Church House, Dean's Yard, London SW1 (01–222 9011)

Offers social services to single women.

Church Welfare Organisations
Contact through Director for Social Services, the National Council for One Parent Families or your local church. Provides assistance to single parent families.

Citizens Advice Bureaux (CAB)
For your local CAB, look in the telephone directory.

Offers legal advice and contact with local organisations.

Citizen's Rights Office
1 Macklin Street, London WC1 (01–405 5942)

Provides information on welfare rights.

Claimants' Unions
The East London Claimants' Union, Dame Colet House, Ben Johnson Road, London E1 (01–790 3867)

Helps with welfare problems.

The Company of Compassion
Mary Sumner House, 24 Tufton Street, London SW1 (01–222–5533)

Offers friendship and advice for single or divorced women and organises holidays for mothers in need of a rest.

Council for Colony Holidays for Schoolchildren
Linden Manor, Upper Colwall, Malvern, Worcestershire.

Organises holidays for children.

Cruse Clubs for Widows
Contact through Headquarters: 126 Sheen Road, Richmond, Surrey (01–940 4818 & 9047)

Offers a variety of services to separated or divorced women.

Department of Health & Social Security
(Address in local telephone directory)

Provides information on financial assistance and accommodation.

Department of Employment
Contact your local Employment Office or write to: Training Services, Agency, 168 Regent Street, London W1 (01–214 6000)

Offers a national training opportunities scheme.

Department of Education & Science
Department E5, Elizabeth House, York Road, London SE1 (01–982 9222)

For information on how to become a teacher.

Depressives Anonymous
50a Masson House, Ruislip, Middlesex

A self-help organisation for people with depression.

Do-It-Yourself Divorce
Do-It-Yourself Services, Free Post, West Drayton, Detford, Nottingham
DM22 8BH

Provides a kit with all the necessary forms and instructions.

Down and Connor Family Welfare Society
43 Falls Road, Belfast 12, N. Ireland (Belfast 43601)

Offers advice on welfare.

Equal Opportunities Commission
Overseas House, Quay Street, Manchester M3 3HN (061–833 9244)

Deals with issues and areas of sexual discrimination.

Scotland: 29ᴬWest George Street, Glasgow G24 (041–226 4591)

Wales: Caerwys House, Windsor Lane, Cardiff (0222 43552)

Families Need Fathers
97c Shakespeare Walk, London N16 (01–254 6680) Evenings and
weekends.

Provides information and aid with access and custody problems.

Family First Trust
The Croft, Alexandra Park, Nottingham (0602–606117)

Provides help with single parent housing, financial and personal
problems.

Family Planning Association
Headquarters at: 27/35 Mortimer Street, London W1 (01–636 7866)

Offers a variety of family planning services throughout the country.

Family Planning Association of Northern Ireland
Headquarters at: Bryson House, 28 Bedford Street, Belfast 2, N. Ireland

For information on contraception and clinics telephone Belfast 662618.

Family Planning Services Limited
4 Lower Leeson Street, Dublin, Ireland

Provides contraception services by mail order.

Family Squatting Advisory Service (FSAS)
2 St Paul's Road, London N1 (01–359 8814, 12–6 pm)

Provides information on short life housing.

Freelance Services
Joan Wilkins Associates Ltd, 37 Maida Vale, London W9 (01–286 0115)

Finds freelance work of all types, requiring considerable competence and professionalism. It specialises in putting teams of women together for a project enabling women to work flexible hours. Pioneers in placing people in part-time work.

Gingerbread
35 Wellington Street, London WC2 (01–240 0953)

Headquarters for Gingerbread self-help groups throughout the United Kingdom, which give practical help and moral support for single parents. Contact for information on local groups.

Government Job Centres
See telephone directory for address.

Provides information on employment opportunities and training.

Government Professional & Executive Register
Details from: Professional & Executive Recruitment, 4 Grosvenor Place, London SW1X 7SB (01–235 7030)

Provides an appointment service for professional, administrative, managerial, executive, technical and scientifically qualified men and women.

Harassment Officer
(Through your local Citizens Advice Bureau. Address in telephone directory)

For help with landlord harrassment problems.

Help
10 Southwharf Road, London W2 (01–937 7687)

Offers assistance to single pregnant women, including abortion referrals. General advice service. Can help with temporary accommodation.

Homeless Action & Accommodation
374 Grays Inn Road, London WC1 (01–278 6349)

Provides assistance for single homeless women.

Housing Aid Centres
(Contact the local Housing Department)

Offers advice and information on housing.

Inquire
85 Chalton Street, Euston, London NW1 (01–388 0094)
Mondays 10am–5pm and 6pm–8pm
Tuesdays & Fridays 10am–5pm
Wednesdays 10am–5pm and 6pm–9pm.

Offers advice (legal and personal) on accommodation, employment, etc.

International Planned Parenthood Federation
18–20 Lower Regent Street, London SW1 (01–839 2911)

Enables British women to obtain contraceptive supplies while abroad.

International Social Service of Great Britain
Cranmer House, 39 Brixton Road, London SW9 (01–735 8941)

Offers advice on legal adoption arrangements to foreign women.

Irish Family Planning Association
10 Merrion Square, Dublin, Ireland (Dublin 63676)

Offers advice on contraception and pregnancies.

The Law Commission
Conquest House, 37 John Street WC1 (242 0861)

Aims to enact reforms in property and magistrate court ruling during and after divorce proceedings.

The Law Society
113 Chancery Lane, London WC2 (01–242 1222)

Provides information on how to obtain a divorce.

Law Society of Northern Ireland
Chichester Street, Belfast BT1 3JE

Provides legal advice and aid.

Law Society of Scotland
26/27 Drumsheugh Gardens, Edinburgh EH3 7YR, Scotland (Edinburgh 226–7411)
Provides legal advice and aid.

Legal Aid Committee
Contact through your local court.

Provides information on legal aid eligibility.

Local Single Parent Groups, (Alphabetically, by location)

Contact local Citizens Advice Bureaus, the National Council for One-Parent Families and Gingerbread for other groups.

Minus One, Belfast
Contact through the Citizens Advice Bureau, Bryson House, Bedford Street, Belfast, N. Ireland (Belfast 43986)

Offers advice and practical help to single mothers or fathers, Protestant or Catholic.

Carlisle Single Parent Family Group
Contact through Council of Social Service, Old Town Hall, Carlisle Cumberland (Carlisle 25517)

Offers practical advice and information, social events for single mothers and fathers and children's activities.

One Parent Family Association, Cirencester
Contact through Citizens Advice Bureau, 11 Gosditch Street, Cirencester, Gloucestershire (Cirencester 2908)

Organises social activities and offers practical information on rights and services.

Association for Deserted & Alone Parents (ADAPT), Dublin
Contact through PO Box 673, Dublin 4, Ireland

Offers legal, practical and personal help for single parents.

Misbourne One Plus Society, Great Missenden
Contact through Missenden Community Centre, Misbourne School, Great Missenden, Buckinghamshire

Offers mainly social contact and mutual help for single parents.

Mums, Harlesden, London
Contact through Harlesden Advice Centre, 25 High Street, Harlesden NW10 (01-965-5480)

Offers baby sitting and social activities for single parent women.

Three Rivers and Watford Association for One Parent Families
Contact Janet Anders, Northall, Stag Lane, Chorleywood, Hertfordshire (Chorleywood 3564)

Offers practical information, help and social activities for single parents.

The Other Branch, Leamington Spa
Bath Place Community Venture, Bath Place, Leamington Spa, Warwickshire (0926 38421)

A family centre set up by a group of women to give advice and information on citizen's rights, nursery services, abortion, contraception, housing, personal problems. It will give support for dealing with the authorities. It is a non-profit making, free, service with voluntary helpers.

Mothers Alone, York
Contact through The Community Council, 10 Priory Street, York (York 21133)

Offers practical information and help, social activities for single parent women.

York Lone Parents
Contact through Mothers Alone

Offers similar services as Mothers Alone to single parent women and men.

London Marriage Guidance Council
76a New Cavendish Street, London W1 (01–580 1087)

Offers marriage guidance counselling services.

London Pregnancy Advisory Service
40 Margaret Street, London W1 (01–409 0281)

Arranges inexpensive abortions.

Marie Stopes Memorial Clinic
108 Whitfield Street, London W1 (01–388 0662)

Provides family planning and abortion services.

Men's Centre
Bread and Roses, 316 Upper Street, Islington, London N1

Provides discussion groups, practical help and information.

National Association for the Care and Resettlement of Offenders
169 Clapham Road, London SW9 (01–582 6500)

Offers information and help for prisoners, ex-prisoners and prisoners' wives and families.

MIND National Association for Mental Health
22 Harley Street, London W1 (01–637 0741)

Provides information about child guidance centres.

National Association for the Welfare of Children in Hospitals
Exton House, 7 Exton Street, London SE1 (01–261 1738)

Provides information on how to care for children in hospital, and help for parents in difficulties with hospital authorities.

National Childbirth Trust
9 Queensborough Terrace, London W2 (01–229 9319)

Offers childbirth preparation classes and information on natural child-birth.

National Childminding Association
Connie Brasted, Westerham, Kent (Westerham 63465) – Secretary Celia Smith

Provides information on childminding.

National Children's Bureau
8 Wakley Street, London EC1V 7QE (278 9441)

Offers services for children.

National Council on Alcoholism
45 Great Peter Street, London SW1

Offers advice on treatment centres.

National Council for Civil Liberties (NCCL)
186 Kings Cross Road, London WC1 (01–278 4575)

Concerned with civil rights, e.g. wrongful dismissal, immigration, problems with the police, with a special interest in women's rights.

National Council for Divorced and Separated People
13 High Street, Little Shelford, Cambridge

Formerly the National Federation of Clubs for the Divorced and Separated.

National Council for One Parent Families
255 Kentish Town Road, London NW5 (01–267 1361)

Offers advice, assistance and information to single pregnant women and single parents.

National Council for the Single Woman and her Dependants
166 Victoria Street, London, SW1 (01–828–5511)

Advice and help for women coping with elderly dependants.

National Federation of Housing Associations
86 Strand, London WC2R 0EG (01-836 2741/4)

Provides information on housing associations.

National Federation of Solo Clubs
Contact through National Council of Social Services, Department of Information, 26 Bedford Square, London WC1 (01-636 4066)

Provides social clubs for single parents.

National Health Service
See 'Your Guide to the National Health Service' NHS2.

National Marriage Guidance Council
Branch Addresses in the telephone directory.

Provides marriage guidance counselling services.

National Society for the Prevention of Cruelty to Children (NSPCC)
Address in telephone directory.

Deals with neglected children and parents with difficulties.

National Union of Students
3 Endsleigh Street, London WC1 (01-387 1277)

Provides information on grants and advice on matters affecting students.

National Women's Aid Federation
374 Gray's Inn Road, London WC1 (01-837 9316)

Offers advice and refuge to battered wives.

Nina West Homes
12 Hampstead Hill Gardens, London NW3 (01-794 2601)

A specialised housing scheme catering for divorced and separated families.

Open University
PO Box 48, Milton Keynes MK7 6AB

Offers degree courses.

Outward Bound Trust
14 Oxford Street, London W1 (01-637 4951)

Organises children's holidays.

Over Forty Association for Women Workers
Grosvenor House, 35/37 Grosvenor Gardens, London SW1 (01–834 0733)

Provides information about job opportunities, and accommodation, for single women.

Oyez Publishing Limited
Oyez House, PO Box 55, 237 Long Lane, London SE1 4PU (01–407 8055)

Provides the necessary forms for a Do-It-Yourself Divorce.

Part Time Careers Limited
10 Golden Square, London W1 (01–437 3103 & 734 0559)

Deals with part-time work for women.

Patients Association
Suffolk House, Banbury Road, Oxford (0865 50306)

Helps people who have complaints about medical services.

Pre-School Playgroups Association
Alfrod House, Aveline Street, London SE11 5DJ (01–582 8871)

Provides information on how to set up a playgroup.

Public Health Inspector
Address through Town Hall.

Deals with health risks in housing.

Release
1 Elgin Avenue, London W9 (01–289 1123) OR for 24 hour emergencies (603 8654) Mondays & Thursdays 10am to 10pm; Tuesdays, Wednesdays & Fridays 10am to 6pm.

Provides services to single pregnant women, single mothers, young people who have run away from home.

Rent Officer
Address from telephone directory.

Assesses fair rents for furnished and unfurnished accommodation.

Rent Tribunal
Address from telephone directory.

Deals with the assessment of fair rent.

Rights of Women (ROW)
374 Grays Inn Road, London WC1 (01–278 6349)

Offers support for single mothers. Free legal advice on Tuesday and Thursday evenings between 7.00 p.m. and 9.00 p.m.

Salvation Army
a) Women's Social Services HQ, 280 Mare Street, London E8 (01–985 1181)
b) Men's Social Services HQ, 110 Middlesex Street, London E1 (01–247 6831)

Offers accommodation for homeless men and women, including units for mothers with small children.

Scarlet Women's Collective
5 Washington Terrace, North Shields, Tyne and wear

Supports single mothers. Publishes *Scarlet Women*, magazine of the socialist feminist current.

Scottish Association for the Care & Resettlement of Offenders (SACRO)
1 Strathmore House, East Kilbridge, Glasgow G74 1LP

Provides help for prisoners, ex-prisoners and prisoners' wives and families.

Scottish Child Poverty Action Group
132 Laurieston Place, Edinburgh (Edinburgh 228 6426)

Scottish Council for Civil Liberties
146 Holland Street, Glasgow 2 (041–332 5960)

Scottish Council for Single Parents
44 Albany Street, Edinburgh 1, Scotland (031–556 3899)

Provides help for single pregnant women and single parents in Scotland.

Secretary of State for Social Services
Alexander Fleming House, Elephant & Castle, London SE1

Deals with complaints and abuses of Social Services Commission.

Shelter
157 Waterloo Road, London SE1 8UU (01–633 9377)

Provides information on housing, homelessness and housing problems.

Shelter Housing Aid Centre (SHAC)
189a Old Brompton Road, London SW5 (01–373 7276)

Provides help with housing problems.

Social Services (Director)
Address from telephone directory or Town Hall.

Provides information on day nurseries.

Supplementary Benefits Appeal Tribunal
c/o Manager, Department of Health & Social Security.

For appeals concerning supplementary benefits.

Supplementary Benefit Office
Deals with supplementary benefits claims, legal aid and the cohabitation rule.

TUC Women's Advisory Council
Great Russell Street, London WC1 (01–636 4030)

Provides information on trade unions, and maternity leave.

Ulster Pregnancy Advisory Association Limited
338A Lisburn Road, Belfast 9, N. Ireland.

Provides assistance for abortions in England.

Women's Forum
26 Bedford Square, London WC1 (01–636 4066)

Publishes a list of women's organisations.

A Woman's Place
48 William IV Street, London WC2 (01–836 6081)

A Women's Liberation information service which provides a list of women's groups and centres throughout the country. Women only.

Women's Royal Voluntary Service
Address in telephone directory.

Provides meals, clothes and furniture to families in need.

Working Association of Mothers
16 Riverview Gardens, Twickenham, Middlesex and 65 Bonnersfield Lane, Harrow, Middlesex

Offers career information for mothers wishing to return to work, playgroups geared to working mothers' needs, babysitting, children's holidays, bulk buying scheme, domestic crisis and illness relief service.

Young Men's Christian Association (YMCA) (local and central)
112 Great Russell Street, London WC1 (01–637 1333)

Offers accommodation information to men and women.

Reading List

Action and Inaction, National Council for One Parent Families, London, 1978
The government's record on implementing the Finer Report with information on what has happened to Finer's 230 recommendations.

Adams, Carol and Laurikietis, Rae, *The Gender Trap: A Closer Look at Sex Roles,* Quartet, London, 1976.

Aries, Philippe, *Centuries of Childhood*, Penguin, Harmondsworth, 1973.

Ashdown-Sharp, Patricia, *The Single Woman's Guide to Pregnancy and Parenthood*, Penguin, Harmondsworth, 1975.
A detailed guide containing chapters on marriage, abortion, contraception, adoption and fostering with a two hundred page section entitled 'Bringing up a child on your own'.

As We See It, National Council for One Parent Families, London, published jointly with Gingerbread, London, 1975.
The problems of one-parent families told in their own words.

Atkinson, Professor A. B., *An Adequate Income,* National Council for One Parent Families, 'Forward From Finer', Number 2, London, 1977.
Argues for inflation-proof benefits for all families, and 'home responsibility payments' for all people caring for dependants, financed by abolishing the married man's tax relief.

Bach, George R. and Wyden, Peter, *The Intimate Enemy*, William Morrow & Co., Inc., New York, 1969.

Barker, Diana Leonard, and Allen, Sheila, (eds.), *Sexual Divisions and Society – Process and Change*, Tavistock Publications, London, 1976.

Battle Royal, Child Poverty Action Group, London, 1977.
Another look at school clothing and maintenance grants.

Beckman, Daniel, *The Mechanical Baby*, Meridian, (New American Library), New York, 1977.

Bernard, J., *The Future of Marriage*, Souvenir Press, London, 1973.

Berne, Eric, *Games People Play*, Penguin, Harmondsworth, 1979.

Biller, Henry B., 'Father absence and the personality development of the male child,' *Developmental Psychology*, 1970a, Volume 2, Number 2, pp. 181–201.

Biller, Henry B., 'The mother-child relationship and the father-absent boy's personality development,' *Merrill-Palmer Quarterly,* 1970 b,- Volume 17, Number 3.

Blake, P., *The Plight of One-Parent Families*, Council for Children's Welfare, London, 1972.

Blishen, Edward, *Sorry, Dad,* Hamish Hamilton, London, 1978.

Blom-Cooper, L., 'From Paternity to Parenthood,' Paper presented at the 'Fathers Alone' Symposium, London, 1973.

Bowlby, John, *Attachment and Loss,* Volume 1, Penguin, Harmondsworth, 1978.

Bowlby, John, *Attachment and Loss,* Volume 2, Penguin, Harmondsworth, 1978.

Bradshaw, Jonathan, and Jane Weale, *Free School Meals: Area Variation in Take-Up*, Child Poverty Action Group, London, 1978.

Bramall, Margaret, 'The single parent family from the unmarried mother's viewpoint', National Council for One Parent Families, London, 1973.
Paper read at the Royal Society of Health Congress 1973.

Bristol Women's Booklist, 59 Lower Union St., Bristol B51 2DU.

Britain's One Parent Families, National Council for One Parent Families, London, 1977.
Some facts and figures. Reprinted from an Annual Report, 1976/77.

Brooke, Rosalind, Field, Frank, Townsend, Peter, *A Policy to Establish the Legal Rights of Low Income Families*, Child Poverty Action Group, London, 1969.

Broughton, M., 'Children with Mothers at Work', *Journal of the Royal Institute of Health and Hygiene,* Volume XXV, May/June 1962.

Bull, David, *Footwear for Families*, Child Poverty Action Group, London, 1978
Memo of evidence to the Price Commission on Footwear Prices.

Burton, R. V., and J. M. W. Whiting, 'The absent father and cross-sex identity', *Merrill-Palmer Quarterly*, 1961, Volume 7, pp. 85–95.

Butterworth, Eric, and Holman, Robert, *Social Welfare in Modern Britain; An Introductory Reader*, William Collins & Sons Co. Ltd., Glasgow, 1978.

Chesler, Phyllis, 'Men Drive Women Crazy', *Psychology Today*, July, 1971.

Chester, R., 'Sex Differences in Divorce Behavior', *Journal of Biosocial Science Supplement,* Volume 2, pp. 121–8, 1970.

Chetwynd, J., and Hartnett, O., 'The sex-role system', *Psychological and Sociological Perspective,* 1978.

Child Benefit – 1978/1979, National Council for One Parent Families, London, 1978.
What the new rates of Child Benefit will mean to lone parents.

Cohabitation, National Council for One Parent Families, London, October, 1976.
Reaction to the Government's report on the cohabitation rule.
Cohabitation: The administration of the relevant provisions of the Ministry of Social Security Act 1966', Report by the Supplementary Benefits Commission to the Secretary of State for Social Services, HMSO, London, 1972.

Compendium Sexual Politics Catalogue, 24 Camden High St., London.

Comer, Lee, *Wedlocked Women*, Feminist Books Ltd., Leeds, 1974.

Cooper, David, *Death of the Family*, Penguin, Harmondsworth, 1972.

Coote, Anna, and Lawrence Grant, *Civil Liberty: The NCCL Guide*, Penguin, Harmondsworth, 1978.

Coote, Anna, and Tess Gill, *Women's Rights: A Practical Guide,* Penguin, Harmondsworth, 1977.
A guide covering work, money, marriage and divorce/separation, housing, children, and sex discrimination.

Coussins, Jean, *Maternity Rights for Women*, National Council for Civil Liberties, London, 1978.

de Beauvoir, Simone, *The Second Sex*, Penguin, Harmondsworth, 1972.

de Mause, Lloyd, (ed.), *The History of Childhood*, Souvenir Press, London, 1976.

de Rham, Edith, *The Love Fraud*, Pegasus, New York, 1965.

Drabble, Richard; Rowland, Mark; Warren, Nick, *Contributory Benefits*, Child Poverty Action Group, London, 1978.
Unemployment, sickness and death, maternity, pensions, and child benefit.

220

Dreitzel, H. P. (ed), *Family, Marriage, and the Struggle of the Sexes,* Collier MacMillan, London, 1972.

Eekalaar, J., *Family Security and Family Breakdown*, Penguin Law and Society, London, 1971.

Ehrenreich, Barbara and English, Deirdre, *For Her Own Good: 150 Years of the Experts' Advice to Women*, Pluto Press, 1979.

Equality for Women, HMSO, London, 1974.

Erikson, Erik H., *Childhood and Society*, Second Edition, W. W. Norton & Co. Inc., New York, 1963.

'Escape From Violence', *Women's Voice*, Issue Number 19, pp. 14–15, London, August 1978.

Etaugh, Claire, 'Effects of Maternal Employment on Children: A Review of Recent Research', *Merrill-Palmer Quarterly*, Volume 17, Number 3, 1974.

Extra Money for Heating, National Council for One Parent Families, London, 1978.
How to claim a heating allowance; for those on Supplementary Benefit.

'Facilities for Women Workers with Home Responsibilities', *International Labor Review, Volume LXIII,* Number 3, March, 1951.

Fairbairns, Zoe, (ed), 'Women's Studies in the U.K.' *London Seminars,* 1975.

Fathers Alone, National Council for One Parent Families published jointly with Gingerbread, London, 1978.
Conference proceedings 1973. Five aspects of male lone parenthood.

Federice, Sylvia, *Wages Against Housework*, Power of Women Collective and Falling Wall Press, London, 1975.

Fenwick, Elizabeth and Peter, *The Baby Book For Fathers*, Angus and Robertson, Brighton, 1978.

Ferri, E., *Growing Up in a One Parent Family*, NFER Publishing company, London, 1976.

Field, Frank, *An Income Policy for Poor Families*, Child Poverty Action Group, London, 1973.

Field, Frank, and Townsend, Peter, *A Social Contract for Families,* Child Poverty Action Group, London, 1974.

Field, Frank, *Children Worse Off Under Labour?*, Child Poverty Action Group, London, 1978.

Field, Frank, *Free School Meals*, Child Poverty Action Group, London, 1977.

Field, Frank, *Priority For Children: A Labour Success*, Child Poverty Action Group, London, 1978.

Figes, Eva, *Patriarchal Attitudes*, Virago, London, 1977.

The Finer Report, Report of the Committee on One-Parent Families, HMSO, London, 1975.

Finklestein, H., Rosenthal, K. & K., 'Fathering After Marital Separation', *Social Work,* Volume 23, Number 1, pp. 11–18, January 1978.

Fisher, Lettice, *Twenty-One Years After: 1918–1946 The Story of NCUMC*, National Council for One Parent Families, London, 1946, 1966.
By the founder member and first chairman of NCUMC.

Fleming, Suzi, *The Family Allowance Under Attack*, Falling Wall Press and Power of Women Collective, London, 1973.

Fogarty, M., and Rapoport R., *Sex, Career and Family*, Allen & Unwin, London, 1971.

Foreman, Ann, *Femininity as Alienation: Women and the Family in Marxism and Psychoanalysis,* Pluto Press, London, 1977.

Faulder, Carolyn, Jackson, Christine, Lewis, Mary, *The Women's Directory,* Quartet Books, London, 1976.
A guide to the issues which concern women individually and collectively, and a full directory of organisations and groups and resources.

Free School Meals, National Council for One Parent Families, London, 1978.
How to see if you qualify.

Friedan, Betty, *The Feminine Mystique*, Penguin, Harmondsworth, 1979.

Friedman, G., *How to Conduct Your Own Divorce in England and Wales*, Wildwood House, London, 1975.

Gavron, H., *The Captive Wife: Conflicts of Housebound Mothers,* Penguin, Harmondsworth, 1975.

George and Wilding, *Motherless Families*. Routledge & Kegan Paul, London, 1972.

Gingerbread Information Leaflets: available from Gingerbread, 35 Willington St., London WC2.
Supplementary Benefits
Exceptional Needs Payments
Family Income Supplement

Coping With High Fuel Costs
Day Care
Appeals
Legal Aid and Advice

Gingerbread Information Sheets:
A Short Guide to the Benefits and Services Available for One-Parent Families.
Direct Payment of Maintenance to Children

Glueck, S., and Glueck, E., 'Working mothers and Delinquency', *Mental Hygiene*, 1957, Volume XLI.

Gordon, Julie, 'We need an adequate living wage for one-parent families . . . now.' *Scarlet Women*, Number 8.
Newsletter of the Socialist Feminist Current, August 1978.

Grant, Judge, *Family Law*, Sweet and Maxwell, London, 1975.

Grassroots Women's Booklist, 109 Oxford Rd., Manchester.

Green, Maureen, *Goodbye Father*, Routledge & Kegan Paul, London, 1976

Greer, Germaine, *The Female Eunuch*, Panther, London, 1971.

Guide to the Finer Report, National Council for One Parent Families, London, 1975.
A summary of Volume 1 of the Report, Finer Joint Action Committee, 1975.

Guze, Henry, 'Marriage – the Death of a Relationship', Mimeographed outline. Summary of presentation at March 1970 joint meeting of the New Jersey Psychological Association and the New Jersey Neurophysical Association, East Orange, New Jersey.

'Battered Women Are Still Homeless', National Women's Aid Federation Report on the Housing (Homeless Persons) Act, 1978.

Hall, Jean Graham, *A United Family Court*, National Council For One Parent Families, 'Forward From Finer', Number 5, London, 1978.
Argues for the abolition of the Matrimonial Jurisdiction of Magistrates' Courts as a step toward independent Family Courts.

Hammer, J., 'Community Action, Women's Aid and the Women's Lib Movement', in Marge Mayo (ed), *Women in the Community*, Routledge & Kegan Paul, London, 1976.

Harbert, W. B., *Social Services for One-Pare]t Families*, National Council for One Parent Families 'Forward From Finer', Number 4, London, 1977.
By the Director of Social Services of Avon. Examines the ways of achieving improvements in the social services to help one-parent families.

Health In Poverty, Child Poverty Action Group, London, 1977.

Hemer, June and Stanyer, Ann, *Handbook for Widows*, Virago, London, 1978.

Herzog, Elizabeth, *Children of Working Mothers*, Children's Bureau Publications, US Government Printing Office, Washington, DC, 1976.

Hewitt, Patricia, *Rights for Women*, National Council for Civil Liberties, London, 1975.
A comprehensive guide to the Sex Discrimination Act, the Equal Pay Act, Paid Maternity Leave, Pension Schemes and Unfair Dismissal.

Hoffman, L. W., 'Effects of maternal employment on children: a review of the research', *Developmental Psychology*, 1974, Volume 10, Number 2, pp. 204–28.

Holes In The Code, National Council For One Parent Families, London, 1977.
Looks at four important gaps in the Code of Practice on Gas and Electricity disconnections.

Holman, Robert, *Inequality in Child Care*, Child Poverty Action Group, London, 1976.

Holman, Robert, *Trading in Children*, Routledge and Kegan Paul, London, 1973.

Holman, Robert, *Unsupported Mothers and the Care of Their Children*, Mothers in Action, London, Second Edition 1972.

Holman, Robert, 'Unsupported Mothers', *New Society*, October 29, 1970.

Human Rights for those Born out of Wedlock, National Council For One Parent Families, London, 1968.
Conference Proceedings 1968. A consideration of needs and how they might be met. Eight papers.

Hurstfield, Jennifer, *The Part-Time Trap (Part-Time Workers in Britain Today)* Low Pay Unit, 9 Poland St., London, 1978.

Ilsley, Professor R., *New Fashions in Illegitimacy*, National Council for One Parent Families, London, 1968.
Sociological analysis of increasing illegitimacy ratio in the 1950s and 1960s.

Infant Health, Child Poverty Action Group, London, 1978.

Janeway, Elizabeth, *Man's World, Woman's Place*, Penguin, Harmondsworth, 1977.

Keep Your Power On, National Council for One Parent Families, London, April 1977, amended November 1977.

224

An explanation of the new guidelines for Gas and Electricity Boards to prevent or delay disconnections.

Laing, R. D., *Conversations With Children*, Penguin, Harmondsworth, 1978.

Lamb, Michael E. (ed), *The Role of the Father in Child Development*, John Wiley & Sons, New York, 1976.

Lambert, L. and Hart, S., 'Who Needs a Father?' *New Society*, 8 July 1976.

Lederer, William J., and Jackson, Don D., *The Mirages of Marriage*, W. W. Norton & Co. Inc., New York, 1968.

Levin, Jenny, *Abolishing Illegitimacy*, National Council For One Parent Families, London, 1977.
A summary of proposals to abolish the legal status of illegitimacy.

Levine, James, *Who Will Raise the Children? New Options for Fathers*, Lippincott, Philadelphia, 1976.

Lister, Ruth, *As Man and Wife? A Study of the Cohabitation Rule*, Child Poverty Action Group, London, 1973.

Lister, Ruth, *Social Security: The Case for Reform*, Child Poverty Action Group, London, 1975.

Lloyd, L., *Women Workers in Britain*, Socialist Women's Publication, 1972.

Lynes, Tony, *The Penguin Guide to Supplementary Benefits,* Penguin, 1975.

McGrindle, Jean and Sheila Rowbotham, *Dutiful Daughters*, Allen Lane, London, 1979.

Mainardi, P., 'The Politics of Housework', in R. Morgan (ed) *Sisterhood Is Powerful*, Wildwood House, London, 1973.

Malos, Ellen, *Housework and the Politics of Women's Liberation*, RSM Publications, Bristol, 1978.

Marsden, Dennis, *Mothers Alone*, Pelican, London, 1973.

Matters of Moment, National Council For One Parent Families, London, 1978.
Conference proceedings 1972. Six papers on adoption, separation and family incomes.

Meacher, Molly, *Rate Rebates: A Study of the Effectiveness of Means Tests,* Child Poverty Action Group, London, 1972.

Mead, Margaret, 'Some theoretical considerations on the problem of mother-child separation', *American Journal of Orthopsychiatry*, July 1954 *XXIV*.

Mead, Margaret, 'The Future of the Family', *Barnard Alumnae Magazine*, Winter 1971.

Means Tests, Child Poverty Action Group, London, 1976.

Mendes, H., 'Parental Experiences of Single Fathers', Unpublished Thesis, University of California, Los Angeles, 1975.

Millett, Kate, *Sexual Politics,* Virago, London, 1977.

Miscellany of Current Care, National Council For One Parent Families, London, 1971.
Conference proceedings 1971. Eleven papers on housing, day care, and groups for one-parent families.

Mitchell, Juliet, *Woman's Estate*, Penguin, Harmondsworth, 1977.

Morgan, D. H. J., *Social Theory and the Family*, Routledge & Kegan Paul, London, 1975.

Moss, Peter, *Jobs For Lone Parents – Towards an Employment Policy*, National Council for One Parent Families, 'Forward From Finer', Number 1, London, 1977.
Assesses the problems of lone parents who go out to work and the need for an employment policy.

Musgrave, Beatrice, and Joan Wheeler Bennett, *Women at Work*, Peter Owen, London, 1972.

National Council for One Parent Families Annual Report 1976/77, London, 1977
'Our most comprehensive Annual Report yet is a source book containing a detailed review of all that happened affecting one-parent families in 1976/77. It also contains comprehensive facts and figures about one-parent families and a series of photographs.'

National Council for One Parent Families Annual Reports of the Previous Five Years, London, 1978.
Except 1973/74 & 75/76. A review of the Council's work and aspects of lone parenthood.

National Council for One Parent Families, *Guide to the Finer Report*, London, 1975.

National Welfare Benefits Handbook, Child Poverty Action Group, London, 1978.
A comprehensive guide to welfare and legal rights. Sections on sup-

plementary benefits, other welfare benefits, rent and rate rebates, local authority and legal aid.

Neubeck, Gerhard, (ed), *Extramarital Relations*, Prentic-Hall Inc., Englewood Cliffs, New Jersey, 1969.

New Rights for the Homeless, National Council for One Parent Families, London, 1978.
A guide to the Housing (Homeless Persons) Act, 1977.

Nicholson, Joyce, *What Society Does to Girls*, Virago, London, 1977.

Nye, F. Ivan, and Lois W. Hoffman (eds.) *The Employed Mother In America*, Rand McNally, Chicago, 1963.

Oakley, Ann, *Housewife*, Allen Lane, London, 1974.

O'Brien, Margaret, *Father Role and Male Sexrole after Marital Separation – Men Coping with Single Parenthood*, Paper presented at the British Psychological Society Social Psychological Conference, University of Wales, Institute of Science and Technology, Cardiff, Wales, September 15–17, 1978.

O'Neill, Nena and George. *Open Marriage, A New Life Style for Couples*, M. Evans and Co., Inc., New York, 1972.

On Top of Your Pay, National Council for One Parent Families, London, 1978.
A guide to Family Income Supplement for lone parents.

'One Parent Families', National Council for One Parent Families, Quarterly Journal, London.

One Parent Families: A Finer Future? Gingerbread, London, 1978
Policy statement of Gingerbread.

One Parent Families – A Guide Book for Children and Young Adults, National Council for One Parent Families, London, 1978.
A list of 38 selected books dealing with aspects of being brought up in a one-parent family.

One Parent Families Bibliography, National Council for One Parent Families, London, 1978.
Selected references of articles about lone parents appearing in popular periodicals in 1977/78.

One Parent Family Housing, National Council for One Parent Families, London, February, 1978.
Response to the Government's Consultative Document on Housing Policy. Thirty-three recommendations are made and proposals to improve the housing situation of one-parent families.

Parker, R. A., *The Housing Finance Bill and Council Tenants,* Child Poverty Action Group, London, 1972.

Parkington, Martin, *The Legal Aid Means Test: A Re-appraisal,* Child Poverty Action Group, London, 1978.

Perry, J. B. Jnr., 'The Mother Substitute of Employed Mothers', *Marriage and Family Living*, 1961, *XXII*.

Piachard, David, *Do the Poor Pay More?* Child Poverty Action Group, London, 1974.

Pilling, Doria and Mia Kellmer Pringle, *Controversial Issues in Child Development*, Elek Books, London, 1978.

Please Ms! National Council for One Parent Families, London, 1974.

Pocketing the Change, National Council for One Parent Families, London, 1978.
The Government's proposals for Child Benefit Payments to one-parent families on supplementary benefit from November 1978.

Poster, Mark, *Critical Theory of the Family*, Pluto Press, London, 1978.

Poyde, Holly, *Superdads: Fatherhood in a Changing Society*, thesis, Department of Extramural Studies, University of Manchester, 1978.

Pregnancy Outside Marriage, National Council for One Parent Families, Facts 2, London, 1977.
The latest figures for conceptions, abortions and births outside marriage.

Puxon, M., *Family Law*, Penguin, Harmondsworth, 1971.

Rappaport, Rhona, Rappaport, Robert N., and Strelitz, Ziona, *Fathers, Mothers, and Others,* Routledge & Kegan Paul, London, 1977.
Contains useful guide to further reading.

Recommendations to the Finer Committee, National Council for One Parent Families, London, 1974.

Reed, Angela, *The Challenge of a Second Marriage*, Plume Press, London, 1975.

Reed, Angela, *Women on the Verge of Divorce*, Ward Lock, London, 1970.

Rennie, S. and Grimstead, K., *The New Women's Survival Catalogue*, Coward, McCann and Georgham, London, 1973.

Rennie, S. and Grimstead, K., *The New Women's Survival Sourcebook*, Knopf, London, 1975.

Rich, Adrienne, *Of Woman Born: Motherhood as Experience and Institution*, Virago, London, 1977.

228

Richman, Joes and Goldthrop, W. O., 'Fatherhood: The Social Construction of Pregnancy and Birth', in Sheila Kitzinger and John A. Davis (eds.) *The Place of Birth*, Oxford University Press, Oxford, 1978.

Rigby, A. *Communes in Britain*, Routledge & Kegan Paul, London, 1974.

Riviere, P. G., 'Rethinking Kinship and Marriage', in Needham, R., *Rethinking Kinship and Marriage,* A. S. A. Monograph. Tavistock Publications, London, 1971.

Rose, Hilary, *Rights, Participation and Conflict,* Child Poverty Action Group, London, 1970.

Rowbotham, Sheila, *Women's Liberation & Revolution: A Bibliography*, Falling Wall Press, London, 1972.

Rowbotham, Sheila, *Hidden from History: 300 Years of Women's Oppression and the Fight Against It*, Pluto Press, London, 1977.

Rudinger, E., *On Getting Divorced*, Consumers Association, London, 1972.

Rutter, Michael, *Maternal Deprivation Reassessed,* Penguin, Harmondsworth, 1972.

Rutter, Michael, 'Parent-child separation: psychological effects on the children', *The Journal of Child Psychology and Psychiatry and Allied Disciplines*, 1971, Volume 12, pp. 233–60.

Sanctuary, Gerald and Whitehead, Constance, *Divorce – And After*, Oyez Publishing, London, 1976.

Sexual Politics – A Basic Reading List, Librarians for Social Change, Release, London, 1975.

Shorter, Edward, *The Making of the Modern Family,* Collins, London, 1976.

Simon, Rosemary, *Breaking Up*, Arrow, London, 1974.
A practical guide to separation and divorce and coping on your own. Information on how to obtain a divorce or separation order, what children may feel about divorce/separation, housing, money 'starting life afresh', and re-marriage.

Simpson, Harry, *The Role of Housing Authorities*, National Council for One Parent Families, 'Forward From Finer', Number 3, London, 1977.
By the Controller of Housing for the Greater London Council, the housing problems of one-parent families and some solutions.

Sixty Years of Caring and Campaigning, National Council for One Parent Families, London, 1978.
A brief history of the National Council for the Unmarried Mother and Her

Child and the future aims of the National Council for One Parent Families.

Social Security Benefits and Other Benefits in 1978/79, National Council for One Parent Families, London, 1978.
Brief guide to all the major benefits to which lone parents are entitled.

Some Books You Might Find Helpful, National Council for One Parent Families, London, 1977.
List of useful books for one-parent families.

Stein, P. J., 'Singlehood: an alternative to marriage', in Sussman, M., *et al* (eds.) 'The Second Experience, Variant Family Forms and Life-Styles', special issue of *The Family Co-ordinator*, (24), 4, 1975.

Steinberg, David, *Fatherjournal: Five Years of Awakening to Fatherhood*, Times Change Press, New York, (62 W. 14th St), 1977.

Sutton-Smith, Rosenberg & Landy, 'Father absence effects in families of different sibling compositions', *Child Development*, 1968, Volume 39, Number 4.

Tax Changes and Child Benefit Changes in 1978/79, National Council for One Parent Families, London, 1978.
How the Budget of 11 April 1978 affects lone parents.

Tunnard, Jo and Wheatlay, Clare, *Rights Guide for Home Owners*, Published jointly by Child Poverty Action Group and Shelter Housing Action Centre, London, 1977.
Guide to mortgages, property law and housing rights with special emphasis on the problems facing lone parents threatened with the loss of their home after marriage breakdown.

The Changing Pattern – Report on the Training of the Older Woman, National Federation of Business and Professional Women's Clubs, London, 1966.

The Cohabitation Rule and the Guide to Supplementary Benefit Appeals Tribunals, Child Poverty Action Group, London, 1970.

The Cost of Raising Children, Child Poverty Action Group, London, 1976.

The Family: What's Happening To It?, Child Poverty Action Group, London, 1978.

The Finer Report, Child Poverty Action Group, London, 1975.

The Finer Report: Recommendations and Response, National Council for One Parent Families, London, 1975.
Conference proceedings 1975. Speeches by Barbara Castle, Prof. O. R. McGregor, Marjorie Proops and others.

230

The Need for a Family Lobby, Child Poverty Action Group, London, 1977.

The One-Parent Family – Possible Effects on Children: Some References, National Council for One-Parent Families, London, 1978.
A list of references about the effects of growing up in a one-parent family.

Tolson, Andrew, *The Limits of Masculinity*, Tavistock Publications, London, 1977.

Toner, Barbara, *Double Shift,* Arrow, 1975, Severn House Publishers, 1976.
A practical guide for working mothers.

Tonybee, P. A., *A Working Life,* Holder and Stoughton, London, 1971.

Trade Union Council Report of The Under Fives, Report of a TUC Working Party, Published by Trade Union Congress, Congress House, Great Russell St, London, WC1, 1976.

Tunnard, Jo, *No Father No Home?* Child Poverty Action Group, London, 1976.

Tunnard, Jo, *The Trouble with Tax*, Child Poverty Action Group, London, 1978.

Undefended Divorce, Gingerbread. Published by the Lord Chancellors Office.
A guide for the petitioner acting without a solictor.

Wastberg, Per, *The Air Cage*, Souvenir Press, London, 1971.

Wear, Stuart and Streather, Jane, *Social Insecurity: Single Mothers on Benefit*, Child Poverty Action Group, London, 1974.

Welfare Rights and Social Action; The York Experiment, Child Poverty Action Group, London, 1974.

Which Way Welfare Rights, Child Poverty Action Group, London, 1975
Discussion paper about the future and direction of the welfare rights movement.

Willans, Angela, *Alone Again,* National Marriage Guidance Council, Little Church St, Rugby CV21 3AP, 1977.
Practical advice to help people with the difficulties of adjusting to life after divorce/separation or the death of a partner.

Willis, Paul, *Learning to Labour; How Working Class Kids Get Working Class Jobs*, Saxon House, London, 1977.

Wilmott, Phyllis, *Consumer's Guide to the British Social Services*, Penguin, Harmondsworth, 1978.

Wilson, Elizabeth, *Women and the Welfare State*, Tavistock Publications, London, 1977.

Wohlford, Santrock, Berger & Liberman, 'Older brothers' influence on sex-typed, aggressive and dependant behavior in father-absent children', *Developmental Psychology*, 1971, *4*, pp 124–34.

Women's Books and Pamphlets List, (H. Rutovitz), 31 Royal Terrace, Edinburgh 7.

Women's Report, Volume 1, Number 2, January-March 1973.
For a list of Women's Liberation Periodicals; and Volume 1, Number 3: rights of husbands, wives and family in marriage and divorce; family allowance.

Women's Report, Volume 3, Number 1, November-December 1974.
The Legal Section: 'Custody is the grumble', and 'On the home front' – no increase in childminding centres compared to the number of working wives over 20 years.

'Woman, Wife and Worker', London School of Economics, HMSO, London, 1960.

'Women's Work and Women's Studies', The Woman's Centre, Barnard College, New York City, New York 10027, 1972.
Over 2,500 entries.

Yo-Yo Children: A Study of 23 Violent Matrimonial Cases, NSPCC, London, 1974.

Yudkin, S. and A. Holme, *Working Mothers and their Children*, Council for Children's Welfare, Michael Joseph, 1963.

Zaretsky, Eli, *Capitalism, the Family and Personal Life*, Pluto Press, London, 1976.

If you would like to know more about Virago books, write to us at 5 Wardour Street, London W1V 3HE for a full catalogue.

Please send a stamped addressed envelope

VIRAGO ADVISORY GROUP

Book Tokens

Give them the pleasure of choosing
Book Tokens can be bought and exchanged at most bookshops